Interrogating the Perpetrator

Set adjacent to "victims" and "bystanders", "perpetrators" are by no means marginalized figures in human rights scholarship. Nevertheless, the extent to which the perpetrator is not only socially imagined but also sociologically constructed remains a central concern in studies of state-authorized mass violence. This interdisciplinary collection of essays builds upon such work by strategically interrogating the terms through which such a figure is read via law, society, and culture. Of particular concern to the contributors to this volume are the ways in which notions of "violation" and "culpability" are mediated through less direct, convoluted frames of corporatization, globalization, militarized humanitarianism, post-conflict truth and justice processes, and postcoloniality. The chapters variously give scrutiny to historical memory (who can voice it, when and in what registers), question legalism's dominance within human rights, and analyze the story-telling values invested in the figure of the perpetrator.

Against the common tendency to view perpetrators as either monsters or puppets – driven by evil or controlled by others – the chapters in this book are united by the themes of truth's contingency and complex imaginings of perpetrators. Even as the truth that emerges from perpetrator testimony may depend on who is listening, with what attitude and in what institutional context, the book's chapters also affirm that listening to perpetrators may be every bit as productive to human rights insights as it has been to listen to survivors and witnesses.

This book was previously published as a special issue of *The International Journal of Human Rights*.

Cathy J. Schlund-Vials is Professor of English and Asian/Asian American Studies, University of Connecticut, USA. She is the author of two monographs: *Modeling Citizenship: Jewish and Asian American Writing*, and *War, Genocide, and Justice: Cambodian American Memory Work*. Her research interests include human rights, critical refugee studies, comparative ethnic studies, Asian American studies, and memory studies.

Samuel Martínez is Associate Professor of Anthropology and Latin American Studies, University of Connecticut, USA. He studies the rights mobilizations of Haitian immigrants and Haitian descendants in the Dominican Republic, North-South human rights knowledge exchange, and contemporary anti-slavery reporting.

Interrogating the Perpetrator

Violation, culpability, and human rights

Edited by
**Cathy J. Schlund-Vials and
Samuel Martínez**

Routledge
Taylor & Francis Group

LONDON AND NEW YORK

First published 2017 by Routledge

2 Park Square, Milton Park, Abingdon, Oxfordshire OX14 4RN
711 Third Avenue, New York, NY 10017

Routledge is an imprint of the Taylor & Francis Group, an informa business

First issued in paperback 2018

British Library Cataloguing in Publication Data
A catalogue record for this book is available from the British Library

ISBN 13: 978-1-138-68931-2 (hbk)
ISBN 13: 978-0-367-02824-4 (pbk)

Typeset in Times New Roman
by RefineCatch Limited, Bungay, Suffolk

Publisher's Note
The publisher accepts responsibility for any inconsistencies that may have
arisen during the conversion of this book from journal articles to book chapters,
namely the possible inclusion of journal terminology.

Disclaimer
Every effort has been made to contact copyright holders for their permission to
reprint material in this book. The publishers would be grateful to hear from any
copyright holder who is not here acknowledged and will undertake to rectify
any errors or omissions in future editions of this book.

Contents

Citation Information

The following chapters were originally published in *The International Journal of Human Rights*, volume 19, issue 5 (June 2015). When citing this material, please use the original page numbering for each article, as follows:

Chapter 1
Interrogating the perpetrator: violation, culpability and human rights
Cathy J. Schlund-Vials and Samuel Martínez
The International Journal of Human Rights, volume 19, issue 5 (June 2015), pp. 549–554

Chapter 2
'Victim/volunteer': heroes versus perpetrators and the weight of US service-members' pasts in Iraq and Afghanistan
Jean Scandlyn and Sarah Hautzinger
The International Journal of Human Rights, volume 19, issue 5 (June 2015), pp. 555–571

Chapter 3
War propaganda, war crimes, and post-conflict justice in Serbia: an ethnographic account
Jordan Kiper
The International Journal of Human Rights, volume 19, issue 5 (June 2015), pp. 572–591

Chapter 4
Refiguring the perpetrator: culpability, history and international criminal law's impunity gap
Kamari Maxine Clarke
The International Journal of Human Rights, volume 19, issue 5 (June 2015), pp. 592–614

Chapter 5
False promise and new hope: dead perpetrators, imagined documents and emergent archival evidence
Michelle Caswell and Anne Gilliland
The International Journal of Human Rights, volume 19, issue 5 (June 2015), pp. 615–627

Chapter 6

The space of sorrow: a historic video dialogue between survivors and perpetrators of the Cambodian killing fields
Susan Needham, Karen Quintiliani and Robert Lemkin
The International Journal of Human Rights, volume 19, issue 5 (June 2015), pp. 628–647

Chapter 7

Perpetrating ourselves: reading human rights and responsibility otherwise
Crystal Parikh
The International Journal of Human Rights, volume 19, issue 5 (June 2015), pp. 648–661

The following chapter was originally published in *The International Journal of Human Rights*, volume 19, issue 1 (January 2015). When citing this material, please use the original page numbering for the article, as follows:

Chapter 8

Victims, perpetrators, and the limits of human rights discourse in post-Palermo fiction about sex trafficking
Alexandra Schultheis Moore and Elizabeth Swanson Goldberg
The International Journal of Human Rights, volume 19, issue 1 (January 2015), pp. 16–31

For any permission-related enquiries please visit:
http://www.tandfonline.com/page/help/permissions

Notes on Contributors

Michelle Caswell is Assistant Professor of Archival Studies in the Department of Information Studies at the University of California Los Angeles, USA. She is the author of *Archiving the Unspeakable: Silence, Memory and the Photographic Record in Cambodia* (2014) and the guest editor of a special double issue of *Archival Science* on archives and human rights. She is also the co-founder of the South Asian American Digital Archive, an online repository that documents and provides access to the diverse stories of South Asian Americans.

Kamari Maxine Clarke is Professor in Global and International Studies, Carleton University, USA. Her research spans issues related to human rights, international courts and tribunals, the export, spread, rejection and re-contextualization of international norms, secularism and religious transnationalism, United Nations and African Union treaty negotiations, and Africa's insertion into international law circuits. Trained in Canada and the US, and formerly a professor at Yale University and the University of Pennsylvania, Professor Clarke has taught multiple generations of students in anthropology, law, politics, the humanities, and social sciences.

Anne Gilliland is Professor in the Department of Information Studies, as well as Director of the Centre for Information as Evidence at the University of California Los Angeles (UCLA), USA. Her recent work examines recordkeeping and archival systems and practices in support of human rights and daily life in post-conflict settings; the role of community memory in promoting reconciliation in the wake of ethnic conflict; and bureaucratic violence and the politics of metadata.

Sarah Hautzinger holds a Masters of Arts and Philosophy Doctorate in Anthropology from Johns Hopkins University, USA. She is Professor and Chair of Anthropology at Colorado College.

Jordan Kiper is a graduate student at the Department of Anthropology, University of Connecticut, USA.

Robert Lemkin is a documentary filmmaker and screenwriter based in Oxford, UK. His work covers investigative journalism, history, drama, and music. He has made around 50 documentaries for television stations worldwide including the BBC, Channel 4, ITV, PBS, and the History Channel. He is co-director with Thet Sambath of *Enemies of the People*, produced with support from EU MEDIA, Sundance Documentary Film Program, Gucci Tribeca Documentary Fund, Worldview.

Samuel Martínez is Associate Professor of Anthropology and Latin American Studies, University of Connecticut, USA. He studies the rights mobilizations of Haitian immigrants and Haitian descendants in the Dominican Republic, North-South human rights knowledge exchange, and contemporary anti-slavery reporting.

Susan Needham, PhD, is Professor and Chair of Anthropology at California State University, Dominguez Hills, USA. She has conducted ethnographic and linguistic research in the Cambodian community of Long Beach since 1988. Her research and publications include the recreation and transmission of Khmer language and literacy, religious practices, and the arts, as well as symbols of community identity. She was the program director for the annual Cambodia Town Culture Festival from 2009–2014. She is a co-founder, with Dr. Karen Quintiliani, of the Cambodian Community History and Archive Project.

Crystal Parikh is Associate Professor in the Department of English and the Department of Social and Cultural Analysis at New York University, USA. In addition to several articles, Professor Parikh has published *An Ethics of Betrayal: The Politics of Otherness in Emergent U.S. Literature and Culture* (2009), which won the Modern Language Association Prize in United States Latina and Latino and Chicana and Chicano Literary Studies. She is currently working on a new book about human rights politics and contemporary American writers of colour titled *Writing Human Rights*.

Karen Quintiliani, PhD, is Professor and Chair of Anthropology at California State University, Long Beach, USA. She has conducted ethnographic and applied research in the Long Beach Cambodian community since 1988. Her research, publications, and community engagement projects include: cultural history of Cambodian immigrant experience; social welfare policy; gender and sexuality; refugee health; youth cultures; and program development and evaluation. She is co-founder, with Dr. Susan Needham, of the Cambodian Community History and Archive Project.

Jean Scandlyn completed a Master of Science (Nursing) at the University of California San Francisco, USA, and a Doctor of Philosophy (Anthropology) at Columbia University, USA. She is Research Associate Professor in the Department of Health and Behavioral Sciences at the University of Colorado Denver, USA.

Cathy J. Schlund-Vials is Professor of English and Asian/Asian American Studies, University of Connecticut, USA. She is the author of two monographs: *Modeling Citizenship: Jewish and Asian American Writing*, and *War, Genocide, and Justice: Cambodian American Memory Work*. Her research interests include human rights, critical refugee studies, comparative ethnic studies, Asian American studies, and memory studies.

Alexandra Schultheis Moore is Associate Professor of English at the University of North Carolina at Greensboro, USA, and works in postcolonial studies and human rights. She is the author of *Regenerative Fictions: Postcolonialism, Psychoanalysis and the Nation as Family* (2004), and co-editor of *Theoretical Perspectives on Human Rights and Literature* (2011), and *Teaching Human Rights in Literary and Cultural Studies* (2015), both with Elizabeth Swanson Goldberg, and the forthcoming *Routledge Companion to Literature and Human Rights* with Sophia McClennen. Moore's current monograph is on embodiment, vulnerability, and security in contemporary human rights literature and film.

Elizabeth Swanson Goldberg, PhD, is Professor of English and Chair of the Arts and Humanities Division at Babson College, USA. Author of *Beyond Terror: Gender,*

Narrative, Human Rights (2007), she is also co-editor of *Theoretical Perspectives on Human Rights and Literature* (2011), and *Teaching Human Rights in Literary and Cultural Studies* (2015), both with Alexandra Schultheis Moore. Dr. Goldberg directs the Women's Entrepreneurial Development Laboratory at Babson College, an innovation space dedicated to testing models for economic empowerment and the restoration of lives for women who have been trafficked or who have experienced other forms of marginalization and exploitation.

Interrogating the perpetrator: violation, culpability and human rights

Cathy J. Schlund-Vials[a] and Samuel Martínez[b]

[a]English and Asian/Asian American Studies, University of Connecticut, Storrs, USA;
[b]Department of Anthropology, University of Connecticut, Storrs, USA

On 9 May 2014, the *Phnom Penh Post* published an article by Poppy McPherson titled, 'Memorial Plan Prompts Debate about Victims and Perpetrators of Genocide'. The story, which was reprinted and reposted in multiple news outlets, focused its attention on two survivors – Bou Meng and Chum Mey – from Cambodia's notorious Tuol Sleng Prison (known more widely as 'Security Prison 21', or 'S-21 detention center').[1] Formerly a high school, Tuol Sleng Prison was repurposed soon after the 17 April 1975 takeover of Phnom Penh by the authoritarian Khmer Rouge. Between 1975 and 1979 – the duration of the Khmer Rouge regime – Tuol Sleng would be home to an estimated 20,000 inmates, the vast majority of whom would perish.[2] Catastrophically, such mass death was emblematic of what those outside Cambodia refer to as the period of 'the Killing Fields' and those within term 'Pol Pot Time'. Indeed, over the course of three years, eight months, and twenty days, approximately 1.7 million Cambodians (21–25% of the extant population) died from disease, starvation, forced labour, torture and execution.

Under head warden 'Comrade Duch' (née Kaing Guek Eav), prisoners were photographed and meticulously catalogued; detained as 'enemies of the people', S-21's inmates were subjected to relentless waterboarding, electrical shock, ruthless beatings, and other modes of torture. The overall intent was to elicit – by brutal force – confessions of regime wrongdoing. These admissions, made under unimaginable and inhumane duress, involved invented accounts of CIA membership, fictitious accounts of KGB affiliation, and fabricated lists of other anti-regime 'collaborators'. From Khmer Rouge cadres, who fell victim to internal purges, to foreign prisoners of war, from returning expatriate intellectuals to pre-revolutionary diplomats, from teachers to students, and from engineers to farmers, the diversity of Tuol Sleng's population underscores geographically expansive and socially voracious regime paranoia. The Khmer Rouge nationalist agenda included not only individuals but also the detention, torture and execution of entire families, making visceral the oft-used Khmer Rouge saying that 'To dig up grass, one must also dig up the roots.'[3]

It is the overall indiscriminateness of the Khmer Rouge regime's search for 'enemies of the people' that is at the root of the aforementioned controversy surrounding how best to memorialise those who died. Put bluntly, not all victims seem equally worthy of memorialisation. The Victims Support Section of the United Nations (UN)/Khmer Rouge Tribunal (officially known as the 'Extraordinary Chambers in the Courts of Cambodia', or 'ECCC')

– in conjunction with Cambodia's Ministry of Culture and Fine Arts – announced plans to construct a memorial *stupa* to commemorate those who died on site and in the nearby Choeung Ek killing field. This memorial, which replaces a similar structure destroyed by a 2008 storm, diverges from its predecessor insofar as prisoner names will be included (inscribed on the *stupa* or via a nearby book display). As McPherson reports, 'While the *stupa* has been widely welcomed', the proposal to incorporate names 'has met with passionate resistance and Khmer Rouge survivors who say that it risks offending families if the names of cadres are listed'.[4] Roughly 70% of S-21's tragic denizens were Khmer Rouge cadres rounded up in periodic internal purges; thus, the majority of those who were detained, tortured and killed were victims of the regime after being interred at S-21 but potential perpetrators of the regime's violence prior to their detention.[5]

This tension – wherein someone can be both victim and perpetrator – along with the mixed feelings that accompany such acknowledgment, is exemplified by Bou Meng and Chum Mey, who represent two sides of the *stupa* debate. Meng, who supports the memorial, stated that he felt 'disappointed because they [opponents] just eliminate the names of victims'; by contrast, Mey disputes the proposed inscription on the grounds that it may upset the relatives of non-Khmer Rouge detainee-victims. As Youk Chhang, the director of the Documentation Center of Cambodia concisely surmises, 'Even though the same person who committed a crime does good later, that does not mean that the crime they have committed can turn them into a victim. At the same time, not all Khmer Rouge are bad people.'[6] Such nuances, at the forefront of present-day reparation debates in Cambodia, unavoidably resonate with other histories of human rights violation, presaging the primary stakes and internationalist interventions at the forefront of this special issue on perpetrator-hood. From Serbian military men to 'War on Terror' United States veterans, from Iraq to Cambodia, from Indonesia to Kenya, inclusive of regime leaders and civilian offenders, perpetrators are – as individual essays make clear – first and foremost transgressive figures who traverse multiple temporalities and inhabit numerous geographies.

Set adjacent 'victims' and 'bystanders', 'perpetrators' are by no means marginalised figures in human rights scholarship. From Hannah Arendt's *Eichmann in Jerusalem* (1963)[7] to Alex Hinton's *Why Did They Kill? Cambodia in the Shadow of Genocide* (2004),[8] the extent to which the perpetrator is not only socially imagined but also sociologically constructed remains a central concern in studies of state-authorised mass violence. This interdisciplinary special issue builds upon such work by 'interrogating' the terms through which perpetrator figures are read via law, society and culture. Of particular interest to the editors of this volume are the ways in which notions of 'violation' and 'culpability' are mediated through less direct, convoluted frames of corporatisation, globalisation, militarised humanitarianism, post-conflict truth and justice processes, and postcoloniality.

Correspondingly, an obvious but perhaps still under-theorised encompassing conceptual context for our discussion is the heterogeneity of 'human rights' when we go beyond foundational concepts to look at human rights as a social process and set of institutions. No responsible critique of human rights is possible, from our standpoint, without pausing at some point to consider the diversity of human rights venues, subjectivities, framings and epistemologies. Consider just some of the venues through which our contributors examine how human rights claims and the contrapuntal or dissonant disclaimers of alleged perpetrators are given voice: truth and reconciliation commissions, video documentaries, motion picture dramas, and memoirs, not to mention conventional fact-finding reports.

Adding further complexity to our discussion is the question of cross-cultural translation, a point of productive confluences and divergences for the literary scholars and sociocultural anthropologists whose contributions we gather together in this special issue. How faithfully can the guiding concepts of universalising human rights frame perpetrator testimony and understandings of perpetratorhood in the Southeast Asian and sub-Saharan African contexts under consideration in some of this issue's articles, and then be translated back again into European realms? It is with great interest that we observe the cultural and historical diversity of the societies and times brought to life by the contributors. Similarly relativised questions relating to historical memory arise in nearly all of this issue's articles. With those questions go overarching possibilities for discussion of what are the effects of culturally particular idioms, social conventions and political economic inequalities on how memory can be voiced, and gender and social class asymmetries regarding who is authorised to speak what kinds of truths.

Even as news of legal proceedings, such as those of the International Criminal Tribunal for the former Yugoslavia (ICTY), the International Criminal Court (ICC) and the hybrid UN/Khmer Rouge Tribunal seem to become more visible with every passing year, public knowledge and opinion about human rights today may be as deeply influenced by representations transmitted through venues other than the courtroom and the legislative chamber. More particularly, dissatisfaction with international legal tribunals' difficulty in doing even what they are designed to do best – executing exemplary punishment of those who ordered and instigated crimes against humanity – casts an uncomforting light on the inadequacies of adversarial, legal/forensic avenues of justice.

Nonetheless, legalism remains dominant in human rights and is a recurrent shadow presence in the articles in this special issue. Points of contrast and coincidence between adversarial, legalist approaches, on one hand, and a spectrum of dialogic, restorative or political agentive approaches to human rights advocacy and justice-seeking, on the other, loom as both a potential source of new insight but also a potential stumbling block to achieving full integration of our insights with human rights' dominant judicial imaginary. Can we escape Nuremburg's shadow, in the form of legalism's dominance in the human rights domain? Should we even try? While recognising that there is room for principled disagreement about whether a prosecutorial imaginary must always hold the centre of human rights discourse, that space for debate can, we hold, be developed most productively only when partisans of legal retribution, reconciliation and restoration each admit to the shortcomings of their favoured approach.

Consider the use of the term 'evil' to characterise perpetrators of crimes against humanity, as 'a preemptive strike against those who might appeal to social conditions in seeking to understand' why people do grievous harm to others.[9] Calling actions evil means that they are beyond comprehension. Consider also some of the questions most asked about perpetrators of intolerable wrongs: Why do they kill? Would we, in their shoes, do the same? Once the killing has been stopped, is our first duty to reconcile with them and reintegrate them into society, or punish them for their wrongs? All these questions situate the perpetrator as a figure of fascination, mixed with dread, but never – not properly, at least – an object of sympathy. A discursive limit is that we may understand his motivations but must never accept his thinking. Whether he appears to have been thrust into evil circumstances or to have stepped into killing and humiliating others willingly, the perpetrator is not 'us' but an inhabitant of a distinct moral universe. Even as it is sure that a measure of human rights' celebrated moral clarity derives from drawing sharp lines between alleged perpetrators and responders, prosecutors and judges, it is less well accepted and understood how the moral distancing of perpetrators from 'us' may reduce the figure of the perpetrator to either monster or puppet.

Of the issues raised above – relating to alternative framings of harm and culpability, questions of cross-cultural translation, asymmetries in access to historical memory, legalism's long shadow, competing dispositions towards individual blame and contextual explanation, and the story-telling values invested in figurations of perpetrators – each enters into one or more of this special issue's articles. One point at which these concerns coincide is the question of how to listen to the perpetrator. As much as perpetrators' accounts may give finer grain and firmer substance to critical scholarly contributions to justice-seeking, it remains difficult to decide what kind of truth and measure of belief to accord to people who have reason to deny and downplay their personal culpability.

The social process and cultural inflections of truth-telling may be a site into which the perpetrator's subjectivity offers particular insight. The question of how certain enunciations and not others come to be accepted as truth was an issue that was easy to ignore for a time via celebratory treatments of victims finding voice; truth's contingency is less easy to overlook when it comes to perpetrators confessing wrong or aiming to reframe wrong as right. Nowhere could this be more apparent than in the retrospective accounts of former combatants, as with the Serbian excombatants and the returning Iraq/Afghanistan veterans interviewed by cultural anthropologists Jordan Kiper and Sarah Hautzinger and Jean Scandlyn. These former soldiers' reticence about any aspect of their perpetration of violence, added to their expectation that civilians would not be able to understand, together erect, in Hautzinger and Scandlyn's view, a kind of tacit contract between soldiers and civilians to just not talk about it. In rejecting the conventional testimonial moulds of the press and the clinic, then, these former soldiers shed a bright light on truth-telling's embedded-ness within particular social processes, in which the listeners' identities and attitudes as well as the context of speech shape the limits of what truths are acceptable to speak and what truths are not.

On the issues of how public discourse and interpersonal dialogues skirt indeterminacies of moral evaluation, in which former soldiers might be deemed perpetrators or victims, or both, Hautzinger and Scandlyn's article provides fine-grained insights. They argue that when discussion of former soldiers' wartime experiences is channelled exclusively through the therapeutically individuated category of post-traumatic stress disorder (PTSD), questions of broader responsibility are evaded. Conveniently avoided through PTSD talk is the question of whether inflicting harm can be as trauma-inducing as fear and pain to one's self and comrades, and with that, whether men conscripted into military service could ask a fuller range of rights of their governments. The experience of former combatants may bring into particularly clear focus what Ariella Azoulay, in *Civil Imagination*, has called 'the right *not* to be a perpetrator'.[10]

Azoulay's characterisation of 'the right *not* to be a perpetrator' is at the forefront of Kiper's previously mentioned contribution. In his Serbian field research, Kiper achieved a level of access and ethnographic rapport with excombatants that amazed Serbian legal and academic professionals. On the basis of that research, Kiper clouds the boundary between victim and perpetrator in importantly different ways. In his contribution to this special issue, Kiper brings forward evidence that throws into doubt all conventional top-down models of wartime propaganda. Specific, widely repeated items of anti-Croat and anti-Muslim propaganda are traceable in their origins to the frontline fighters and not to the Serbian nationalist politicians and media figures who are now the targets of Serbian war crimes prosecution. If propaganda is to continue to be prosecuted as a war crime, Kiper concludes, it will have to be on the basis of a more sophisticated concept of perpetratorhood than that currently held by war crimes prosecutors, who assume that propaganda has a clearly specifiable source and target. The value of patiently seeking out and listening to perpetrator-centred accounts is confirmed by Kiper's research. Troubling, by contrast, is

Kiper's finding that Serbian prosecutors think that they are barred by their rules of legal engagement from interviewing excombatants. With that, other significant doubts are raised about legal prosecution as a justice strategy in relation to propaganda crimes.

Kamari Clarke's contribution also interrogates legal prosecution for its reductions and exclusions in relation to seeking justice at the ICC against the Kenyan politicians Uhuru Kenyatta and William Rutu, for organising widespread acts of interethnic violence and terror in the aftermath of the contested presidential election of 2007. The ICC's focus on holding commanders accountable leaves open an 'impunity gap', in Clarke's words, which leaves many Kenyans' aspirations for justice unsatisfied. At its high end, the impunity gap consists of failures to consider the responsibility of colonial officials for laying down structures of exclusions and violence within Kenyan society, which would later be the lines along which the blood-letting would unfold. At its low end, and felt in more proximate and quotidian ways, the impunity gap leaves unquestioned and unpunished the foot soldiers and neighbourhood people who inflicted, if not organised, the physical and emotional violence. In Clarke's account, then, international legalism's long shadow obscures responsibility and obstructs justice-seeking for wrongs at both distal and proximate ends of the 'joint criminal enterprise' doctrine used to prosecute crimes against humanity in international courts.

Whereas Clarke's contribution is focused on a particular *legal* gap and envisions a new way of comprehending perpetratorhood, Michelle Caswell and Anne Gilliland consider by way of comparative archive the imagined possibilities and limitations of accessing intangible forms of evidence. Opening with the provocative and all-too-real question of what happens when perpetrators die before giving legal testimony, Caswell and Gilliland recast such subjects as imagined and alternative archival sites. Accessing the juridical and archival legacies of the Khmer Rouge in Cambodia and the Yugoslav wars, Caswell and Gilliland consider first how survivors and victims' families construct such figures as *unavailable* documents; they then evocatively evaluate the ways in which such narrative absences make possible – through reimagination and recontextualisation – creation of new archives and records that complicate rather than essentialise histories of state-sanctioned violence.

Such narrative reframing – particularly with regard to the Khmer Rouge and more generally in terms of perpetratorhood – analogously presages the emphases found in Susan Needham, Karen Quintiliani and Robert Lemkin's co-authored contribution. Beginning with Lemkin and Sambath Thet's 2010 documentary film, *Enemies of the People*, which featured candid interviews with two Khmer Rouge cadres and Nuon Chea ('Brother Number 2' and Khmer Rouge chief ideologue), Needham, Quintiliani and Lemkin detail an intergenerational and international video conference which brought together victims of the regime and Khmer Rouge perpetrators. Intended to instantiate dialogue and engender post-conflict healing, Needham, Quintiliani and Lemkin draw upon the literary idea of a 'chronotope' as a flexible means of understanding exchanges between victims, perpetrators and bystanders.

The use of literature as a site of perpetrator contemplation is considerably more overt in Crystal Parikh's concluding evaluation of diasporic Chinese-Indonesian writer Li-Young Lee, whose poetry is circumscribed by the postwar history of political violence in postcolonial Indonesia. Arguing for a more nuanced conception of the figure of the 'perpetrator', Parikh uses the ethical theory of Emmanuel Levinas and considers how relations of responsibility necessarily extend beyond individual agents of violence. Integral to Parikh's critique of dominant human rights discourse is a serious evaluation of how the interpretative dimensions of the literary imagination enable alternative, non-state sanctioned ways to contend with past violence, loss and repression.

Set against these summaries and in drawing to a close, our final motivation in bringing together this special issue is to suggest – like our contributors – that listening to perpetrators may prove to be every bit as productive of human rights insight as it has been to focus on victims, and more recently protectors, as emblematic subjects of human rights. It is through the eyes of victims, witnesses and protectors that audiences of human rights reportage are typically asked to cognise and weigh the gravity of wrongs; even more surely, it is with victims, and not perpetrators, that audiences are expected to identify emotionally. Yet the figure of the perpetrator, while more shadowy, is indispensable in all human rights representations, including monitor group investigatory reports, documentary and dramatic films, and fiction.

Notes

1. See Poppy McPherson, 'Memorial Plan Prompts Debate about Victims and Perpetrators of Genocide', *Phnom Penh Post*, 9 May 2014. http://www.phnompenhpost.com/7days/memorial-plan-prompts-debate-about-victims-and-perpetrators-genocide (accessed 2 July 2014).
2. On 17 April 1975, the Khmer Rouge rolled into Cambodia's capital (Phnom Penh), signalling the start of the regime; it would eventually be deposed on 7 January 1979 by the Vietnamese Army, signalling the end of both the regime and the Cambodian-Vietnamese War (1977–1979).
3. See Alexander Laban Hinton, 'A Head for an Eye: Revenge in the Cambodian Genocide', in *Genocide: An Anthropological Reader*, ed. Alexander Laban Hinton (Malden, MA: Blackwell Publishers, 2002), 273.
4. McPherson, 'Memorial Plan Prompts Debate about Victims and Perpetrators of Genocide'.
5. Ibid.
6. It should be noted that another critique of the proposed memorial involves its connection to Western modes of memorialisation.
7. Hannah Arendt, *Eichmann in Jerusalem: A report on the Banality of Evil* (New York: Penguin Books, 1963).
8. Alexander Laban Hinton, *Why Did They Kill? Cambodia in the Shadow of Genocide* (Berkeley, CA: University of California Press, 2004).
9. Terry Eagleton, *On Evil* (New Haven, CT: Yale University Press, 2011), 2.
10. Ariella Azoulay, *Civil Imagination: A Political Ontology of Photography* (New York: Verso, 2012), 243.

'Victim/volunteer': heroes versus perpetrators and the weight of US service-members' pasts in Iraq and Afghanistan[1]

Jean Scandlyn[a] and Sarah Hautzinger[b]

[a]Department of Health and Behavioral Sciences, University of Colorado Denver, USA; [b]Department of Anthropology, Colorado College, USA

How might military service members figure as perpetrators of human rights violations? The question remains a taboo, painful and suppressed topic in United States' face-to-face communities with strong veteran and active-duty presences. Our 2008–2014 ethnographic, team-based anthropological fieldwork focused on a mid-sized American city and its adjacent army base. We argue that the ambiguities and contradictions between soldiers-as-perpetrators and more common and public designations for soldiers and veterans – as heroes, protectors and volunteers, but also as victims of circumstance and injury – impede such exploration. War as a framework for legitimising lethal force complicates what constitutes perpetration, as do the implications of all-volunteer forces fighting protracted campaigns. The legacy of the Vietnam War brings key historicity to civilians' efforts to not repeat the *a priori* victimisation of veterans as presumed perpetrators, alongside recognition that the signature, psychological and moral injuries of the post-9/11 wars also can render veterans as victims in the public's perspective. Finally, as counterpoint to the generalised avoidance of confronting rights violations, we draw on a journalist's account of a veteran who sought to face an Iraqi victim who lost family members directly; their mutual victimhood is sharply qualified by the civilian's innocence and the veteran's willing volunteerism.

'If someone needs to pay in blood for the things we're doing over there, let it be one of us', BJ, the former Green Beret, said to the small circle of people clustered on the stage of an old theatre in downtown Colorado Springs. 'Over there' referred to the war in Iraq. 'Because', he added, 'we're okay with it'. By 'one of us' BJ meant the small Bible study group, just himself and two other recent veterans, who met nightly.[2] If anyone would be called to account, if actions intended to 'do bad things to bad people' were themselves deemed bad or wrong in some final judgement, then these self-fashioned spiritual warriors were there to take responsibility.

It was only through a difficult process that BJ had reached this place of tentative, ongoing reconciliation with what he had seen and done in Iraq. When he first came back to the United States (US), his relationships with his five siblings suffered painfully.

'I'm not liberal, but they are', he explained. 'The things I'd done, out on patrol picking up bad guys every night, became a problem for us.' He felt 'deeply damaged' and 'unable to compartmentalize' or respect 'taboos on violence' upon returning home, especially with his wife and sister, he intimated. 'You go there to free Iraqis, and come home and you're captive to your own mind.'

We listened to BJ's account at a veteran-civilian dialogue aimed at encouraging conversation on veteran reintegration and addressing gaps in the transition from '"battlefront to homefront", "uniform to university", or "combat to corporate"', as the sponsoring organisation's press release stated.[3] In stating that there might be things to account for, or indeed to 'pay for in blood', for US military actions in Iraq, BJ spoke directly to the topic of the moral stains of these wars, campaigns in which the US and its allies represent overpowering military force and act as invading forces. It was as specific a confrontation with morality and transgressions in the post-9/11 wars as one was likely to hear in a face-to-face, community setting, in Colorado Springs, a quintessentially military town. BJ raised the spectre, if only tentatively, and immediately refuted it with 'We're okay with it.'

At the time of the event in 2010, wars in Iraq and Afghanistan were both still raging. We were two years into fieldwork (2008–2014) on the relationship between the urban community of Colorado Springs, Colorado and neighbouring Fort Carson, one of the largest military installations in the US. In the midst of unprecedented multiple deployments spanning a decade, we interviewed active-duty combat veterans in the self-named 'Lethal Warrior' battalion (eight of whose soldiers were soon to be revealed as disproportionately responsible for a rash of local murders[4]), and immediately post-deployment to Afghanistan, shadowed them as they 'processed through' mental health screening and attended 'reintegration university'. We began with a focus on post-traumatic stress disorder (PTSD) and other psychological injuries related to combat stress, then expanded our project with participant observation at a variety of settings off-post, focused on 'deployment stress' more generally: homes, schools, health care providers' offices, and other service institutions. We studied dialogues like the one above, as well as more formal town hall meetings about military impact and reintegration challenges, as sites where military and civilians negotiated their relations and constructed their narrations of the wars.

Across these many sites, direct references like BJ's to the issue of soldiers[5] as prospective perpetrators of human rights violations were relatively rare. Glaringly absent was any semblance of balanced attention to the effects of the wars on Iraqi and Afghan lives; attention to us-and-ours dominated. Soldiers occasionally wound around to witnessing or participating in the maiming or killing of children and other innocents, but these stories emerged slowly. In most exchanges people avoided going there, having learned the conventions of how civilians are admonished for talking about war. Direct questions about what a combat veteran has seen or caused regarding killing are taboo, and soldiers anticipate them with fear. Rules for events that brought veterans and civilians together, typically unstated, but occasionally quite explicit, made it clear that judgement was off limits. At a 'Veterans Remember' event, the organiser, a Vietnam veteran, offered three explicit guidelines for the event. First was the exchange of stories between 'older guys' and 'younger guys'. Second, there needed to be a 'place of receptivity for the stories to be heard'. Finally, was 'the importance of a nonjudgmental, civilian audience', which would not politicise the sharing, but simply offer acceptance. Discussing the moral aspects of war would definitely violate the injunction not to politicise the event.

Why do we find ourselves so daunted and shackled when it comes to facing the possibility that among our military personnel are some who might have perpetrated war crimes and caused unnecessary suffering? We argue that historical and sociocultural dynamics combine to repress examination about responsibility and lessons to be learned from the post 9-11 wars, in large part because soldiers necessarily challenge definitive, either/or categorisation as perpetrators versus heroes, or as volunteers versus victims. Critically, however, none of these categories is homogeneous or mutually exclusive – one act of heroism or transgression may appear negligible against another, and the same individual or unit might justifiably be considered both heroic and perpetrators, in turns. Though we construct the article in terms of 'versus' contrasts, far from wishing to dichotomise, we wish to expose the instabilities between the poles. Variability within categories and unclear boundaries between them complicate efforts to recognise, confront and reconcile illegitimate and unnecessary force, that is: violence.[6] Though this article draws largely from reflections by soldiers and their community members on these matters, we note that these in fact capture, and in turn construct, the contours of how the nation as a whole witnesses and grapples with issues of shared complicity – or avoids doing so – during the post-9/11 wars.

We can note at least four factors that complicate clear identifications of illegitimate perpetration of violence in war, each related to frameworks that justify use of force as legitimate.

First, there is the nature of contemporary war itself. Framing a conflict as 'war' legitimates the use of force between states or groups and valorises sacrifice and heroism. But war also demands rules to contain violence and keep it focused on its military mission. The Geneva Conventions institutionalise this tension in modern legal terms by defining who can be attacked and who must be protected in war on the one hand, and making it possible to charge individual soldiers with war crimes on the other.

Second, there is the legacy of the Vietnam War, what we call 'post-Vietnam paralysis'. As the war became increasingly unpopular at home, stories of hero's welcomes were replaced with stories of US soldiers returning from Vietnam only to be spit upon by outraged civilians. At the same time, the public began to realise that young, poor men of colour who could not escape the draft bore an unfair burden of injury and death on the front lines.[7] This, coupled with the obvious suffering of many Vietnam veterans who ended up homeless, unemployed and addicted to drugs and alcohol, led to the cultural dictum that while it is the duty of citizens to oppose wars they feel are unjustified, it is not fair to attack the soldier who does the fighting. This may be an instance where we are doomed to 'fight the last war'. In public conversations we observed or participated in, the question of whether refraining from criticising soldiers might have had more validity in the Vietnam era, when soldiers were drafted, compared to the post-9/11 wars, where they all ostensibly volunteer, never arose.

Third is another legacy of the Vietnam War, coupled with the psychological turn in US cultural understanding of trauma: PTSD. In 1980 the American Psychiatric Association, under pressure from Vietnam veterans and their advocates among other groups, adopted PTSD as a psychiatric diagnosis. Its adoption represented a significant shift in public policy that provided access to mental health services and compensation for many veterans. As a medical diagnosis, PTSD shifts the focus away from military personnel as actors in an international conflict – war – towards the neurobiological mechanisms of injury. Soldiers become victimised individuals suffering from a disorder. In the decades since its adoption, mental health providers and lay people, especially in the US, have used PTSD to explain an ever-expanding range of suffering. Thus those who kill and those who are killed, by sharing a common humanity, may both qualify as victims of trauma. The concept of trauma also links individual suffering to the collective acts of violence and inhumanity that produced it, but less as actors than as mutual victims of these larger social forces.[8] This may be why deployment-based PTSD diagnoses have emerged as the central focus, the sole publicly permissible critical discourse and key symbol of the post-9/11 wars, something we explore at length elsewhere.[9]

Finally, the stand-out feature of the post-9/11 wars is that these are the first large-scale, protracted engagements fought and serviced exclusively by the professionalised, all-volunteer force (AVF) implemented in response to social dissent and subsequent abolition of the draft in 1973.[10] To volunteer for a job, especially one as dangerous and difficult as war, is to be the agent of one's destiny. Being a volunteer precludes soldiers from being victims of a nation that drafted them or of the trauma that might come from willingly putting themselves in harm's way. And yet many recruits who fought in the post-9/11 wars might be viewed as economic draftees, volunteers in name only.

All wars have their singularities and distinctions, and the engagements that the US and its allies[11] undertook in Afghanistan and Iraq are no exceptions. As a consequence, soldiers' varied roles can only be understood in historical context. An important particularity of *this* decade of American warfare is the open-ended, uncertain nature of what the military calls GWOT, the Global War on Terror. As many have pointed out, the inherent ambiguity of declaring a war on terror, an emotion, or terrorism, a political tactic and practice, has obscured what 'mission accomplished', or ultimate success in either Iraq or Afghanistan would look like (short of removing all risk of terrorism, an impossible goal). For service members on the ground, the diffuse geographical nature of the wars finds them battling in low-intensity, urban- and village-based exchanges of fire, in which civilians can be indistinguishable from the enemy and where counter-insurgent combatants are typically not uniformed or aligned with a localised nation-state. The absence of clear battle lines means that supposed non-combatants, including women, may find themselves in the line of fire or subject to blasts from IEDs (improvised explosive devices).[12]

Also distinctive about the post-9/11 wars is the high survival rate of the wounded, and the unique profile of the injuries sustained. Due to medical advances, far more soldiers are surviving multiple injuries, which frequently include severe damage to the head, face and extremities. For these wars, 9.2 wounded service members survive for every service member who dies (as compared to 2.2 to 1 for all US wars 1775–1991).[13] These large ranks of survivors face learning to recover or cope with injuries at the same time they confront reintegrating with family and friends, and for those able, retooling their skill sets to find new employment.

Heroes versus perpetrators: lethal force in war

Military officers we spoke with frequently cited Carl von Clausewitz, a General in the Prussian Army, whose theory of war guided their thinking in the current conflicts. One component of Von Clausewitz's 'remarkable trinity' of war is 'primordial violence, hatred, and enmity', which he regarded as a natural force that is 'inherent in the people' and 'kindled in war'.[14] Gwynne Dyer argues that until recently 'most people' have accepted the legitimacy of war and its attendant killing because they are willing to be killed. 'There is a heightened humanity, both good and bad, about the way soldiers behave in battle which seems to transcend ordinary morality and place them in a special category'.[15] The state's monopoly on the use of force[16] sets war apart as a social institution that sanctions and legitimates soldiers' use of lethality, defining them as combatants. As combatants acting under the state's authority and international laws governing armed combat, they are explicitly *not* perpetrators, i.e., persons who commit crimes against the state or against humanity. War's exceptionalism is the foundation for the soldier as hero, but more recent changes in social attitudes towards war and the state's legitimate use of force have complicated heroism and introduced the possibility that soldiers can be perpetrators.

The magnitude of killing and wounding in World War I (WWI) and the large number of civilian casualties compared to previous conflicts initiated a significant shift in public discourse surrounding war and international law governing war. The authors of the Treaty of Versailles sought to make this the 'war to end all wars'. Although the treaty failed to prevent World War II (WWII), included in the United Nations Charter in 1945 was 'a general rule that prohibits recourse to force in international relations, qualified by a small group of exceptions'.[17] The Nuremberg Trails following WWII stated that 'Crimes against international law are committed by men, not by abstract entities, and only by punishing individuals who commit such crimes can the provisions of international law be enforced'.[18]

The UN Charter also set the stage for the Geneva Conventions of 1949, which mandated that military personnel and governments distinguish between combatants and therefore legitimate targets of lethal force and non-combatants,[19] whom the conventions not only specifically prohibited as targets of violence, but commanded that combatants protect from harm. As a consequence, the Geneva Conventions institutionalised the tension between soldiers as heroic combatants and protectors whose duty was to preserve life. If soldiers failed to protect or harmed innocent non-combatants, they were perpetrators who could be individually charged with war crimes or murder. While only defeated German military personnel were tried for war crimes at Nuremberg, incidents such as the My Lai massacre in 1968 showed that public sentiment was changing and that violations of the rules of war, when and if they became publicly known, would be prosecuted. One effect of the focus on the actions of individual soldiers instead of the state and its leaders is that the responsibility for interpreting and enforcing the rules of engagement and determining the legitimacy of military orders in specific situations increasingly falls on individual soldiers and units.

One of the interview questions our team asked of infantry soldiers was, 'In terms of being adequately recognised and honoured, on return, do you think this affects coping with combat stress and other problems?'

The soldier who called himself Daniel Quest was back from his first deployment to Iraq, extended to 15 months because of heavy fighting with insurgents and a shortage of troops to send, and preparations for a second deployment to Afghanistan monopolised his thoughts.

'Probably not', he told student interviewer Caroline McKenna. 'I don't think it helped me. People just brought it up constantly, every day. I would just get pissed off. I'm a freaking hero because I was shooting 50-caliber rounds through families' living rooms and shit? How does that make me a hero?'[20]

Quest's delivery, peppered by a dry, rattling laugh, conveyed his ambivalence about his own diagnosis of PTSD that he had received between deployments, for which he resisted treatment: 'I'm just not wanting to sit in group counseling', said with a touch of ridicule, 'because I killed people'.

As team leader he tried to ensure that one of his soldiers got mental health attention because of his risk for violence. Quest's commander, however, ' ... was always giving Flores [the soldier] shit – "What; why do you *always* got an appointment?" and stuff like that. Then they started giving *me* shit: "You need to fix Flores." What? I'm not a doctor. What are we supposed to do? Sit around and talk about the – we did the same shit!' Flores eventually managed to 'get himself into enough trouble that he also got help', Quest said.

But this got Quest to think aloud about the difficulties of compartmentalising violence more generally: 'I guess people beat their wives and stuff, I don't know, because they got used to beating *hadjis*, I guess. I don't know; I wasn't one of the guys out there pulling people's fingernails out of their hands, so I really … '

Caroline, surprised, asked, 'Was that done by infantry? I mean, torture?'

'It can be', Quest replied. 'It can be anyone. I'm not gonna say we did worse than anyone else, but I know people who were guilty of it, yes', he affirmed with the nervous laugh. He clarified,

> But I mean this usually didn't happen to people [Iraqis] unless we *knew* that it was them. Unless we busted some dude just obviously doing something, you know? We were not going to just pick people off the street. Or, doing a house raid. I mean, half the time you're in the wrong house, anyways. You know, people realize that, so … Unless there was like beyond a reasonable doubt that this person was, you know, the bad guy, yeah, it usually didn't happen. I've seen seen soldiers pester detainees with fly swatters and stuff. But unless they seriously got busted. Red hands,[21] all the way.

Quest's intention here, to show that tactics involving what could be considered torture or other human rights violations did not happen at random, or often, is at least in part belied by his need to qualify, twice, with the word 'usually'. It is what happened, perhaps not usually but enough that he feels called to account. The fog-of-war indeterminacy clouds interpretation, making summing up his own experiences as 'heroic' such a difficult fit.

The myth of the fallen soldier can feel similarly imposed for soldiers, erasing individual particularities as something they have overcome through their military service and death, and as anthropologist and former service member Andrew Bickford puts it, 'transforming everyday citizens into something more than mere mortals'. Bickford calls heroism 'the balm we use to soothe the suffering of family and friends' left behind, observing that this is a shallow remedy that many 'heroes' and their families reject. At the memorial for Pat Tillman, an Army Ranger and former professional football player killed in action in Afghanistan, as it turned out by friendly fire, politicians and public figures lined up to say, 'Pat, you are home. You are safe.' His brother, Richard Tillman, 'refused that glory, standing up to say this: "He's not with God. He's f- - - - - - dead. He's not religious. So thanks for your thoughts, but he's f- - - - - - dead"'.[22] Not only might the myth not offer comfort, it shrouds in mist the social forces leading less than 1% of the US population to join up and strongly affects how soldiers see and understand their own roles and their experiences in war. Frontline combatants are central to the fallen soldier myth, further obscuring the role of and danger faced by the six-of-seven deployed who provide support in the 'tail' at heavily secured forward operating bases in theatre[23] and those working from air-conditioned, domestic bases. Thus the myth of the soldier as hero, though ostensibly giving us a simple and coherent image of the costs and benefits of war, actually obscures the public grasp of the realities of altered and injured survivors who do not feel heroic.

Listening to soldiers' resistance to being framed as heroes may hold the keys to many cases of combat stress injuries (i.e., PTSD) and suicidality in multiple-deployment situations as a whole. Numerous soldiers have expressed annoyance and anger at being asked by civilians 'Did you kill anyone?' or 'Did you get shot at?' Expectations that one can broach such topics in a facile or casual manner fill soldiers with contempt for civilians' remove from their worlds. Such questions, too, may cleave uncomfortably close to fears of being called 'baby killer' and worse, as Vietnam veterans reported hearing upon their return from war. These aspersions, be they actual or imagined, may intersect with soldiers' difficult memories, their doubts and questions, the things they lose sleep over. They circle not only around what they witnessed, but around what they did or failed to do, and what they were commanded to do, and why.

Protectors versus perpetrators: war and nation-building

The dual nature of the US and its allies' mission in the post-9/11 wars – both to subjugate the enemy but also to rebuild functional civil societies – brings an additional impediment to determining when the use of force is legitimate. David Riches offered an open-ended way to conceptualise violence, calling it the use of force whose legitimacy could be questioned by a (at least hypothetical) witness, and situating it in a performer-victim-witness triangle.[24] But how do the active-duty soldiers we interviewed identify performer, victim and witness? While in theatre, an apt metaphor, soldiers see themselves as performers first and foremost, focused on whatever mission their superior officers have issued. Soldier Wilson Lemmons described military training to us, 'The Army's culture, especially in the infantry, it's like a man's … It's all guys. "Steely-eyed killers", that's who you're supposed to be. Hard as nails. They beat it into your brain that when you go over there you're indestructible. I don't want to say brainwash, but they kind of do it.' Tim Vincent is a solidly built man in his mid-20s who served as a truck driver for an infantry battalion in Afghanistan and is now enrolled in a master's programme in geography paid through the GI Bill. 'When I am in combat, I can't think about pulling the trigger. I am trained to see targets, not people. I cannot have remorse … [the] MOS [Military Occupational Specialty] in 11th Bravo; our primary job is to kill.' While Vincent is particularly direct, other soldiers repeated this message – that hesitation is likely to end in your own or your fellow soldiers' injury or death.

Despite this sanction to use lethal force against an enemy, most of the enlisted soldiers we interviewed saw themselves primarily as protectors rather than perpetrators of Iraqi or Afghan civilians but especially of their fellow soldiers. Bradley Kay reported a conversation he had with a radio operator and gunner: '"I can't wait to go to Afghanistan so I can do my job. I didn't do my job the first time." I asked "What were you? Did you shoot people; did you shoot your weapon?" He was like, "Yeah." I said, "Then you did your job. You protected people. You protected your guys, you're done."' Soldier Scott Roberts' description illustrates the conflation of the purpose of war to injure the enemy with the issue the contest of war is to decide.[25] 'We aren't just going over there and saying, "Bang, you're dead, ha ha." No, we go over there, and we help the culture … At first no one would talk to us, but then we started bringing them blankets, and helping them, giving them money, help them start shops. And then the word spreads, and then you have a population who loves you, and they will help you identify who is shooting at you, who has bombs or weapons.' Many of the soldiers we interviewed talked about the humanitarian side of their work; in part this reflects the particular time and place during the war when this unit was in Iraq (or any of three subsequent Afghanistan tours), in part perhaps a desire not to identify the Iraqis (or Afghans) as victims of US aggression. Brian Turner remarked, 'People back here say we're not doing anything good over there. They just don't know what they're talking about. We had local nationals crying and hugging us. I still talk to five or six guys on the Internet that I became really good friends with over there. It's really cool. I see now the difference that we made.' At later junctures, with setbacks in Afghanistan or the resurgence of fighting in Iraq in 2014, the same highly personalised engagement could generate feelings of despair.

Tim Vincent describes this aspect of the war in Iraq as the necessity to hold, simultaneously, two incompatible perspectives:

Both U.S. and Afghan soldiers are telling their kids the same thing. When an Afghan insurgent who is a father gets up in the morning and puts on his gun and the explosives to plant an IED he doesn't say, 'I'm going out to kill Americans and do evil.' No, he says, 'I'm going to kill American soldiers who are trying to steal our way of life.' He's going out to make a better life for his children just the way we are. Really, nobody's wrong, nobody's right. Regardless, when you are in combat, you must believe that you are in the right. There is no choice of right or wrong – you just must be right to do what you have to do.

The paradox of according *a priori* legitimacy to one's own side's use of force, even while understanding that opponents do the same, suggests inherent instability in balancing the two views.

Quincy Stevenson expressed this as the need to move between different behavioural codes, one for combat and another for civilian life:

It's like a switch. I was over there and had the mindset I needed to get it done, came back here and totally turned it off, came back here and enjoyed myself, had a good time. There's no need to worry about what happened over there, because, you know, it's done, there's no need to worry about it. It hasn't really affected me. Two totally different mindsets, and I'm pretty good at separating, flipping them on and off when they need to be.

Stevenson may be able to turn the switch on and off and leave behind what happened in Iraq, but many others cannot compartmentalise and codeswitch behaviourally with such flexibility.

Which brings us to the third element of Riches' performer-victim-witness triangle of violence: the witness. While in theatre, the soldier's primary witness, aside from the highly vilified press, which most soldiers reject as a valid witness, is the military itself. Military culture supports action, focus on mission, and loyalty to one's fellow soldiers above all else. When action is equivalent to following orders passed down the chain of command, military culture exonerates, in theory, individuals from having to weigh the moral, ethical or functional effects of their actions.

Performers versus witnesses: at home things quickly get more complicated

When soldiers return home, the witnesses to their performance immediately change. In place of battle buddies, officers and support staff, on returning to the US they face witnesses who may not have consented to the contest of war or who may have changed their minds. As military personnel are quick to point out, a mistake civilians make is to assume that all military personnel agree with the war. As soldier Connor Guinness said, 'Civilians are very removed. They only see them [soldiers] out of town, in uniform. They don't see the human being. We may or may not have the same opinions as someone who is anti-war, but they don't see that. They associate the soldier immediately with the larger institution.' Several soldiers, including Chris Stimpert, said that they felt generally supported by the civilian community. 'Everyone in Colorado has been supportive. In Texas in particular, everyone makes the military feel welcome and supported. Some people can be against the war, but still show him respect.' Quincy Stevenson noted, 'Having people that care and appreciate definitely makes us feel better about the stuff we've done ... ' Nonetheless, there is still apprehension about civilian attitudes and responses. Brian Turner observed, 'Most civilians don't really get it; they don't understand. And then they treat guys like crap when they come back.' Or as Tiger Woodsman put it, 'I'll see that anti-war propaganda, and I'll get pretty ticked, but it's their right.' Chris Stimpert had a friend who was doing recruiting in

Washington State – 'the worst place to be a soldier.' And people would spit on him, throw drinks on him. 'I don't know how he didn't, like, kick anyone's ass, like really, really, I would.'

In the context of civilian life, the Geneva Convention and human rights, anyone who is not an official combatant and injured by military personnel is a victim. US civilians opposed to these wars or to wars on principle may point out the number of innocent Iraqi and Afghan civilians, women and children in particular, who have been killed. Soldiers may be distressed by decisions they made which resulted in Iraqi or Afghani civilians being injured or killed, especially when facing their own children. When soldiers spoke of their interactions with Iraqis, they often pointed out how women and children were victims in their own society, thus needing the protection of US military personnel. One soldier told us about Iraqi insurgents opening fire when their wives and children were present and thus knowingly put them in harm's way. A therapist in Colorado Springs who works with many combat veterans told us the story of a soldier manning a checkpoint who, following protocol, shot and killed the driver of a car, an unarmed civilian who would not stop. He was unable to forgive himself for his action. Several soldiers spoke of the rage they felt towards Iraqis when someone in their unit was killed, and journalist David Philipps reports that units often retaliated with a 'death blossom' of gunfire directed at anyone or anything within range.[26]

Dawn Weaver, a psychiatric nurse who treated hundreds of combat veterans at Fort Carson, said that many soldiers have had to kill children, whom insurgents have trained to point weapons at US soldiers to provoke them, 'because they know that Americans will forever be damaged by that'. She adds that not all of soldiers' actions in war are rational, but may arise from the primal brain that has been released in training so that soldiers can kill. One soldier she worked with had beaten his wife, saying 'I can't live with my wife 'cause I don't know that I'm not gonna kill her. I don't know what the fuck happened to me.' Dawn adds that 'And these guys are deeply ashamed of what's going on with them. And when they're not deeply ashamed, it's because their rage has them so poisoned that they're tapped into their rage.' Nor are they always able to unburden themselves. 'And part of the reason that it is so bad is that they will not discuss that with their therapist. Because they don't trust their therapist to respond correctly to that.' For Weaver, the correct response is non-judgemental listening and assessment of whether soldiers can now control their primal, violent urges.

Although the stories of soldiers returning home to accusations of 'baby killer' may be largely mythical,[27] soldiers' fears about how civilians will react to them are not unfounded. Kathleen Dougherty, a professor of psychology who is married to a special forces' veteran, tells of bursting into tears during a presentation about the rape of Iraqi women, wondering if her husband, and she herself, and all of us, were not complicit by association. She also has had a recurring dream of her husband, Kurt, 'being the swamp monster, where he's coming out of the swamp and there's all these fires smoldering out in the distance and smoke and ash and all that and the sky is red and black and I know it's because of him. I know that he was the cause of it all. He set all those fires.' We ask her, as a loving wife, a US citizen and social justice activist, how she deals with these images and thoughts:

The thing is that I refuse to tell a story in which he is fully separate from, or that his multiple deployments are unrelated to, the bigger political picture. The way that I have to resolve that crisis is to assign him exactly no more blame than he merits and no less blame either. It's really easy to say, the Americans have nothing to do with that. They didn't walk in there and hit these people's wives. I can't really tell that story either. But then I also know, it's kind of an *ad nauseum* argument to some extent because if he's to blame then we're all to blame for filling our cars up with oil and everybody who didn't try to get George W. impeached is to blame, then if we're all to blame, then, you know.

Kathleen stopped, her sentence unfinished, saddened and frustrated at her inability to find a way to apportion responsibility that made sense, that she could live with. Both of these women, and others working with veterans we spoke with, emphasised the need for civilians and the nation at large to take responsibility for the actions committed during war.

Volunteers versus victims

The wounds of war raise yet another impediment to viewing soldiers as perpetrators. The veteran who returns from combat with disabling physical wounds yet goes on to succeed in business, politics or in athletic competitions is still a hero, undefeated by the enemy despite great personal sacrifice. But running parallel to wounded heroes are veterans who return with the invisible wounds of PTSD, traumatic brain injury (TBI) or depression.

Military personnel spoke about PTSD in particular, as a medical diagnosis, as some-thing that happened *to* soldiers, not something that they may have brought on through their own actions. Soldiers' roles as protectors were eclipsed as they, too, come to share vic-timhood with the civilians traumatised by living in a war zone. Although therapeutic treat-ments for PTSD do not prevent therapists from helping veterans deal with moral doubts and questions, treatment generally focuses on providing relief from symptoms, and therapists, especially if they are civilians, may not feel entitled to explore those waters. Thus prohibi-tions against broaching issues of remorse, anguish, shame, guilt or anger, particularly as connected to constraints from or violations of Rules of Engagement, or of questions about the legitimacy or necessity of the campaigns overall, appeared enforced through unspoken rules. It appeared as if a tacit consensus obtained that confronting events in their contextual and intrinsically political aspects could only serve as salt in wounds of com-batants who were already, in important senses, themselves victims of the campaigns.[28] In our efforts to forge relationships of confidence and trust with soldiers, their families and those in the service and treatment community that work with them, we did not typically raise the topic of what soldiers had done in theatre directly, although a number of post-deployment active-duty soldiers did provide details in response to various questions we asked them. It is just these questions of individual and collective agency in the use of vio-lence in war that haunt veterans and contribute to the chronicity of PTSD, as Young, Bracken, Tick, Finley, and others have also noted.[29] While we expect far greater attention to the issue in years to come, we have perceived it still to be too soon, for many of those in military communities, for it to be taken up directly, particularly with service members who were still deploying, and for whom the spiritual and moral injuries were still fresh.

Soldiers' resistance to the diagnosis and wariness about engaging civilians in dialogue about war experiences show that there are limits to a trauma framework in aiding veterans with their reintegration into civilian life. A diagnosis of PTSD offers soldiers compensation, disability benefits, access to a host of services, and a widely accepted label for what troubles them. So we were surprised at how often and how vehemently many active-duty soldiers resisted PTSD as a legitimate cause of suffering. The diagnosis of PTSD marked a soldier as a victim: weak, abnormal, and violating the highly masculinised military code of toughness, readiness for action, aggression, camaraderie and attention to mission above all else. As a consequence, having PTSD could be a source of stigma, shame and often roused suspicion that a soldier was faking symptoms to get out of the military.

It is while attempting reintegration, where past confronts present and combatants face the civilians they purport to serve, that soldiers are most likely to confront their simultaneous ties to both victim-hood and perpetrator-hood. Soldiers fend off identification as perpetrators by subscribing to nationalistic notions of 'fighting for our freedoms', securitisation (security building through increased legitimisation of force[30]), humanitarian intervention and promoting economic and social development, but these ideas may compete with concomitant feelings of disillusion, anger and shame.[31] For this reason, we argue, PTSD acts as a screen onto which subjects project the conflicts and distress created by reentry. To some extent PTSD lets soldiers and civilian society alike 'off the hook' – allowing non-military citizens to believe and act as if they live outside of the web of a nation at war and are not complicit in the actions of individual veterans. PTSD provided legitimate recognition of the suffering of Vietnam veterans and explained their struggles with reintegration into civilian life. Thus, it marked the 'end of suspicion' that soldiers experiencing psychological distress from combat were malingering cowards who wanted to escape combat. But by casting veterans as victims, in particular victims of a state that sent them to an unpopular and highly contested war, PTSD contributed to making the nation shy of judging or assessing the moral actions of soldiers and the nation, of censuring and silencing public and private conversations that reckon the costs of war.

Compounding the hardships of combat, the conditions of the post-9/11 wars placed many recruits in positions of hardship not faced by previous generations of soldiers. The Department of Defense created the AVF during a time of relative peace[32] when the US military 'downsized, outsourced, and privatized'.[33] But when the quick victory of overcoming Hussein's forces in Iraq or the Taliban in Afghanistan led to protracted, violent conflicts, the AVF faced shortages of manpower, leading to repeated tours of unprecedented number.[34] Maintaining the needed numbers of troops in combat has also meant that the rotation of deployments accelerated, while dwell time (time at home in between deployments) shrank accordingly.

The recent scandal about the Veterans Administration's cover-up of months-long wait times and inadequate services to veterans dramatically shows how the victim-hood of the soldiers is arguably *under*stated. As we go to press, lines between victims and perpetrators twist and bleed together with cruel irony. A recent newspaper column reveals that the Veterans Administration has 'patient record flags (PRFs)' to monitor those with 'difficult', 'annoying' or 'noncompliant behavior'. Offenses include venting frustration about VA services and/or wait times', complaints or threatening lawsuits, or excessive visits or calls to VA staff. 'Disruptive Behavior Committees' are secret panels which can then restrict veterans' right of access to care without prior notice. Veterans may be flagged for being 'too expensive', or 'trouble-makers' who pursue their rights too assertively. And the Department of Homeland Security provides the 'muscle to deter sick vets from protesting in front of VA hospitals'.[35]

That battle turns upon our own would-be champions, metaphorically, is not a new insight. Veterans have to battle for benefits, as Monahan and Connolly's 2010 title, *The Battle for Veteran's Benefits*, shows.[36] And when benefits are inaccessible or denied, neglect itself can be reconfigured as battle: Aaron Glantz called his 2009 book *The War Comes Home: Washington's Battle against America's Veterans*.[37] But the battle metaphors go much further: the pre-deployment 'Battlemind™' trainings combine meditation and visualisation with body-based techniques of relieving battle stress. Families of deploying service members consult *Battlebook IV* to weather their own enlistments at home, and social workers speak of 'deploying' here at home, performing counselling 'surges' on returning brigades and call their fellow social workers 'battle buddies'. Why should it be surprising, then, when our Veterans Administration facilities identify and manage threats through the primary, profoundly militarised, paradigm they know, war?

Today's soldiers are volunteers, a designation so underwritten by notions of agency it becomes difficult to reconcile with also being, in some sense, victims. If they have PTSD it is because they willingly exposed themselves to trauma and violence. If they endured multiple deployments it was part of the job they took on. If they violate codes of military conduct and rules of engagement, they may be prosecuted in courts-martial. On a personal level, they may judge their actions by cultural or religious moral codes whose prohibition against the use of violence and killing one's fellow human beings may conflict with the state's authority and may be significant sources of distress and suffering when soldiers return from combat. Though they volunteered, many recruits are arguably economic draftees, enlisting to obtain a college degree, find full employment with benefits, or escape small rural towns with limited opportunities. Volunteering bleeds into victimhood, heroism blurs with perpetration, and war comes home – are these twists not inevitable?

Volunteers-made-victims versus *victims*

As we have stated, the domestic settings of our fieldwork are largely marked by silence around American implication in human rights violations in Iraq and Afghanistan. They afford only partial, fragmented views of soldiers' struggles with deeds and events in which they may have figured, at least in part, as perpetrators. To explore this theme further, then, we turn to an account by journalist Dexter Filkins, which appeared in the September 2012 issue of the *New Yorker*.[38] This case invites us to ponder how veterans-as-victims relate to other categories of victims of war – in this case, a family of Iraqi civilians innocent of the fact that they would barrel through a US Marine checkpoint.

Marine Lu Lobello posted a video via Facebook to a young Iraqi woman named Nora Kachadoorian, in which he explained that his unit crossed paths with her family on 8 April 2003. 'I have been trying to learn what happened that day, I think, since that day ended.' His unit had killed her father, brother and a baby nephew on a fateful day outside Baghdad. The family was almost home after evacuating, and had no idea as they roared past a checkpoint and into an intersection the Marines were trying to hold that, from the unit's perspective, they were likely suicide bombers, leaving them little choice but to open fire. Nora's ethnic Armenian and Christian mother, Margaret, had held up her baby grandchild's body by his bloody foot, imploring through her tears, 'We are the peace people; why did you kill us?'

On the Facebook video, Lobello said to Nora, 'Lots of people I was with that day, they don't do too good sometimes.' Later, he cried, then composed himself, saying, 'I'm so sorry for your loss. I just think that talking to you guys will help me out so much. I know it seems really selfish. I hope it helps you, too, but really I can't – I can't go on not trying to say hello to you.'

A week after Lobello posted the video, Nora Kachadoorian wrote back: 'Me and my mother we both forgive you, we know we will see them in the kingdom of Jesus', then quoted from the Bible, 'Do not marvel at this, because the hour is coming in which all those who are in the memorial tombs will hear his voice and come out.' Lobello's initial relief at receiving the message eroded as he realised she had left off the second part of the verse, which consigned 'those who committed the evil deeds to a resurrection of judgment'.[39]

Lobello had been searching for articles 'memorializing Fox Company's deeds' and found one Filkins had written on the Kachadoorians. 'What was so weird is that it wasn't about us. It was about them – the Iraqis. It just kind of hit me. Oh, my God, these are the people we killed.' As he set about trying to contact the surviving Kachadoorians, Lobello also wrote Filkins, wanting to enlist the journalist's aid. 'I think it would ease my PTSD', he wrote. This was in the wake of Lobello's Other-than-Honorable discharge after positive drug tests, followed by his denouncing his commanders and leaving base without permission. He had eventually received help from the Veterans Administration only by lying down on the floor and refusing to leave.[40]

Filkins helped arrange a meeting; Nora, now married with children, had immigrated to the US with her mother and was living near Los Angeles. Nora's mother, Margaret, showed Christian compassion and forgiveness for Lobello's suffering, but also underlined her own: they shared about their mutual sleeplessness and depression, and when Lobello cried, she said 'I cannot cry. My eyes have no tears left.' Though Lobello had said he was 'sorry for your loss' on the video, he wanted to be clear he was not there to apologise for his actions, that they had had no choice but to shoot.[41]

'There is not a day or a week that goes by that I don't think about what we went through', Lobello said. Filkins wrote, 'He seemed to be positing a kind of equivalence between him[self] and his victims. If this was self-serving, there was also an undeniable truth to it: of all the people in the world, no one else could better understand what had happened.'[42]

Here we arrive at the crux of Lobello's search for what Filkins calls both 'absolution' and 'atonement'. Both combatants and civilians caught in crossfire may indeed be victims, of intrinsically inextricable sorts. Yet only when veterans-as-victims face innocent-civilian-victims – whose representation is so conspicuously absent from the domestic discourse that constructs veterans with PTSD as victims – can we grasp both the parallels and their stark limits. For there are striking differences between the suffering of a voluntary combatant, an active agent and performer of violence, and those who stumble into its path in comparative innocence. In this example, which does not even involve a human rights violation proper but circumstances that force service members' hands, it is the performer of 'legitimised' force-gone-wrong, become violence,[43] who seeks atonement, not the recipient-victims. The moral wound needing balm is arguably caused by the performer's internal witness. And just as violence and legitimate force have a way of bleeding together, so do protectors and perpetrators, volunteers and victims, in dizzying spirals of variability, contrasts and contradictions. It is in this context, we argue, that critical differences between veterans' victimhood and suffering and those shouldered by victim recipients are thrown into relief. Pain and suffering may be shared, but they are not equivalent. To understand veterans plagued by PTSD, depression and suicidality, we must factor in how their role as victims is shaped by their earlier roles as volunteers, sometime heroes, sometime victims, and, for too many, in key, fateful moments, as occasional perpetrators of acts that rest on their own consciences as 'wrong'.

Conclusion

In this article we argue that our collective abilities to identify, face and share responsibility for acts of human rights violations or other war crimes are grievously constrained. Impediments to this process include our sanitising frameworks for contemporary war itself, our post-Vietnam fear of wrongly blaming veterans, our individually based medicalisation of deployment-based trauma, and the volunteerist ethic that insists upon individual choice and agency even while submitting to a chain of command or economic necessity. PTSD in particular, as a diagnosis-turned-framework for public discourse, evacuates crucial context and moral content from the excombatant's psychic anguish, particularly if it becomes a collective historical narrative and not just a tool for tending to individual suffering. Exclusive attention to the individual soldier's prolonged exposure to mortal danger, injury and death, while ignoring the broader contexts and the acute loss and suffering exacted from innumerable souls in these conflicts' 'host' countries, inhibits the collective reckoning and resultant learning that can follow in war's wake. Lost too is any conscious consideration of moral hazard (that soldiers might be one decision or action away from depriving non-combatants of life or wholeness) or of the collective, inherently and inescapably political nature of war itself. The moral consequences of war, based in individual and collective actions, cannot be solved through more and better treatments for PTSD and TBI.[44] While the post-9/11 campaigns have been fully engaged, US civilians have been actively enjoined in larger, tacit contracts of silence as they interact with active-duty military and veterans. The US withdrawal from Afghanistan at the same time that Iraq re-erupts into civil war compels us to move beyond these coping mechanisms of silence.

We open this article with a soldier stating that if there is moral blame to be apportioned for US violence in Iraq, he and his brethren were there to shoulder that. Such a clean 'resolution' seems yet another attempt to enjoin the civilians in a compact not to talk about, or to shoulder, responsibility more collectively. That said, our findings also suggest that the soldiers are within limits willing to talk, particularly when accorded the means to mitigate the gravest threats of such interactions by naming areas of inquiry off limits – something we have heard called 'controlling the environment'.

Funding

This work was supported by the National Endowment for the Humanities Exploring the Human Endeavor [grant number RZ 51459-12]; Social Science Division, Research and Developmental Grant, Colorado College; Jackson Fellowship, Southwest Studies, Colorado College; Cultural Attractions Program, Colorado College; Southwest Summer Community-Based Research Internships, Colorado College, Summer Faculty-Student Collaborative Internship, Venture Grant Program, Colorado College; Graduate Research Assistantship, Health and Behavioral Sciences Program, University of Colorado Denver.

Disclosure statement

No potential conflict of interest was reported by the authors.

Notes

1. 'Victim/volunteer' borrows from Christine Lavin's song title, http://www.christinelavin.com/index.php?page=songs&category=Attainable_Love&display=281.

2. We use 'veteran' inclusively, as applied to any service member who has served in theatre for at least one day, thus including both active-duty and former military.

3. Active-duty soldiers who participated in our initial set of interviews chose their own pseudonyms. We assigned other participants in the project pseudonyms unless they expressly asked to be identified by their real names, and we assigned pseudonyms to some organisations to protect individual participants' privacy. Colorado College's Internal Review Board approved the study.

4. David Philipps, *Lethal Warriors: When the New Band of Brothers Came Home* (New York: Palgrave Macmillan, 2010).

5. 'Soldier/s' frequently appear as including active-duty members from non-army branches in this article, for ease of speech, following a broad convention but one rarely used within military circles.

6. David Riches, 'The Phenomenon of Violence', in *The Anthropology of Violence*, ed. David Riches (Oxford and New York: Blackwell, 1986), 1–27.

7. Douglas L. Kriner and Francis X. Shen, *The Casualty Gap: The Causes and Consequences of American Wartime Inequalities* (New York: Oxford University Press, 2010).

8. Didier Fassin and Richard Rechtman, *The Empire of Trauma: An Inquiry into the Condition of Victimhood*, trans. Rachel Gomme (Princeton, NJ and Oxford: Princeton University Press, 2009).

9. Sarah Hautzinger and Jean Scandlyn, *Beyond Post-Traumatic Stress: Homefront Struggles with the Wars on Terror* (Walnut Creek, CA: Left Coast Press, 2014).

10. Bernard Rostker, *I Want You!: The Evolution of the All-Volunteer Force* (Santa Monica, CA: The Rand Corporation, 2006); Mark F. Cancian, 'The All-Volunteer Force: After 10 Years of War, It's Time to Gather Lessons', *Armed Forces Journal* (2010), http://www.armedforcesjournal.com/2011/10/7691489; Glen H. Elder, Lin Wang, Naomi J. Spence, Daniel E. Adkins, and Tyson H. Brown, 'Pathways to the All-Volunteer Military', *Social Science Quarterly* 91, no. 2 (2010): 455–75. Reliance on National Guard and Reservist forces have also exceeded any other wars. These units make up 28% of the service members deployed to Iraq and Afghanistan with 37% deploying more than once (http://hiddensurge.nationalsecurityzone.org/nsjihs_special_pages/changing-of-the-guard/). Outsourcing much of the work performed in support of military campaigns to the private contractors is also at an all-time high: At the height of the Iraq war in 2007, for example, contractors in Iraq were counted at over 160,000, outnumbering the uniformed troops in-country, despite strong arguments that overreliance on private sector services undermines strategic goals and the legitimacy of that campaign (P.W. Singer, 'Can't Win With 'Em, Can't Go to War Without 'Em: Private Military Contractors and Counterinsurgency', *Foreign Policy at Brookings*. Policy Paper No. 4 (September 2007): iii–21, http://www.pwsinger.com/pdf/FPS_paper_4_revise.pdfSinger; cf. Deborah Avant, 'Mercenaries', *Foreign Policy* 143 (2004): 20–2, 24, 26, 28).

11. 'Allies' has different implications for the two wars: the 19 March 2003 invasion of Afghanistan was led by North Atlantic Treaty Alliance forces, while that of Iraq was by a 48-member Multi-National Force to which Great Britain, Australia and Poland contributed troops and other countries later supplied with support troops post-invasion.

12. http://en.allexperts.com/q/Military-Policy-Weapons-346/2009/9/Support-Troop-Combat-Troop.htm. See also J. Collicutt McGrath, *Ethical Practice in Brain Injury Rehabilitation* (Oxford: Oxford University Press, 2007); Kirsten Holmstedt, *Band of Sisters: American Women at War in Iraq* (Mechanicsburg, PA: Stackpole Books, 2007). The ban on women in frontline combatant roles was lifted in January 2013, in recognition that women were already serving, de facto, in such roles (Tom Vanden Brook, 'Pentagon Makes Women in Combat Rule Change Official', *USA Today*, 24 January 2013, http://www.usatoday.com/story/news/nation/2013/01/24/women-combat-change-panetta/1861995/Vanden).

13. As of May 2011; http://www.infoplease.com/ipa/A0004615.html. Sources: Department of Defense and Veterans Administration.

14. Edward J. Villacres and Christopher Bassford, 'Reclaiming the Clausewitzian Trinity', *Parameters* 25, no. 3 (1995): 9–19, 2–3.

15. Gwynne Dyer, *War* (New York: Crown Publishers, Inc., 1985), xi.

16. Max Weber, 'Politics as a Vocation', in *From Max Weber: Essays in Sociology*, ed. H. H. Gerth and C. Wright Mills (Abingdon, Oxon: Routledge Sociology Classics, 1991[1984]), 77–128.

17. Christopher Greenwood, 'International Law and the Conduct of Military Operations: Stocktaking at the Start of New Millennium', in *International Law across the Spectrum of Conflict:*

Essays in Honor of Professor L. C. Green on the Occasion of His Eightieth Birthday, ed. Michael N. Schmitt, *International Law Studies*, Volume 75 (Newport, RI: Naval War College, 2000), 180. The two major exceptions were the right to defend oneself, individually or collectively, from armed attack and the use of force when the United Nations (UN) Security Council sanctions such action under its Charter.

18. Kevin Jon Heller, *The Nuremberg Military Tribunals and the Origins of International Criminal Law* (Oxford: Oxford University Press, 2011), 3.
19. Non-combatants include civilians and non-military humanitarian workers, wounded and sick soldiers, and prisoners of war.
20. Gutmann and Lutz share a similar reaction by a former soldier: 'You have no idea what you're thanking me for. You don't know what I did' (Matthew Gutmann and Catherine Lutz, *Breaking Ranks: Iraq Veterans Speak Out Against the War* (Berkeley: University of California, 2010), 145.
21. As in, only those caught 'red handed', in the act of committing counterinsurgent acts, would be subjected to torture.
22. Andrew Bickford, 'Shadow Elite: Pat Tillman & Why Soldier Hero Worship Serves the Powerful … Not the Soldiers', *Huffington Post The Blog*, 30 September 2010, http://www.huffingtonpost.com/andrew-bickford/emshadow-eliteem-pat-till_b_744890.html?view=screen.
23. Referred to derogatorily as 'fobbits'; see also David Abrams' novel, *Fobbit* (David Abrams, *Fobbit* (New York: Black Cat, 2012)).
24. Riches, 'The Phenomenon of Violence'. See also Pamela Stewart and Andrew Strathern, *Violence: Theory and Ethnography* (London and New York: Continuum, 2002); Sverker Finnström, '"Today He Is No More": Magic, Intervention, and Global war in Uganda', in *Virtual War and Magical Death: Technologies and Imaginaries for Terror and Killing*, ed. Neil Whitehead and Sverker Finnström (Durham, NC: Duke University Press, 2013), 111–31.
25. Elaine Scarry, *The Body in Pain: The Making and Unmaking of the World* (New York: Oxford, 1985), 152.
26. Philipps, *Lethal Warriors*, 68.
27. Jerry Lembcke, *The Spitting Image: Myth, Memory, and the Legacy of Vietnam* (New York: New York University Press, 1998); Jerry Lembcke, *PTSD: Diagnosis and Identity in Postempire America* (Lanham, MD: Lexington Books, 2013).
28. Hautzinger and Scandlyn, *Beyond Post-Traumatic Stress*, 247–56.
29. Allan Young, *The Harmony of Illusions: Inventing Post-Traumatic Stress Disorder* (Princeton, NJ: Princeton University Press, 1995); Patrick Bracken, *Trauma: Culture, Meaning and Philosophy* (London and Philadelphia: Whurr Publishers, 2002); Edward Tick, *War and the Soul: Healing Our Nation's Veterans from Post-Traumatic Stress Disorder* (Wheaton, IL: Quest Books, 2005); Erin P. Finley, *Fields of Combat: Understanding PTSD among Veterans of Iraq and Afghanistan* (Ithaca, NY: Cornell University Press, 2011).
30. Bernazzoli and Flint (Richelle M. Bernazzoli and Colin Flint, 'From Militarization to Securitization: Finding a Concept that Works', *Political Geography* 28, no. 8 (2009): 449–50) build on Enloe's (Cynthia Enloe, *Globalization and Militarism: Feminists Make the Link* (Lanham, MD: Rowan and Littlefield, 2007)) depictions of 'militarizarization', but favour 'securitization' for its emphasis on military-civil society relationships and the extension of legitimised force into non-state (e.g. corporate or militia) hands. Human security theory, by contrast, reminds us of numerous non-violent forms of security creation (Enloe, *Globalization and Militarism*; Sakiko Fakuda-Parr and Carol Messineo, 'Human Security', in *Elgar Companion to Civil War and Fragile States*, ed. Graham Brown and Arnim Langer (Northampton, MA: Edward Elgar Publishing, 2012); S. Neil MacFarlane and Yuen Foong Khong, *Human Security and the UN: A Critical History* (Bloomington, IN: Indiana University Press, 2006)).
31. Ashwin Budden, 'The Role of Shame in Posttraumatic Stress Disorder: A Proposal for a Socio-Emotional Model for DSM-V', *Social Science & Medicine* 69 (2009): 1032–9.
32. Catherine Lutz argues that the era between the end of the Cold War and the post-9/11 wars was not one of peace, but instead one of 'Hot Peace: training other people's armies and police, drug interdiction, hurricane relief, hostage rescue, the quelling of civil disorder, and what it called nation-building assistance' (Catherine Lutz, *Homefront: A Military City and the American 20th Century* (Boston, MA: Beacon Press, 2001)).
33. Ibid.
34. Paul Yingling, 'Breaking Ranks?' *Small Wars Journal* (2010), http://smallwarsjournal.com/jrnl/art/breaking-ranks.

35. Michelle Malkin, 'Exposed: How the VA Red-Flags "Disruptive" Vets' (2014), http://michellemalkin.com/2014/06/25/exposed-how-the-va-red-flags-disruptive-vets/.
36. K. David Monahan and Alex Connolly, *The Battle for Veteran's Benefits* (Bloomington IN: Xlibris Corporation, 2010).
37. Aaron Glantz, *The War Comes Home: Washington's Battle against America's Veterans* (Berkeley: University of California Press, 2009).
38. Dexter Filkins, 'Atonement: A Troubled Iraq Veteran Seek Out the Family He Harmed', *The New Yorker*, 29 October and 5 November 2012, 92–103.
39. Ibid., 98b.
40. Ibid., 96–7.
41. Ibid., 102.
42. Ibid.
43. Kelman and Hamilton refer to instances of this sort as crimes of obedience. Herbert C. Kelman and V. Lee Hamilton, *Crimes of Obedience: Toward a Social Psychology of Authority and Responsibility* (New Haven, CT: Yale University Press, 1989).
44. Recent advances in the treatment of PTSD yield hope that its symptoms can be effectively alleviated (Finley, *Fields of Combat*).

War propaganda, war crimes, and post-conflict justice in Serbia: an ethnographic account

Jordan Kiper

Anthropology, University of Connecticut, USA

Recent international criminal trials of incitement have brought about a novel precedent for prosecuting war propagandists that not only moves incitement from being inchoate to causally proven but also neglects the voices of perpetrators. Following recent ethnographic research in Rwanda, this article examines the new precedent and suggests that incitement should return to being inchoate. The discussion centres on interview data collected among Serbian veterans of the Yugoslav Wars about the degree to which wartime media motivated them during the breakup of Yugoslavia and interview data collected among Serbian prosecutors about the alleged influence of Serbian wartime media. Serbian veterans report that they were not motivated by wartime media but rather former conflicts, peer-to-peer stories on the frontline and evident threats to Serbs. Moreover, prosecutors' assumptions about the influence of war propaganda and the unwillingness to interview 'perpetrators' about their motivations illuminate the complexities of post-conflict justice in Serbia.

Introduction

While carrying out fieldwork and conducting interviews with Serb veterans of the Yugoslav Wars (1991–1995, 1998–1999) in Belgrade, Serbia, I was struck by how different veterans' accounts of war propaganda were from those of human rights lawyers. The former charac-terised war propaganda as 'wartime media' that, in the Serbian case, was more or less a byproduct of already occurring violence and hardly influential on combatants. Lawyers, on the other hand, are nowadays prone to argue that war propaganda causes collective vio-lence (ethnic cleansing, mass rape, massacres, or genocide), especially in environments where there is an impoverished marketplace of ideas, economically depressed population or history of ethnic conflict.[1] According to Richard Wilson, this outlook reflects an emer-ging trend in recent speech-crimes trials at the International Criminal Tribunal for Yugosla-via (ICTY) and the International Criminal Tribunal for Rwanda (ICTR).[2] In those trials several journalists, politicians and media figures have been prosecuted for disseminating hate-media and causing collective violence.[3] Yet these cases, and the respective legal outlook they inspire, unblushingly presume that there is a direct link between the illocutions of war propaganda and its perlocutionary force on perpetrators.[4] This article draws from interviews with Serbian military personnel of the Yugoslav Wars to shed light on their motivations for participating in war and, to some degree, the cultural structuring of violence, which challenge recent legal theoretical notions of war propaganda.

To illustrate, the ICTY judges maintained that Ferdinand Nahimana, the owner of the notorious Hutu 'hate radio' or Radio Television Libre des Mille Collines (RTLM), 'caused the deaths of thousands of innocent civilians'.[5] Despite this assertion, Hutu perpetrators told a different story: ethnographers Charles Mironko and Scott Straus interviewed hundreds of confessed genocidaires and found that most perpetrators neither listened to RTLM nor reported being influenced by it. Most were instead guided by fellow soldiers or peers whose rhetoric about the duty to support one another, even in the reluctant practice of killing, made participation in genocide obligatory.[6] Such ethnographic results are not only externally valid but also corroborated by other perpetrator studies that deemphasise the significance of war propaganda but stress the importance of peer-to-peer influence on acts of collective violence.[7]

In my own fieldwork, I am gathering similar accounts from Serbian veterans who participated in notorious military campaigns during the Yugoslav Wars, including sieges at Vukovar, Sarajevo and Kosovo. Most veterans claim that they were willing to engage in violence to defend Serbia before the dissolution of Yugoslavia, and thus before the onset of alleged Serbian war propaganda.[8] As soldiers they strove to emulate historical Serbian warriors who defended Serbia from Ustaši, Turks and Albanians. They also stressed that wartime media coming out of Belgrade meant little to them, but stories coming from fellow soldiers meant a great deal. One veteran told me, for example, that he relinquished his non-combatant role for a combative one at the Battle of Vukovar after hearing stories from soldiers that Croatian physicians were scavenging Serbian corpses and harvesting their organs for profits. Such stories, which seem incredible to outsiders, were nonetheless credible for combatants. This can be attributed to several wartime factors, but Serb veterans today provide their own explanations. They claim to have believed frontline stories because they were circulated among soldiers, never denied by military leaders, and, most remarkably, reported to journalists who then reported them as facts to wider audiences. Quite literally, then, veterans' accounts suggest that the presumed relationship between war propaganda and collective violence held by lawyers may be backwards. In the Serbian case, war propaganda did not motivate collective violence but rather the two shared a cyclical relationship that was not linear, as recent speech-crime trials purport.

In bringing these issues to light, this article aims at reconsidering the notion of culpability in international criminal law as it concerns the assumed effects of wartime media and the alleged – but oftentimes neglected – motivations of perpetrators when considering those effects. By drawing from interviews with Serb veterans, I will suggest that the outlook inspired by recent cases of incitement in international criminal law is questionable and incomplete without the voices of so-called perpetrators who were allegedly motivated by war propaganda. In the end, I suggest that incitement should remain an inchoate crime proven by the intent of the war propagandists and not by the effects of his or her propaganda. I also draw from interviews to show that the accounts of Serb veterans and human rights lawyers vary in terms of the Yugoslav Wars and post-conflict justice in Serbia, which highlight the cultural repercussions of the legal precedent in question.

It should be stressed at the outset that my goal is not to absolve perpetrators of criminal responsibility. I wish to illustrate instead the significance of multiple viewpoints, especially those of combatants from notorious wars, when dealing with issues of culpability, perpetrator behaviour and democratic life in post-conflict regions such as Serbia. Furthermore, while such in-depth interviews provide reliability, they can neither confirm nor reject the hypothesis that war propaganda causes violence. Rather, my interviews with Serb veterans show the importance of former combatants' views and that without them the legal narrative on war propaganda in international law is insufficient.

Incitement, war propaganda and international law

An inclusive account of war propaganda could never be constructed solely in terms of legal theory. But the very issue of war propaganda at issue here is rooted in the legal history of culpability as it relates to incitement in international criminal law. War propaganda that falls within the set of incitement is defined as any message (proximate to the conflict in question) that directly and deliberately attempts to bring about violence against another group as such, regardless of outcome.[9] War propaganda is thus prosecutable as incitement whenever it is a persecutory message with the intention of shaping perceptions, manipulating cognition and directing behaviour towards collective violence.[10] The key here is the intentionality of the propagandist and the persecutory nature of incitement: if the war propagandist publically and directly calls for collective violence, he or she signifies his or her intention to incite such violence and is thus guilty of doing so, whether collective violence ensues or not.[11]

For example, in *J.R.T. & W.G. Party* v. *Canada* (1983) the United Nations Human Rights committee (UNHRC) upheld the conviction of a man known only as Mr T., accused of leaving anti-Semitic messages on people's answering machines throughout Canada. According to the UNHRC, Mr T. was guilty of incitement not because his messages resulted in violence but rather he made direct calls for violence that deliberately exposed others to hatred and contempt for Jews.[12] Juxtaposing this case with another, the international military tribunal at Nuremburg (IMT) acquitted the Nazi war propagandist Hans Fritzsche of incitement because his 'war propaganda' was nothing more than a set of war reports. In fact, those reports appeared to lack any purpose on the part of Fritzsche, who reported what his superiors, such as Goebbels, demanded of him.[13]

Contrary to Fritzsche, the IMT convicted Julius Streicher – whose case thereafter served as the legal precedent for incitement until the ICTR. Streicher was found guilty of using his anti-Semitic newspaper *Der Stürmer* to make 'frequent, public and direct' calls for the eradication of Jews; Streicher's associates testified that he continued making calls for extermination even after he learned about the realities of the Holocaust, thus underscoring his intent.[14] The IMT convicted Streicher of incitement on the grounds that his incessant calls for collective violence reflected a genocidal intent, regardless of his causing genocidal acts.[15] Incitement under the *Streicher* precedent made persecutory war propaganda an inchoate offence in international law, meaning that the *mens rea* was not the effects of the message but rather the intention of the propagandist.[16]

The *Streicher* precedent was nevertheless overturned by the ICTR, where several Hutu war propagandists were convicted of intending *and* causing collective violence. The turning point came with Jean-Paul Akayesu, a Hutu politician who was convicted for his anti-Tutsi speeches at Taba, a commune where Tutsis were later massacred.[17] Remarkably, Akayesu was not accused of motivating the subsequent massacre – a trope that would have echoed legal liability in negligence cases, whereby the accused is found guilty based on a counterfactual ('but-for') argument or NESS test.[18] Rather, the judges took it upon themselves to prove that Akayesu actually caused the massacre, telling the prosecution: 'there must be proof of a possible causal-link [between Akayesu's speeches and subsequent violence]'.[19] Not surprisingly the prosecution argued that a causal link was evident in so far as Akayesu called for massacres and a massacre eventually took place.[20]

Talk of causation in the *Akayesu* case redefined war propaganda as incitement, changing it from an inchoate offence to a causally proven crime, which was then written into legal precedence by several immediate cases.[21] The most important of which was the so-called 'Media Trial' in which Ferdinand Nahimana and Jean-Bosco Barayagwisa, the co-founders of RTLM, and Hassan Ngeze, a Rwandan journalist, were collectively charged. Despite never wielding a weapon, these war propagandists were found guilty of 'causing the deaths of thousands of Tutsis' through their hate-media and inflammatory remarks.[22] In relying on the *Akayesu* precedent, the Media Trial made legal history: instead of being an inchoate offence proven by intent, war propaganda that incites violence became a causal offence proven by effect.

This has important consequences for Serbian war propagandists. This is due to the fact that the ICTY has brought charges against Radoslav Brđanin, Radovan Karadžič, and Vojislav Šešelj using the *Akayesu* precedent. In the case of Brđanin, it was claimed that ethnic cleansings in northern Serbia were linked to his war propaganda and would not have transpired without it.[23] The tribunal has likewise claimed that Karadžič's war propaganda, including his war poetry, caused Bosnian Serbs to participate in a joint criminal enterprise that resulted in ethnic cleansing and genocide.[24] In the Šešelj case, too, the tribunal has maintained that his political rhetoric about a 'Greater Serbia' caused paramilitary units to commit war crimes in Serbia's Krajnia region.[25] Because the ICTY is closing its doors in 2015, the Serbian Prosecutor's Office of War Crimes (SPWC) in Belgrade is inheriting the remaining trials of war propagandists, along with the *Akayesu* precedent and its notion of culpability. The SPWC has recently used 'Akayesu' to launch a criminal investigation of former Serbian journalists who allegedly propagated inflammatory news reports during the Yugoslav Wars.[26]

While international law tends to operate in its own sphere of logic, social scientists and media scholars argue that the *Akayesu* precedent is problematic on several fronts. First, because international courts have neither defined what 'causation' is nor how to prove it forensically, it is difficult to pinpoint what is meant by the term.[27] Second, judges have been rather easily persuaded by what Nenad Fiser calls 'top-down' arguments that tend to overgeneralise causation rather than 'bottom-up' arguments that demonstrate a link between perpetrators and war propagandists.[28] Third, lawyers have presumed a linear notion of causation and shared culpability, such that war propagandists directly cause perpetrators to engage in collective violence, making them equal participants in a joint criminal enterprise.[29]

To avoid the many pitfalls of 'causation', my focus here will be on perpetrator motivation since, regardless of what international courts mean by the term, causation in municipal criminal law tends to imply that the perpetrator was at least partially motivated by the accused instigator. With that said, my in-depth interviews with former combatants cannot affirm or disconfirm a valid connection between war propaganda and collective violence. For war propaganda often operates below the conscious awareness of individuals; changes social environments and not the motives of isolated individuals; and cannot thoroughly be assessed post hoc. However, like other ethnographers working in post-conflict regions I am alarmed by the legal narrative on incitement being built on the exclusion of perpetrator voices. As I show in the next section, interviews with perpetrators reveal surprising motivations for participating in collective violence and thus expose the incompleteness of the *Akayesu* precedent without incorporating perpetrator views.

Ethnographic challenges to the *Akayesu* precedent

After the Rwandan Genocide, expert witnesses and regional specialists testified at the ICTR that Hutu media was an influential factor in the genocide, causing machete-wielding genocidaires to kill Tutsis en masse.[30] Such motivation was presumably evident in the fact that war propagandists called for mass murder and genocidaires enthusiastically responded.[31] However, when this 'top-down' line of argumentation became the touchstone for several convictions, such as Akayesu's, media scholars interjected. Richard Carver, for instance, worried that the ICTR was proceeding negligently. Albeit justified in convicting war propagandists, it neglected perpetrator views – the so-called puppets of the propagandists were excluded from telling their side of the story – and courts adopted a faulty account of causation, namely that wherever war propaganda preceded collective violence, the former caused the latter.[32] However, post hoc reasoning of this kind is of course fallacious and begs the question of what motivated perpetrators.[33] Spurred by such criticisms, four ethnographers undertook research among confessed perpetrators in Rwanda after the ICTY. Their shared goal was to gather perpetrator self-reports and to determine whether war propaganda, in fact, motivated their participation in collective violence and, if so, to what degree.

The first was Darryl Li who conducted hundreds of open-ended interviews with both Hutu perpetrators and bystanders.[34] Based on self-reports, Li found that war propagandists manipulated three aspects of Hutu culture to motivate Hutus: valuing service to others, performing for the state and honouring in-group relationships.[35] Because Hutus value serving one another and working for the state, war propagandists framed attacks on Tutsis as state 'service'. The killings were also characterised as difficult yet necessary 'work' for the good of Hutus. Friends and families were likewise called upon to 'serve one another' and 'work together' to rid Rwanda of its 'pests' and to usher in its long-awaited peace. And because Hutus admitted to trusting RTLM, one of the few media resources in Rwanda, they believed its reports about imminent Tutsi threats and participated in the killings, trusting it was the right thing to do. For Li, then, the ICTR's judgments were sound: war propagandists, especially those on RTLM, such as Nahimana and Barayagwisa, motivated perpetrators and thus played a causal role of sorts.

Shortly after Li's fieldwork, Charles Mironko conducted structured interviews with hundreds of confessed perpetrators in Rwandan prisons.[36] Contrary to Li, Mironko found that the impact of RTLM was minimal at best. This finding was rooted in the fact that Rwandan culture produced two kinds of perpetrators based on its rural and urban divides. Rural perpetrators claimed to have rarely or never listened to RTLM because they found its urban sensibility too foreign. Urban perpetrators claimed to have listened to RTLM but did not find it motivating. Urban perpetrators further claimed to have been organised into militias and prepared for collective violence long before RTLM made calls for it. Once genuine threats to Hutus were evident, would-be perpetrators were ready to strike and RTLM simply shared their desires for military offensives. Mironko thus echoes Li's weaker claim that RTLM might have motivated some genocidaires but it did not cause genocidal violence; in Mironko's words, 'RTLM alone did not cause them [Hutus] to kill.'[37]

At about the same time Scott Straus independently conducted over 200 structured interviews with Rwandan perpetrators who claimed to have never listened to RTLM and not to have been motivated by it.[38] Most claimed instead that they were motivated by tangible threats to Hutus, such as economic and political insecurities, and most of all peers. Straus found that peer pressure took the following forms: soldiers demanding bystanders to participate in murders, neighbours encouraging Hutus to share the burden of killing, and friends and family framing collective violence as a necessary self-defence against Tutsis. Straus further discovered that peer pressure was more likely an influence than RTLM since most Hutus lacked steady radio transmissions or radios altogether. Straus thus concludes that war propaganda was not as strong as the ICTR presumed, and not a central motivator as reported by perpetrators.[39]

Another influential study of RTLM and its impact on collective violence was David Yanagizawa-Drott's radio coverage analysis.[40] By comparing regional radio coverage and the number of individuals prosecuted for genocide therein, Yanagizawa-Drott found that no more than 20% of Hutus possessed radio sets during the genocide. However, perpetrators must have shared radios, for wherever there was radio coverage there was an increase in violence by 65–77%, suggesting that RTLM increased genocidal deaths by 9% overall, which corresponds to 45,000 murdered Tutsis.[41] As significant as these statistics may be, there is nevertheless a fundamental shortcoming: Yanagizawa-Drott used radio coverage and locations of perpetrator prosecution as proxies for RTLM's causal influence on perpetrator violence. Yet broadcast coverage and trial location should overlap, given that both measure populated areas of Rwanda, which would yield a statistically significant but theoretically insignificant correlation.[42]

Taken together the above studies show that the link between war propaganda and collective violence is much more difficult to prove than courts presumed. When it comes to motivations for the Rwandan Genocide they also yield an impasse: Li and Yanagizawa-Drott affirm a significant motivational link, while Mironko and Straus refute it. However, while these studies speak to the *Akayesu* precedent in light of the ICTR, they do not speak to the precedent in light of the ICTY. Moreover, when it comes to studies on war propaganda in the Yugoslav Wars, the motivations of perpetrators are often neglected. This is important because the *Akayesu* precedent and its notions of culpability have been inherited by the ICTY. Yet similar interviews have not been undertaken in Serbia, which is surprising given the imminent closing of the ICTY and the ongoing criminal investigation of war propaganda by the SPWC.

In what follows I build on the above studies by discussing the working results of my own snowball-sampling semi-structured interviews with non-veteran Serbs, SPWC lawyers and Serb veterans of the Yugoslav Wars living in Belgrade. Eleven veteran interviews shall occupy my interest here because they are cases in which veterans openly discussed motivations for fighting in campaigns involving war crimes, including Vukovar, Sarajevo and Kosovo, and witnessing collective violence. The 11 also represent an average sampling of the different kinds of veterans of the Yugoslav Wars (four were enlisted soldiers, four were volunteers, and three were draftees)[43] and exemplify three themes: the history of ethnic conflict in Serbia, the cyclical nature of war propaganda on the frontline, and genuine threats against Serbs in the Yugoslav Wars. After focusing on these, I will then discuss my interviews with Serbian lawyers at the SPWC.

Our land is our curse

The interviews I conducted with Serb veterans unfolded more or less in the same way. After discussing the veteran's military history, such as the campaigns, battles or sieges he witnessed, I then asked: Did you or other veterans participate in collective violence, and, if so, what motivated you or them to do so and were you or they persuaded by media reports?

When Yugoslavia began to 'break-up' in 1991, Serb nationalists dedicated to creating a 'Greater Serbia' consolidated power under Slobodan Milosevic, a former socialist who portrayed himself as the defender of Serbia. From 1991 to 1999, the Milosevic regime transformed Serbia, an otherwise open society, into a media-controlled state and launched attacks characterised as 'strength' and 'self-defence' upon Croatia and Bosnia-Herzegovina, bringing about the worst European atrocities since World War II. Hundreds of villages were ethnically cleansed; 50,000 women were systematically raped; thousands were massacred; millions were displaced; 140,000 perished; and genocide took place at Srebrenica. Although dozens of perpetrators have been brought to justice by the ICTY, most combatants of the Yugoslavian Wars maintain somewhat ordinary, if not troubled, lives today. In Serbia, combatants of all stripes have received little governmental support because of the shadow cast by the wars. Consequentially, veterans have networked with one another to form veterans' associations. Most of these organisations are not recognised but are independently designed to provide the social and psychological support that veterans need. Besides being scapegoats for the Yugoslav Wars, veterans in Serbia face numerous hardships, especially compared to veterans elsewhere.

Since 2010 I have networked with these organisations to interview veterans about their present circumstances, wartime experiences and motivations. When I began my interviews, very few veterans openly discussed the wars with me, and none admitted to partaking in collective violence. Moreover, most of the men who voluntarily spoke to me ended up interrogating me about American injustices committed abroad but especially in Serbia, including the extensive NATO bombings in 1999 and the removal of Kosovo in 2008. Nevertheless, after becoming an honourary member to one of the associations, I gained the trust of many veterans and was able to speak with them about their military experiences.

One veteran in particular, who I will call Vladimir, approached me one afternoon at a Slava,[44] telling me he was aware of my research, had spoken to few people about his wartime experiences, but was willing to answer my questions about the Yugoslav Wars. We thus arranged to meet a few days later. I knew Vladimir had fought in several battles, including Vukovar, and his reputation as a quiet person, who seemed very cold, made me somewhat apprehensive about the interview. Yet, like most of the veterans I got to know throughout my fieldwork, Vladimir was not what I expected. When I visited him, he greeted me with warm eyes, treated me hospitably as all Serbs treat guests, and talked with me for hours over Turkish coffee, as friends in Serbia do. After speaking together for an hour or so, I asked Vladimir about his experiences in the Yugoslav Wars. He denied being motivated to fight in the wars by Serbian wartime media, but he openly admitted to engaging in violence for other reasons. He was prepared to fight for Serbia ever since he was a boy, when his father taught him about the generations of Serbian heroes, including those at the Battle of Kosovo and World War II. He then explained that Serbia is a vulnerable land often caught between political forces impinging upon it. He thus emphasised that Serbian defenders have always needed to face such forces, which have often been genuinely threatening regimes, including the Ottoman Turks and, worst of all, the Ustaši (that is, Croatian Nazis) who executed thousands of Serbs at the death camp Jasenovac in World War II. That is why, when the Yugoslav Wars began, and he found himself facing threatening Croatians in the Battle of Vukovar, he exercised brutality. He said:

> My father was in WWII and I had seen those [Nazi] uniforms and weapons, and the Ustaši [Croatians] in Vukovar were wearing them again. And they would shout 'Srpske krvi!' [i.e., 'Serbian blood'] ... They were killing Serbs: men, women, and children, the old and the young, they didn't care. They wanted to kill off the Orthodox people. And we, the Orthodox, had to fight to keep the Orthodox people alive ... That is why I fought as I did, I had to do it.

Vladimir recounted how, amid the Battle of Vukovar, he and two other Serbian soldiers were captured and tortured over the course of one night by 'Ustaši'. Vladimir thought he would surely be killed, so when only one guard was left with him and his companions,

Vladimir attacked the man. Vladimir claimed that the experience confirmed for him that Croatians were inhumane Nazis (hence his broad application of the term 'Ustaši'). He returned to battle and, to his admission, stormed into Croatian homes or buildings, killing (and sometimes apprehending) any Ustaši he came across, and thus 'eliminating the Ustaši threat and protecting innocent Serbs'.

How do combatants like Vladimir come to commit such violence? One of the main reasons is that cultural models of previous conflicts combine with genuine threats and intensive combat to serve as templates for seeing the 'enemy' as deserving of brutality. Unfortunately, the Croatians at Vukovar were mostly civilians under attack from militarised Serbs and there is little evidence that the majority of Croatians had realigned with the political ideologies of World War II. Yet Serbs saw themselves as once again fighting Ustaši. How did this happen?

Like many regions of the world, Serbia is a land scarred by ethnic conflict, and like many ethnic groups, Serbs have repeatedly been the victims of collective violence.[45] A common outcome of such generational persecution is the psychological phenomenon known as 'accusation in a mirror'.[46] Fearing that they will once again be victims, an ethnic group at the onset of a new conflict accuses its opponents of intending to recommit past brutalities, which the defensive ethic group ends up committing themselves in the course of fighting.[47] This phenomenon occurred in both Rwanda and Yugoslavia where Hutus and Serbs, respectively, did not see their own people as possibly being aggressors, since generations of victimisation left them feeling vulnerable, innocent, and justified in their defensive (if not retaliatory) violence. It is not very surprising, then, that Serbian brutalities of the Yugoslav Wars mirrored those of previous Balkan wars, such as World War II, where Serbs experienced horrendous brutalities at the hands of Croatians.[48] Another way to describe accusation in a mirror is using Mamdani's expression 'when victims became killers' – that is, victims of generational violence become perpetrators in renewed conflicts.[49]

By extension we can see from Vladimir's remarks that he saw the Croatians of the 1990s as the Ustaši of the 1940s and himself along with fellow Serbs as targets of reoccurring persecution. Once Vladimir found himself in combat, his fears were confirmed: testimony from Serb fighters on the frontline fixed his views of Croatians as Nazis and the violent experience of war fixed his sense of being targeted. Vladimir thus exercised a type of brutality that he saw as being necessary – and justified – but from an outside view, without knowing Serb history, looks like wanton aggression.

Being enculturated to view Serbia as a land of conflict and the Serbs as a persecuted yet innocent people began at an early age for most veterans. From a young age they were taught to value Serbian history, which is replete with battles and uprisings, throughout which Serbs have protected their people, religion and land from would-be invaders. Veterans learned that Serbs may occupy a vulnerable territory that is prone to invasion but they have admirably challenged – and oftentimes defeated – notorious world empires. One veteran, when reflecting on Serbian uprisings against the Ottoman Turks and Nazis, told me: 'In defending Serbia, we Serbs have defended Europe.' Other veterans spoke the same way, seeing themselves as contiguous with generations of European defenders, stretching all the way back to the Battle of Kosovo (1448). In fact, veterans often referred to the Battle of Kosovo to frame their understanding of Serbia as a land coveted by empires and neighbours, and Serbs as a persecuted but innocent or 'heavenly people'. The latter saying reflects, on the one hand, Prince Lazar's decision at the Battle of Kosovo to forsake an earthly kingdom for martyrdom and heavenly reward.[50] On the other hand, it represents Serbia's defence of Orthodox

Christianity from persecutory invaders, beginning with Lazar and continuing to the present day.

For instance, veterans often told me that they fought just as Serbs before them to defend 'Orthodoxy', regardless of whether or not they won the war. I also found that most veterans used religious terms to refer to themselves and their enemies. One veteran explained that, 'Catholics [Croats] and Muslims [Bosnians] were trying to rid their lands of Orthodox Christians [Serbs].' Built into this cultural frame is the outlook that Catholics and Muslims are known to persecute Orthodox Christians, while the latter are known to defend the innocent. Along these lines one veteran told me: 'We Serbs are entirely innocent – we have never done anything wrong. We have only defended ourselves in every single war and every single battle.'

When I asked veterans why Catholics or Muslims persecuted Serbs, I was often told a number of conspiracies that illustrated accusation in a mirror. Most veterans said that conspirators within the Vatican or Muslim world wanted to ethnically cleanse the Balkans of Serbs and Orthodoxy. With each of these explanations, veterans expressed the sentiment that persecution is more or less tied to the land itself. As the so-called 'powder keg of Europe', Serbia has often been caught between competing political forces that have pulled the small country into large-scale wars, and veterans recognise this. Yet they also see Serbia as sacred land, making it something they will fight for, despite the powers they face or the suffering it causes.[51]

For example, one veteran echoed several others when he told me: 'My people are always ready to defend Serbia ... One thing you must also understand, we will never, never, never give up Kosovo. We will always fight for it, even if it destroys us.' This kind of idealism over protecting Serbia, especially Kosovo, is both heartening and disheartening for veterans. It is a source of patriotism in so far as veterans recognise the need to protect Serbia from threatening opponents in virtually every generation. On this very point one veteran told me that Serbs, conditioned by generational warfare, make great soldiers and great athletes: 'It's natural selection. We have survived centuries of oppression and warfare protecting our lands. Those that survive are smart and strong.' However, having to protect Serbia is a source of desperateness, as one veteran lamented: 'Perhaps that is our fate – to be invaded, persecuted, and bombed. It happens every generation here. We sometimes say, "when China becomes the world power, they will bomb us too".' Hence, the cultural narrative of persecution and Serbian innocence is a rationalisation of the fact that Serbia is, in fact, at one of the most vulnerable crossroads in Europe where war and persecution has unfortunately been a generational occurrence.

Thus, as many historians note,[52] the explosion of collective violence during the break-up of Yugoslavia was not unique to the Balkans of the 1990s. Such violence had occurred in previous Balkan wars and, with the break-up of Yugoslavia, reoccurred in the generation of veterans of the Yugoslav Wars. Yet beyond accusation in a mirror, what motivated the violence? Self-reports from former combatants suggest that histories of collective violence in the Balkans – combined with cultural notions of victimisation and heroism – prepared them to see entire groups of people as opponents and longtime enemies who deserved little respect. Of course, Serbian war propagandists could have easily manipulated such views to encourage collective violence, without veterans taking notice or reporting it today. But for most veterans, motivation was born out of their historical experience. As one veteran explained, Serbs carry the heavy burden of having to protect their lands and people because of their historic vulnerability. Thus he commented: 'Our land is our curse.'

Rumors on the frontline

Of course, fear also contributes to collective violence. This became apparent when I asked veterans, such as Vladimir, why they thought they had to kill as opposed to negotiate with their neighbours. The answer was somewhat akin to what Mironko and Straus were told by perpetrators in Rwanda.[53] Although veterans denied killing non-combatants and were admittedly inspired by honour to defend Serbia, many said they were motivated by peers – and the fears they instilled – to engage in collective violence.

One of the most illustrative interviews along these lines took place with a veteran named 'Nikola', a veteran of nearly every major battle in the Yugoslav Wars. Nikola was once again not what I expected. He was a white-haired man in his 50s, who was carrying a stack of recently acquired books when we first met. When I finally got the chance to ask Nikola about Serbian wartime media, he refuted its effects on soldiers but acknowledged its potential influence on frightened volunteers. He said that on the frontline volunteers and reserves often said they joined after watching the news or hearing political speeches and wanting to defend Serbia, fearing that more battles and attacks were imminent. He went on to explain that the media might have raised men's concerns but it was soldier-to-soldier conversations about the enemy on the frontline and firsthand violence that influenced men the most. 'Anyways', he said, 'the news was blocked from us [on the frontline]. There were no televisions, radios, or newspapers … But we surely knew what was happening to Serbs.' Nikola then claimed that he initially went to war 'to protect Serbs within Serbian territory'. But he came to support aggressive attacks on Croatian and Bosnian strongholds, such as ethnic cleansings, given the atrocities that Croatians and Bosnians were committing against Serbs, which he heard about or witnessed personally.

I asked Nikola whether by 'Serbian territory' he meant the territory within the 'Karlobag-Ogulin-Karlovac-Virovitica' (KKV line). The KKV was a concept used by Serbian war propagandists, such as Vojislav Seselj, to describe the extent of an irredentist nationalist Serbian state. If Nikola consented, it would be evidence of what linguist Predrag Dojcinovic calls a 'mental fingerprint' – a word or phrase that is coined by a propagandist and later used by a perpetrator, thus linking the instigator with the instigated.[54] However, Nikola replied: 'No, I mean the Serbian Republic and Serb villages just outside of it.' Perhaps reading into my question, he went on to say: 'You should know that Seselj wasn't the first to use it [the KKV line]; he borrowed it from Nikola Pasic[55] who designated the *rightful* borders of Serbs between Ottoman and Austro-Hungarian rule.' Nikola then said 'Seselj attempted to define Serbia within these borders – he had to, you see.' When I asked why, Nikola retorted: 'To protect Serbs! The Croatians had strategized for some time to rid the land of Serbs … they were halted under Tito, thank goodness, but they began again in earnest once the war started. Seselj was tired of the injustices, just like everyone else [in Serbia].' Although Nikola denied fighting for the KKV line or 'Greater Serbia', he admitted to initially fighting to defend Serbs but eventually to attacking Croatians and Bosnians.

Given Nikola's enthusiasm for Seselj, I then asked: 'So, throughout the war and between battles you never read the news or listened to political speeches – for example, from Seselj?' Nikola hesitated. 'Of course', he said, 'I would read or listen to the news when I could. But that was rare and it didn't influence me … Most of the time, actually, it was the reporters who came to us, asking about the war, what we had seen; we'd tell them and they'd report it.' Nikola went on to say, 'Sometimes we [soldiers] later read or heard about it in the news [what soldiers had told reporters]. But we didn't think much of it; [for] we already knew what was happening [in the war].' Although Nikola's contradictory remarks made me think his denial of frequent media exposure or its influence on soldiers was somewhat disingenuous, I decided not to press him on the matter, fearing he would avoid talking about the wars all together. Instead, I asked Nikola to explain what kinds of things he told reporters on the frontline. He replied: 'Foreign journalists asked about how many soldiers were with us, our weapons, locations, strategies – I never answered these questions, because they were meant to aid the enemy.' He then said that Serbian journalists 'wanted to know about Serbs – what was happening to them – were they safe? And what were we doing, as soldiers, to protect them?' In what remained of the interview, it became evident that what Nikola and other soldiers told reporters during the wars were stories that were then propagated by reporters as facts to larger Serbian audiences. Yet most of these stories were rumours that gained credibility by circulating among soldiers. Three kinds of stories, which I heard from Nikola and other veterans, deserve mentioning.

First, Nikola claimed to have learned about the severity of Serbian persecution when he arrived on the frontline, where he heard stories about the disappearance, torture and massacre of local Serbs. In virtually every city under siege or pillaged village, 'one-third of the Serbs had gone missing, one-third had been killed, and the other third had left for Serbia'. Another veteran, who I will call Zoran, had previously told me that when he arrived at the Battle of Vukovar, he learned from fellow soldiers how local Croatians instigated assaults on Serbs prior to the war, resulting in countless disappearances and deaths. 'Before the battle, strange things happened … there were several cars without license plates, no one knew why. Then, Serbs started to disappear.' Zoran continued: 'It turned out that the Ustaši told Croats [living in Vukovar] to drive in unmarked cars, making it easier to identify Serbs, to kidnap them, and to kill them … before the war, even, they were killing Serbs.' Rarely did I challenge such stories, for when I asked Zoran how he knew the stories were true, he replied: 'What the fuck!?! How does a doctor know someone is sick? He just fucking knows! I knew, I was there!' However, Nikola told me a similar story about Vukovar, which he validated by saying, 'several of them [missing Serbs] were later found maimed in Croatian homes'. However, what Nikola and fellow soldiers seemed to have found were the unrecognisable corpses of civilians inside damaged buildings or homes, which they interpreted as the remains of slaughtered Serbs. Instead of suggesting this I asked Nikola if these instances were what influenced him to fight, especially in making attacks on Croatians. He said, 'Yes, I knew I had to protect Serbs from being wiped out.'

Second, Nikola mentioned that he was motivated by stories from other soldiers about how 'the Ustaši massacred Serbs'. Such stories were common and persuasive for soldiers, as several veterans mentioned them as being motivators of collective violence. For instance, in a very brief interview one veteran told me that hearing from other soldiers that Serbs were being 'butchered' not only morally enraged him but also confirmed the importance of his fighting. Remarkably, he also said: 'these were real things [attacks on Serbs]. We [soldiers] knew and the Serbian people knew', and they were credible stories because 'they were being reported in the news'. Likewise, Nikola explained to me that such stories were legitimated by the fact that they were supported by eyewitness testimony, never denied by higher ranking officers, and conveyed to reporters who came to the frontline. As Nikola explained, when taken together 'these were facts' – in other words, the combination of testimony, reoccurrence and record made the stories true. Furthermore, their seeming truth justified the escalating levels of collective violence in which veterans found themselves throughout the wars, as Nikola's earlier comments indicate. The truth of such stories is nevertheless doubtful. To illustrate, another veteran told me that Croatians in Vukovar had massacred over 40 Serbian children in an elementary school, a story that circulated among soldiers, made its way into Serbian media, but was later proven to be entirely fabricated.[56] Nikola also commented that Bosniaks not only had the audacity to torture Serbs but also to bomb their own people to make it look like Serbs were attacking innocent Bosnians. Although such stories seemed credible, they have since been proven false.

Third, when discussing unjust attacks on Serbs, Nikola mentioned how fellow soldiers went missing throughout the wars. At that point in our conversation, he paused for an extended amount of time and I could tell he was wrestling with painful memories. Sensing that I should end the interview, I said: 'Please, Nikola, we do not need to talk about this any further.' Nikola replied, 'No, I want you to know that they [Croatians and Bosnians] killed whoever they captured. I doubt that those crimes were reported in the States, were they?' Despite his apparent frustration, Nikola went on to say that I might also be surprised to know that Serbs 'fought combatants and protected the innocent'. He then said, 'Muslim fighters in Bosnia', on the other hand, 'invited Mujahidin [into their country] to help target all Serbs' and 'beheaded captured Serbian soldiers, as trophies'. He also explained how the many soldiers who 'would disappear over the course of battles' must have faced a similar fate, which was another common topic of conversation and motivation for violence among soldiers. I wanted to ask Nikola whether some of the soldiers could have simply deserted their post, as hundreds of disillusioned Serbian soldiers were reported to have done.[57] For the remainder of our interview, however, Nikola turned to the portrayal of Serbs as aggressors within Western media, a common source of unease for Serbian veterans.

Many of my interviews with veterans about the influence of wartime media paralleled Nikola's comments. Veterans claimed that the media had little influence on them and was often blocked from them. However, it would later be seen or heard and repeat a story that circulated among soldiers on the frontline days, weeks or months earlier. Whenever this occurred, it further confirmed for soldiers the validity of stories they heard about Serbian persecution. One veteran told me that he 'learned about the armed uprising of the Kosovo Liberation Army from the news', but when he heard reports from fellow soldiers that the KLA were abducting and murdering Serbs, he 'wanted to fight like hell in Kosovo'.

In sum, veterans openly admitted to being motivated by peer-to-peer stories. Although this reaffirms Mironko and Straus's findings on peer influence,[58] it does not disprove the effects of war propaganda, a conclusion that could only be drawn after more extensive studies. It nevertheless shows how oversimplified the *Akayesu* precedent is without perpetrators' views. Similar to the self-reports of Rwandan genocidaires, Serbian veterans illustrate that international criminal lawyers underappreciate the complexities and dynamics of collective violence. Comments like Nikola's suggest that, contrary to the ICTR and ICTY, war propaganda functions less like a bullhorn that calls soldiers to engage in collective violence and more like an echo chamber that initially rationalises violence but allows it to escalate over the course of war. Remarkably, war propaganda can sometimes originate among soldiers who, in their cognitive dissonance over collective violence, produce misinformation or inflammatory stories about the people they target, which later finds itself in circulated wartime media.

We defended our country – that is not a crime

Throughout my interviews it became apparent that the concept of post-conflict justice is as important to veterans as it is to human rights lawyers. The two differ, however, with regard to who bears the ultimate responsibility for the Yugoslav Wars. In this section, I wish to examine and compare comments of legal actors and Serbian veterans about post-war culture and the ongoing investigation of war propaganda in Serbia.

As I have suggested, the ICTY and SPWC's notions of war propaganda are simplistic because they neglect the long history of media studies on propaganda and neglect perpetrator self-reports. Besides focusing solely on the latter, I recognise that perpetrators are unaware of all their motivations and that the principle valence of war propaganda is not restricted to the relationship between mass media and isolated individuals. However, like other ethnographers, especially those who undertook similar fieldwork in Rwanda, I believe interviews with former combatants can expose many of the primary motivations for collective violence.

Yet this presumption is not recognised by the SPWC, who has neither interviewed veterans in Serbia nor are its members intending to do so, even to assess the potential effects of war propaganda during the Yugoslav Wars. My interviews with the SPWC reveal that they are instead following the ICTR and ICTY, assuming the *Akayesu* precedent that a 'possible causal link' is evident whenever the former precedes the latter. On more solid ground, a clerk at the SPWC did tell me that there is, in fact, direct evidence linking Serbian war propaganda to violence in the Yugoslav Wars. He said 'there is a video of a soldier being interviewed by reporters at the Battle of Vukovar' and 'the reporters ask the soldier why he is fighting' to which the solder responds: 'because of what I saw on the news'.[59] 'Evidence such as this', the clerk told me, 'could be used to prove the link between war propaganda and collective violence'. Being familiar with the video he referenced, and knowing that there is only one other video like it, where a woman claims to be volunteering for service in light of the news,[60] I asked: 'But how many instances are there of men admitting to the news that they were influenced by war propaganda? Moreover, in these videos the perpetrator doesn't say what exactly in the news influenced him. And does that kind of "confession" prove causation?' He responded, 'I really cannot tell you any more than what is public ... the two examples [his video reference and mine] are public.'[61] The clerk went on to say that all that is required under the *Akayesu* precedent is a 'possible causal link', meaning any potential evidence linking war propaganda to a perpetrator, a point that I challenge in the next section.

Besides ignoring the legal difficulties inherent to the *Akayesu* precedent,[62] the clerk also classified all Serbian perpetrators as one and the same. I asked him, being a Serb himself, 'How do you think the war propaganda influenced people during the Yugoslav Wars?' He replied, 'I don't know ... but it only worked on the uneducated.' He then explained how he and many other Serbs were either multiethnic or educated, which made them less prone to believing the war propaganda or supporting the war. Distancing himself and other Serbs from perpetrators, the clerk said that perpetrators were neither ordinary Serbs nor ordinary people. 'These people came out of nowhere; they crawled out from under a rock ... They were poor villagers, hoodlums, gang members, even convicts who were promised freedom to defend Serbia. These kinds of people came out of no where – who were they, I asked?' After pausing for a moment, he went on to say, 'It was these men who committed crimes, not just anyone.' Wanting to know how he viewed former combatants today, I asked whether he had interviewed any veterans. He explained that he had not and that the SPWC was not planning to undertake any interviews. Somewhat shocked, I reminded him that the bulk of my ethnographic research in Serbia involved veterans and that some were very eager to share their wartime experiences. After being asked whether I would share my findings, I told the clerk somewhat tongue-and-cheek: 'I will share whatever becomes public through my publications.'

The outlooks of Serbian veterans expectedly conflict with the views of the SPWC. Though what is perhaps surprising is that many veterans have sophisticated opinions about what influenced them, and their comments highlight the complexities of establishing culpability. For instance, one veteran named Mihailo explained with prescience how few veterans would admit to being influenced by wartime media even if it was influential. 'We did not fight because of what the news reported or what some politician said. We fought because of real threats facing Serbia ... [we fought] because it was the right thing to do, not because we wanted to.' Looking into my eyes, Mihailo then said, 'Serbs were being killed, cleansed ... our monuments were being destroyed.' And finally, 'We defended our country – that is not a crime.' After that, he explained how he never fully trusted the Serbian media, how he despised Serbian war propagandists, and how he regrets the war crimes committed by fellow Serbian soldiers. Because veterans like Mihailo fought to protect compatriots, they would not reduce their motivations to the violent calls of war propagandists. Whether this corroborates ethnographic findings in Rwanda, and thus prioritises other motivators above war propaganda, is an open question. My inclination is that former combatants believe – or need to believe – that their fighting in unjust wars was not in vain but was necessary and, all things considered, the right thing to do.

Like other veterans, Mihailo nonetheless expressed surprising views about the difficulties of living and establishing justice in post-war Serbia. He longed for the days of Yugoslavia when 'everyone had a job, education was free, and life was good'. Such 'Yugo-nostalgia' was common for most veterans who saw former Serbian politicians, such as Milosevic, as most responsible for the break-up of Yugoslavia. One veteran told me that he could not stand Serbian politicians and wanted to see them punished because 'they lied to us about the war and now they blame us for the wars'. When I asked how they lied, he said: 'they kept saying we were winning [the war]; Milosevic even said we won – that we won!?!' The veterans thus see themselves as victims of wartime and post-war governments. While the previous Serbian government created the conditions for war or found war thrust upon it, the current government refuses to recognise the veterans of the Yugoslav Wars. In other words, veterans made a sacrifice to what they now see as a corrupt regime but nevertheless are the ones paying the price for that regime today. Veterans lamented that the international and local communities blame them for the wars and, as I observed at the SPWC, put all veterans into one category. They are denied benefits, honour and monuments because they are not 'veterans' but 'perpetrators' writ large. However, as Mihailo complained, it was the paramilitary units – 'a few bandits' – who committed most of the war crimes. 'They were bandits!' Mihailo explained, 'They were profiting from the war while we [soldiers] were fighting it.' Hence, most veterans today see themselves as scapegoats and portrayed as an indiscriminate class of perpetrators, even though they consider their service to have been 'right and honourable' and not motivated by war propagandists.

International law and post-conflict justice

What can we infer from comments made by veterans of the Yugoslav Wars? The simplest conclusion is similar to what Mironko and Straus inferred: the self-reports of former combatants suggest that war propaganda is a weak motivation for collective violence. Yet unlike the Rwandan interviews, there are even further limitations to what can be said here. Establishing a causal link would require a much larger sample, and it cannot be assumed that the 11 veterans I interviewed were aware of all the factors influencing their wartime activities. When it comes to motivation, conclusions are nevertheless a bit more promising. The interviews are similar to those conducted in Rwanda in so far as both show surprising motivations for violence. For Serbian veterans those are longstanding ethnic tensions, religious divides, peer influence and apparent threats to conspecifics. As anthropologists of war and media researchers observe, it is often the interaction of similar factors that combine with war propaganda to motivate collective violence.[63] Contrary to the legal narrative, then, it is unlikely that war propaganda could be a direct cause of collective violence. And motivations cannot be inferred on temporality alone since, in the Serbian case, some forms of war propaganda emerged out of conflict and even originated with combatants, not reporters or politicians.

Furthermore, in-depth reports from former combatants complicate the legal narrative about war propaganda and collective violence but bring a more nuanced picture into focus. Comments by Serbian veterans suggest that war propagandists acted less as 'top-down' opinion-makers and more like 'parallel' inoculators. By not dispelling historically inculcated fears or being more critical of rumours from the frontline, Serbian nationalists and their controlled media outlets appear to have used fear and cultural norms of heroism to bolster justifications for war. Yet the responsibility for carrying out collective violence does not lie entirely with war propagandists – there are, after all, cases where war propagandists called for violence and it did not occur. Moreover, the fact that commanders and soldiers on the frontline did not dissipate hatreds but instead engaged in collective violence is yet another factor that needs to be considered in the set of conditions that contributed to collective violence.

Several questions of culpability thus remain unresolved. What was the chain of communication on the frontlines and how did it relate to war propagandists in Belgrade? How does that chain of communication influence the retributive agenda of the ICTY and the SPWC? And, finally, does it further complicate pinning the blame on perpetrators? While I cannot fully answer these queries, I suggest the following.

First, veterans' accounts suggest that communication between war propagandists and soldiers was not a chain of command, as lawyers presume, but rather a tangled knot of soldier-to-soldier rumours, uncritically reported journalism, and fervent nationalistic rhetoric. The result was an overlapping chain of information with multiple forms of wartime communication that made the fog of war even less penetrable. Amid such chaos and confusion collective violence grew like an uncontrolled firestorm, eventually consuming several military operations. Because national leaders had the best vantage point for seeing the repercussions of wartime communications, they should have been more critical of information, quicker to lessen longstanding hatreds through political messages, and more aggressive in diminishing historical and cultural sentiments that contributed to violence.[64] Second, soldiers in campaigns involving heavy fighting or collective violence were not automatons but rather conscious human beings forced to come to terms with, and justify, their violent acts. For many former combatants, it was in the act of justification that war propaganda seems to have had its strongest influence. Recall, for instance, how Vladimir entered the war with biases towards Serbian 'enemies' and enculturated ideas about Serbian 'innocence'. Yet it was his experience of war – and only after engaging in violence – that he embraced propagandistic outlooks. The same can be said of other veterans, such as Nikola and Mihailo, who believed frontline rumours and incorporated news reports and political speeches into their beliefs that they were doing the right thing. Third, perpetrators are not just 'trigger men' as recent international trials of speech crimes suggest. Based on my interviews with Serbian veterans, former combatants were not blind killers but rather, using Christopher Browning's term, 'ordinary men'. Once in war their historical experiences and fears contributed to their violent behaviour. Self-reports and my own observations suggest that veterans were motivated primarily by peers and secondarily by the 'power of the situation',[65] where collective violence became the norm. This norm came about because military leaders neither discouraged collective violence nor questioned stories or viewpoints that endorsed it.

Hence, it is perhaps tempting to dismiss ethnographic findings and maintain a prosecutorial frame that assumes a direct link between war propagandist and an oversimplified characterisation of perpetrators. Doing so would make prosecutions under the current precedent simple but would ignore the ambiguities and interactive dimensions of perpetration. Under the current precedent these complications are unavoidable since incitement in the form of war propaganda now demands proof of a possible link. This is indeed significant in so far as the UN has recently condemned war propaganda in several countries, indicating that additional war crimes trials involving war propaganda are imminent.[66] However, if defenders challenge the *Akayesu* precedent on empirical grounds, the precedent may prove to have raised the bar too high for prosecutions. Richard Carver observed this long ago and ethnographers working with former combatants have supported his scepticism.[67] Although my interviews with Serb veterans are not conclusive, they do show that the motivations for collective violence are more complicated than what the *Akayesu* precedent recognises. As a tentative conclusion, then, international courts may have to return to the *Streicher* precedent or include perpetrators' views within more methodological investigations of the effects of war propaganda in future trials.

Conclusion

I have framed my discussion around the *Akayesu* precedent because it is the impetus of ethnographic research among perpetrators in Rwanda and my own fieldwork in Serbia. For the precedent states that former combatants in these countries were motivated to engage in collective violence because of war propaganda – but tribunals and prosecutors relying on the precedent have neglected the voices of alleged perpetrators. As my interviews with Serbian veterans demonstrate, former combatants were motivated by a host of factors that often violate a priori assumptions about wartime motivations and contradict legal narratives about war. Indeed, the narrative at issue here is the one about war propaganda in international law, and though an argument about propaganda cannot be constructed solely on the basis of this single narrative, it is the one that has created a questionable and incomplete frame without interrogating the perpetrator. Like other ethnographers, I have attempted to include those neglected voices since there is real value in the personal accounts of former combatants of military campaigns involving collective violence. Although such data cannot affirm or deny the cause-and-effect of war propaganda, it can tell us about the motivations of those who participated in notorious wars, and in so doing what some of their central motivators were.

As a final point, in societies of post-conflict justice where accountability is necessary for democratic life, legal culpability cannot be limited to a few war propagandists and social blame cannot be attributed to a broadly defined set of perpetrators. In the Serbian case, doing so has obscured the deeper xenophobic and nationalistic currents that contributed to collective violence. Interviews with veterans reveal that such currents persist because of their being excluded from post-conflict discourse. To illustrate, believing the United States (US) and international community has pressured Serbia to exclude veterans, Mihailo told me that he has taught his sons to 'to hate the US and pray for its destruction'. Additionally, survey data indicate that nationalism is on the rise in Serbia, especially among 18 to 24-year-olds.[68] If Serbia is going to maintain its burgeoning democracy, it cannot blame the wars on a few while ignoring the many politicians of the Milosevic regime who still remain in power. Yet the international community cannot expect Serbia to achieve post-conflict justice without addressing widespread animosities expressed by Serbs regarding the role of the US and UN during and after the Yugoslav Wars, respectively. Serbs have experienced a great deal of social and economic hardships, rendering them with little hope in the post-conflict environment. All of these issues underscore the importance of including the many voices of persons who experienced the wars, including former combatants, in legal investigations and post-conflict narratives. Doing so will not only identify the many complex motivations for war, but also prevent such motivations in future conflicts and achieve a permanent peace in the Balkans.

Acknowledgments

I wish to thank Samuel Martínez and Cathy Schlund-Vials for offering feedback on several versions of this article, Richard Sosis for providing comments on an earlier version, and Richard Wilson for his innovative research on speech-crimes and introducing me to many of the issues discussed in this article. Moreover, I am extremely grateful for the very helpful comments provided by the anonymous reviewer of this manuscript.

Disclosure statement

No potential conflict of interest was reported by the author.

Notes

1. Susan Benesch, specifically, outlines such a criteria for predicting the likelihood of war propaganda leading to collective violence. See Susan Benesch, 'The Ghost of Causation in International Speech Crime Cases', in *Propaganda, War Crimes Trials and International Law: From Speakers' Corner to War Crimes*, ed. P. Dojcinovic (New York: Routledge, 2012), 254–68.
2. Richard Wilson, 'Inciting Genocide with Words', *Michigan Journal of International Law* 36, no. 1 (2014).
3. See I. Boljevic, D. Odavic, V. Petrovic, S. Rabrenovic, B. Stankovic, J.S. Jankovic, N. Vuco, and D. Vukotic, *Reci I Nedela: Pozivanje ili Podsticanje na Ratne Zlocine u Midijima u Srbiji 1991–1992.* Beograd: Studija Tuzilastva za Ratne Zlocine Republike Srbije, 2011. See also the following ICTR cases: *Prosecutor* v. *Akayesu*: Case No. ICTR-96-4-T; *Prosecutor* v. *Simon Bikindi*: Case No. ICTR-01-72; *Prosecutor* v. *Ferdinand Nahimana, Jean-Bosco Barayagwiza, and Hassan Ngeze*: Case No. ICTR-99-52-T; and *Prosecutor* v. *Georges Ruggiu*: Case No. ICTR-97-32-I. And see the following ICTY cases: *Prosecutor* v. *Radoslav Brđanin*: Case No. IT-95-10; *Prosecutor* v. *Radovan Karadžič*: Case No. IT-95-5/18-PT; and Prosecutor v. *Vojislav Šešelj*: Case No. IT-03-67.
4. See Wilson, 'Inciting Genocide'; see also Jordan Kiper, 'Towards an Anthropology of War Propaganda', *Political and Legal Anthropology Review* (In Press).
5. Nahimana et al., 1099. This was based on the evidence that Akayesu told the crowd in his speeches to fight the Tutsis and the use of euphemistic language, which for Hutus was a direct call to genocide.
6. Charles Mironko, 'The Effect of RTLM's Rhetoric of Ethnic Hatred in Rural Rwanda' in *The Media and the Rwandan Genocide*, ed. A. Thompson (London, UK: Pluto Press, 2007), 125–

35; Scott Straus, *The Order of Genocide: Race, Power, and War in Rwanda* (New York: Cornell University Press, 2006); Scott Straus, 'What Is the Relationship between Hate Radio and Violence? Rethinking Rwanda's "Radio Machete"', *Politics & Society* 35, no. 4 (2007): 609–37; Darryl Li, 'Echoes of Violence: Considerations on Radio and Genocide in Rwanda', *Journal of Genocide Research* 6, no. 1 (2004): 9–28.

7. See Christopher Browning, *Ordinary Men: Reserve Police Battalion 101 and the Final Solution in Poland* (New York: HarperCollins, 1992); Alex Hinton, *Why Did They Kill? Cambodia in the Shadow of Genocide* (Berkeley, CA: University of California Press, 2005); Anthony Oberschall, 'Volislav Seselj's Nationalist Propaganda: Contents, Techniques, Aims and Impacts, 1990–1994', *An Expert Report for the United Nations International Criminal Tribunal for the Former Yugoslavia* (2010); Anthony Oberschall, 'Propaganda, Hate Speech and Mass Killings', in *Propaganda, War Crimes Trials and International Law: From Speakers' Corner to War Crimes*, ed. P. Dojcinovic (New York: Routledge, 2012), 171–200.

8. See Boljevic et al., *Reci I Nedela*.

9. Michael Kearney, 'Propaganda in the Jurisprudence of the International Criminal Tribunal for the Former Yugoslavia', in *Propaganda, War Crimes Trials and International Law: From Speakers' Corner to War Crimes*, ed. P. Dojcinovic (New York: Routledge, 2012), 235.

10. Predrag Dojcinovic, 'Introduction', in *Propaganda, War Crimes Trials and International Law: From Speakers' Corner to War Crimes*, ed. Predrag Dojcinovic (New York: Routledge, 2012), 1–29. See also Kiper, *Anthropology of War Propaganda*.

11. Benesch, 'Ghost of Causation', 254.

12. Joshua Wallenstein, 'Punishing Words: An Analysis of the Necessity of the Element of Causation in Prosecutions for Incitement to Genocide', *Stanford Law Review* 54, no. 2 (2001): 351–98.

13. Ibid., 357–8.

14. Gregory Gordon, 'A War of Media, Words, Newspapers, and Radio Stations: The ICTR Media Trial Verdict and a New Chapter in the International law of Hate Speech', *Virginia Journal Law* 45, no. 139 (2005): 1–60, 143–4.

15. Telford Taylor, *The Anatomy of the Nuremberg Trials* (New York: Little Brown & Company, 1992), 376–80.

16. Margaret Eastwood, 'Hitler's Notorious Jew-Baiter: The Prosecution of Julius Streicher', in *Propaganda, War Crimes Trials and International Law: From Speakers' Corner to War Crimes*, ed. P. Dojcinovic (New York: Routledge, 2012), 203–30, 221.

17. Wilson, 'Inciting Genocide'; Kiper, *Anthropology of War Propaganda*.

18. The 'But-for' rule is used to demonstrate a counterfactual in a case of liability, such that 'but-for' x then not y, where x is the conditional and y is the consequence.

19. See *Akayesu*, 349.

20. Ibid., 673.viii.

21. See *Prosecutor v. Georges Ruggiu*: Case No. ICTR-97-32-I; *Prosecutor v. Simon Bikindi*: Case No. ICTR-01-72.

22. *Nahimana* et al., 1101.

23. *Brdanin*, 80.

24. *Karadzic*, 14.

25. *Seselj*, 10.

26. For an overview of such stories, see Boljevic et al., *Reci I Nedela*.

27. See Benesch, 'Ghost of Causation'.

28. See Dojcinovic, 'Introduction'; Dojcinovic, *Word Scene Investigations*; Nenad Fiser, 'The Indictable Propaganda: A Bottom-up Perspective', in *Propaganda, War Crimes Trials and International Law: From Speakers' Corner to War Crimes*, ed. P. Dojcinovic (New York: Routledge, 2012), 33–70; Michael Kearney, 'Propaganda in the Jurisprudence of the International Criminal Tribunal for the Former Yugoslavia', in P. Dojcinovic, ed., *Propaganda, War Crimes Trials and International Law: From Speakers' Corner to War Crimes* (New York: Routledge, 2012), 231–53.

29. Benesch, 'Ghost of Causation'.

30. Jean-Pail Chretien, *Rwanda: les Medias du Genocide* (Paris: Karthala, 1995).

31. See ibid.; Allison Des Forges, *Leave None to Tell the Story: Genocide in Rwanda* (New York: Human Rights Watch, FIDH, 1999).

32. Richard Carver, 'Broadcasting and Political Transition: Rwanda and Beyond', in *African Broadcast Cultures: Radio in Transition*, ed. R. Fardon and G. Furniess (Oxford: James Currey, 2000), 188–97.
33. Ibid., 190.
34. Li, 'Echoes of Violence'.
35. Ibid., 10.
36. Mironko, 'Effect of RTLM's Rhetoric'.
37. Ibid., 134.
38. Straus, 'Relationship between Hate Radio and Violence'.
39. Ibid., 615.
40. David Yanagizawa-Drott, 'Propaganda and Conflict: Evidence from the Rwandan Genocide', Unpublished Paper, 6 December 2010, Harvard University, david_yanagizawa-drott@harvard.edu.
41. Ibid., 33.
42. See Kiper, 'Towards an Anthropology of War Propaganda'; Wilson, 'Inciting Genocide'.
43. Moreover, their ages averaged out to 48, all were from Serbia (five rural, four urban), and all identified as Serbian Orthodox.
44. Slava is a Serbian Orthodox ritual and celebration dedicated to a particular family or organisation's saint.
45. Misha Glenny, *The Balkans: Nationalism, War and the Great Powers 1804–1999* (New York: Viking, 2000).
46. See Kenneth Marcus, 'Accusation in a Mirror', *Loyola University Chicago Law Journal* 43, no. 2 (2012): 357–93.
47. Ibid.; see Mahmood Mamdani, *When Victims Become Killers: Colonialism, Nativism, and the Genocide in Rwanda* (Princeton, NJ: Princeton University Press, 2001).
48. Vjekoslav Perica, *Balkan Idols: Religion and Nationalism in Yugoslav Wars* (New York: Oxford University Press, 2002).
49. Mamdani, *When Victims Become Killers.*
50. Legend has it that before the Battle of Kosovo, the leader of the Serbs, Prince Lazar, had a vision where told the the prophet Elijah that he would either win the battle and secure an earthly kingdom or lose the battle and secure a heavenly kingdom. According to many epic stories, Lazar opted for the latter.
51. Scott Atran, *Talking to the Enemy: Faith, Brotherhood, and the (Un)Making of Terrorists* (New York: HarperCollins Publishers, 2010); Scott Atran and Jeremy Ginges, 'Religious and Sacred Imperatives in Human Conflict', *Science* 336 (2012): 855–77.
52. Perica, *Balkan Idols.*
53. Mironko, 'Effect of RTLM's Rhetoric'; Straus, 'Relationship between Hate Radio and Violence'.
54. Dojcinovic, *Word Scene Investigations*, 95.
55. Nikola Pasic (1845–1926) was a Serbian politician and diplomat who was the most important leader of the People's Radical Party in Serbia until his death.
56. After the Battle of Vukovar, Serbian Reuters and Radio Television Serbia reported that 41 Serb children were slaughtered in a school in Borovo Naselje. Although the story was never verified, it was reported on 20 November 1991. The Serbian media used such stories to create the political agenda for an expansive Serbian state. See Renauld La Brosse, 'Political Propaganda and the Plan to Create a "State for all Serbs": Consequences of Using the Media for Ultra-Nationalist Ends', Office of the Prosecutor of the International Criminal Tribunal for the Former Yugoslavia (2003). Retrieved 21 April 2012.
57. Nebosa Bugarinovic, 'Yugoslavia: UN Seeks Refuge Status for Serbian Deserters', Radio Free Europe (1999). http://reliefweb.int/report/serbia/yugoslavia-un-seeks-refugee-status-serbian-deserters.
58. See Mironko, 'Effect of RTLM's Rhetoric'; Straus, 'Relationship between Hate Radio and Violence'.
59. Anes Alic, 'Balkans: Media and War Crimes', International Relations and Security Network. http://www.isn.ethz.ch/Digital-Library/Articles/Detail/?ord633=grp1&lng=en&id=102376. See also Boljevic et al., *Reci I Nedela.*
60. Boljevic et al., *Reci I Nedela.*

61. They are considered public in so far as they were included in a compilation of Serbian war propaganda put together and published by Boljevic et al., *Reci I Nedela*, to bring about the current investigation at the SPWC.
62. Gregory Gordon, 'Formulating a New Atrocity Speech Offense: Incitement to Commit War Crimes', *Loyola University Chicago Law Journal* 43 (2012): 281–316.
63. Hinton, *Why Did they Kill?*
64. Boljevic et al., *Reci I Nedela*.
65. Philip Zimbardo, *The Lucifer Effect: Understanding How Good People Turn Evil* (New York: Random House, 2007).
66. Kearney, 'Propaganda in the Jurisprudence', 232–3.
67. Carver, 'Broadcasting and Political Transition'.
68. Kiper, 'Towards an Anthropology of War Propaganda'.

Refiguring the perpetrator: culpability, history and international criminal law's impunity gap

Kamari Maxine Clarke

Global and International Studies, Carleton University, Canada

This article is about the ways that the notion of the African perpetrator and notions of 'culpability' are mediated through a distinct colonial–postcolonial continuum. These different assessments for assigning and comprehending guilt result in what I term an 'ICC impunity gap'. Epitomising this gap is the case against Kenya's William Ruto and the recently dropped case against Uhuru Kenyatta, whose indictments by the International Criminal Court (ICC) cohered with and confirmed the image in the international imagination of the perpetrator – an image of an African commander whose actions are in need of international judicial management. I consider the historical and juridical frames through which Kenyatta and Ruto were indicted and the resultant disjuncture in recognition by analysing the historic circumstances surrounding the violence that erupted following the 2007 presidential election alongside legal arguments made by the ICC about ways to determine culpability for mass atrocities. Though not new to legal anthropology, notions of legal time are scarcely interrogated in western jurisprudential circles, particularly with regard to differences in international law (which limits how notions of legal time are conceptualised). The goal is to make visible a particular 'gap' in the legal and popular senses of criminal responsibility, especially as it relates to the temporality and proximity of legal responsibility. By reflecting on temporal determinants for parsing guilt, I suggest that we consider the way that new modes of criminal liability shapes new narratives that determine the way that the perpetrator figure is constructed in international criminal law circles.

To be sure, the notion of the perpetrator indicted by an international tribunal has – since the Nuremberg Tribunals and Adolf Eichmann in Jerusalem – propelled a particular international imaginary of those whose actions or inaction contributed to vast crimes against humanity, war crimes and crimes that shock the human conscience. These perpetrators – military leaders, co-conspirators, heads of state and warlords – embody a presence that is at large in various post-violence situations today. This article is concerned with the ways the African perpetrator – conceived of and indicted by international bodies such as the International Criminal Court (ICC) – and notions of 'culpability' are mediated through a distinct colonial–postcolonial continuum. In this context, entities such as the ICC base culpability for contemporary violence in a narrow, ahistorical time frame that adheres to notions of 'command responsibility' which places responsibility in the hands of those who gave the orders or encouraged the violence. Others take the long history of colonial and postcolonial injustices into account when assigning guilt for present-day actions. As important, there are still others, often those who experienced or lived through the violence themselves, who are more likely to hold accountable the proximate actors who inflicted the physical and emotional violence, including the police, the head of the police, the military and the foot soldiers.

These different assessments for assigning and comprehending guilt result in what I term the 'international criminal law (ICL) impunity gap'. This ICL impunity gap is the gap between the assignments of guilt that draw their meaning from the individualisation of criminal responsibility distinguished from modes of liability for parsing guilt that go beyond the individual. Though the impunity gap has been invoked traditionally to refer to the gap in adjudication mechanisms between the international, regional, national and/ or local mechanisms that shield some individual perpetrators from adjudication and enable the pursuit of adjudication for others, going beyond the individual analyses of guilt allows us to consider how and why collective and continuing crimes may trump new individualised conceptions of guilt in certain situations. Such examinations of the way that people parse guilt differently allow us to examine the differences that social time and legal time might offer; they likewise attend to the ways in which proximate actors are contradistinguished from commanders responsible for the actions of their subordinates and have implications for a substantial difference in how large portions of the Kenyan population are rethinking the popular international image of the perpetrator of crimes against humanity. For in the Kenyatta and Ruto cases under analysis, despite charges of culpability on the international stage, in 2013 a majority of the Kenyan people democratically elected them to be Kenya's president and deputy president respectively. Both Kenyatta and Ruto remained in power, notwithstanding ICC indictments, and among various constituencies they took on a hero status which calls into question the gap between the international court and Kenya's domestic imaginary.

In the remaining article I consider the historical and juridical frames through which Kenyatta and Ruto were indicted: specifically, I analyse the historic circumstances surrounding the violence that erupted following the 2007 presidential election alongside legal arguments made by the ICC about culpability. To clarify, a democratic election in 2002 deposed then-president, Daniel Moi, ending a 22-year dictatorship and resulted in the election of Mwai Kibaki (and not Uhuru Kenyatta Moi's desired successor). In the 2007 elections, Kibaki was again declared the winner. This electoral result was contested by Kibaki's opponent, Raila Odinga of the Orange Democratic Movement as well as Odinga's supporters who accused Kibaki of electoral manipulation. Nevertheless, Kibaki was sworn-in immediately after the declaration of his electoral victory. The rushed nature of the ceremony held during night hours led to further suspicion, incitement and targeted regional and ethnic violence. The violence was first directed against various Kikuyus–Kibaki's ethnic group–and then from the Luo and Kalejin ethnic groups. At stake in the ICC case against Kenyatta and Ruto was their alleged roles in the post-election violence following the election in which responsibility for the 2007-8 post-election violence was individualised and attributed to only a few constructed as key perpetrators. In this sense, the article shows that this logic of the African perpetrator figure is also contravened through a distinct colonial–postcolonial continuum in which affective relationships to perceived historical and ethnic injustices shape the way that people grapple with contemporary notions of individualised culpability.

Making sense of the perpetrator

Where all are guilty, no one is.[1]

In his opening statement as one of the prosecutors of the Nuremberg Military Tribunal in November 1945, Justice Jackson stated: ' ... the idea that a state, any more than a corporation, commits crimes, is a fiction. *Crimes always are committed only by persons.* While it is quite proper to employ the fiction of responsibility of a state or corporation for the purpose of imposing a collective liability, it is quite intolerable to let such a legalism become the basis of personal immunity. This statement forms the cornerstone of modern-day international criminal justice. Article 25 of the Rome Statute of the ICC – developed over half a century after the Nuremberg Tribunal started its first case – solidifies this position, determining that the court shall have jurisdiction over natural persons. While historians of ICL often take Nuremberg as the staring point and trace the genealogy from there, the concept of individual criminal responsibility or culpability has long existed in national jurisdictions. Efforts to ascribe liability for collective crimes are a key feature of (international) criminal law. Liberal legalism (a key feature of Anglo-Saxon legal systems) dictates that individuals must be held accountable for their own crimes and not for those of others – it follows that the Western legal profession has a preference for direct, individual criminal responsibility. However, criminal trials (both domestically and internationally) have had to find ways to account for crimes that may have been collective in nature or have had collective elements.

On a national level, modes of liability such as aiding and abetting, conspiracy, etc., have long existed. However, due to the particular nature of international crimes, the tensions have been more pronounced. Prosecutors and judges have grappled with ways to establish the linkages between a particular accused's actions (or failure to act) and a given set of acts. This tension in ICL – the matter of how to attribute individual guilt for collective crimes – remains among the most problematic issues of ICL. Yet, the figure of the perpetrator of violence in the international imagination represents the imagery of an individual actor and/or high-ranking leader who is mercilessly engaging in maiming and murdering thousands through their relentless commands. This figure is often described in human rights reports as an actor lacking feeling and brutally engaging in relentless prosecution. It often stands for a figure of violence, representing African politics to the world embedded in irrational violence. In this light, this perpetrator imagery is often seen as a figure of African tragedy and uncivilised violence, uncontrollable by reason and without respect for the sanctity of human life.

But the reality is that there is a gap between the individualisation of criminal responsibility and collective conceptions of guilt. Epitomising this gap is the ongoing case of Kenya's William Ruto and the recently dropped case against Uhuru Kenyatta, whose indictments by the ICC cohere and cohered for some with the international image of the African perpetrator. For others it contradicted such depictions. Such international characterisations operate in ostensible contrast to in-country politics in which it is clear that conceptions of culpability are lived not as permanent, synchronic or diachronic temporalities but in what Achille Mbembe (2001) has referred to as embodying multiplicities and synchronicities in their presences and absences. Set against a backdrop in which Kenyatta and Ruto were cast legally as perpetrators notwithstanding an extensive history of colonial violence, this chapter makes visible a particular 'impunity gap' with regard to the office of the prosecutor's alleged perpetrators and popular sense of responsibility. This gap is evident via the *longue durée* of colonial violence which operates simultaneously and in opposition to the proximity of violence; such spaces lay bare the problem of legal time and the resulting implications for how culpability is imagined differently.

Culpability and the challenge of legal time

The cornerstone of criminal law – national or international – is culpability. Culpability refers to the degree to which one can be held responsible for a particular act or set of results. Measuring culpability then, can be said to be the prime objective of criminal justice. Rooted in American and European legal traditions, individual culpability treats individuals as autonomous agents able to either obey or violate the law, and to bear the consequences of a violation of the law. In Anglo-Saxon legal tradition, known as the liberal justice model, culpability requires the existence of a criminal act (*actus reus*) coupled with the intentional commission of such an act (*mens rea*).[2] Elies van Sliedregt's work on individual criminal responsibility[3] approaches individualism as a concept rooted in Western legal traditions, stemming from the understanding that a person is only culpable to the extent of his own free will or guilty mind (*mens rea*). Chrisje Brants, in her essay 'Guilty Landscapes' argues that individual guilt permeates Western legal culture, and that criminal law takes individual guilt as its sole domain, rather than concepts such as collective guilt (a peoples' guilt) or even metaphysical guilt (the notion that man is guilty simply by being, which Brants argues have been banished to the terrains of art and philosophy).[4]

The modern-day usage of individual criminal culpability can be considered an effort to pierce two traditional 'shields' from criminal culpability – the defence of superior orders and the principle of immunity for heads of state and senior state officials. While there is a tendency within international criminal legal scholarship to describe the development of ICL, and the modern-day international criminal justice system as merely another step in creating global law, a simple transplantation of domestic legal norms to the international level, the reality is more complex. Key proponents of ICL such as the late Cassese insist that 'international criminal law, to a great extent results from the gradual transposition on to the international level of rules and legal constructs proper to national criminal law or national proceedings'.[5] The choice to reject collective responsibility was seen by Cassese as the central idea behind individualised liability decided in the *Tadic* decision, he argued that a 'defendant ought not to be punished for the acts of others'.[6]

The rejection of collective guilt in the international criminal legal system is both a matter of practicality in that it is not feasible to prosecute all who played a role, as well as a matter of principle and ideology with distinct historical roots.[7] While prior to the twentieth century the response to collective guilt was collective punishment (i.e. military retaliation and war), after World War I the victorious allies addressed the matter of settling accounts with the 'aggressors' (Germany and the Ottoman Empire) in the Treaty of Versailles. While mention of criminal trials was made (a solution favoured by the British and to a lesser extent the American), the Treaty provided for criminal trials in national courts Brants writes, but little came of this. Instead, she argues that the Treaty of Versailles resulted in the collective punishment of the German people, creating economic malaise, poverty and hunger. For many, the agreement reached at Versailles represented 'the first *de facto* criminalization of a pariah state in international legal history'.[8] Many historians and other scholars have reflected that these conditions after World War I created the ideal circumstances for the rise of the Nazi Party and World War II. And among some, the Versailles example of collective responsibility fell into disrepute, leading to the renunciation of state criminality and the invocation of a model of individual responsibility.[9]

Ultimately, through discussions amongst the victors of World War II on the way forward, a criminal procedure based in the Anglo-American tradition of fair trial, due process and, by extension, individual culpability, was favoured as the solution most likely to contribute to durable peace following the Nazi regime and the development of a legitimate regime in Germany.[10]

Justice Jackson, in his opening statement, employs similar reasoning. A famous quote from his opening statement reads: 'That four great nations, flushed with victory and stung with injury stay the hand of vengeance and voluntarily submit their captive enemies to the judgment of the law is one of the most significant tributes that Power has ever paid to Reason. Throughout his speech, Jackson makes the case that individual responsibility is the most reasonable and necessary approach. 'This principle of personal liability is a necessary as well as logical one if international law is to render real help to the maintenance of peace.' He then insists that 'an international law which operates only on states can be enforced only by war because the most practicable method of coercing a state is warfare … Only sanctions which reach individuals can peacefully and effectively be enforced.'[11] Thus, the Nuremberg solution is often taken to represent the 'triumph of liberal legalism and individual responsibility over vengeful politics and collective guilt.[12] To date, the Nuremberg precedent heavily influences ICL.

ICL is strongly influenced by humanitarian law and international efforts to regulate armed conflict. Even where, as is the case with the development of the legal definition of crimes against humanity, the contextual requirement that the crime took place during an armed conflict has been removed, international crimes by their nature require that the conduct took place systematically, was organised and occurred on a large scale. War crimes, for instance, as in Article 8 of the Rome Statute, fall within the jurisdiction of the ICC 'in particular when committed as part of a plan or policy or as part of a large scale commission of such crimes'.[13] Some, like Mark Drumbl, have argued that there is an element of collectivity in all international crimes. This collective element is the 'essence' of international crime.[14] In this sense, there is an inherent conundrum present in ICL – the jurisdiction is triggered by collectivity, but once a court is seized of jurisdiction, individual perpetrators – 'those most responsible' – are to be prosecuted. In short, the conundrum ICL presents is that the very acts which are criminalised (war crimes, crimes against humanity, genocide, aggression) are least suitable to individualised accounts of blame or guilt.[15]

Ascribing the guilt of many to a few results in evidentiary challenges when attempting to link an accused to the crimes (and prove this beyond a reasonable doubt).[16] Simpson has reflected that though putatively individualistic, ICL 'cannot escape into individualism entirely' and finds itself 'perpetually drawn back to group responsibility and communal guilt'. However, this challenge of communal guilt is also tied to the forces of history that drive communal action'.[17] Though not new to legal anthropology, the notion of legal time is scarcely interrogated in Western jurisprudential circles, particularly with regard to how notions of culpability are conceptualised.

Scholars of international law like Simpson and Brants have explored questions of liability as a way to understand criminal responsibility but they, among many scholars of critical international law, have hardly examined how notions of legal time are not only conceptualised in particular ways but serve to restrict the analytic space in which criminal law can operate. To examine legal time through its strict understandings and demarcations in criminal law is to reflect on other temporal modes – such as continuing crimes – for addressing collective crimes. Continuing crimes (such as colonialism or apartheid) present us with less stable questions of *perpetratorhood* and create multivalent legal dilemmas. These dilemmas involve questions of jurisdiction, admissibility and evidence, and further the parameters of an 'impunity gap' through which the notion of Kenyatta and Ruto as perpetrators is imagined as viable or unacceptable.

Foundations for continuing crimes in the Kenyan postcolonial imagination

On 1 July 1895, the region that is now known as Kenya was declared to be a British-East African Protectorate.[18] British colonialism in Kenya produced a situation of uneven land distribution and a related problem of elite patronage. The colonial government forcefully evicted Africans from their ancestral lands and relocated them onto what became known as the 'Native Reserves'. The confiscated lands were referred to as the 'White Highlands', and represented some of the most fertile regions of Kenya. The British colonial administration imposed laws that also forced Kenyans to labour on European farms with poor social services. They imposed taxation laws, instituted racial segregation, restricted movement through the *kipande* identification system and curtailed basic freedoms.

Despite their displacement, land and ritual oathing continued to be important for the unification of various Kenyan social groups. Land was not merely a means of economic production but was seen as a divinely inherited blessing that connected them to their ancestors. But as a result of the dispossession of Kenyans from their land, the Mau Mau struggle broke out in order to reclaim their land and promote equality in the region. The majority of the Mau Mau members were from the Kikuyu, Embu and Meru communities, other Kenyans from various groups – such as the Akamba, Maasai, Abaluhya, Abagusii and Luo, as well as various Kenyan Indian trade unionists – also participated in the struggle.[19] This struggle began as early as the late 1940s. It was most intense between 1952 and 1957 as its members intensified their mobilisation to establish the conditions for Kenyan independence in 1963. With Jomo Kenyatta, a former Mau Mau combatant,[20] as the new post-independence prime minister, there were great expectations that Kenyatta's government would sufficiently address the land question through a new land redistribution policy. Hundreds of thousands of Africans – mainly Kikuyu – were either living as squatters on European farms in the Rift Valley or in relatively unproductive 'Native Reserves' away from their ancestral lands. Many hoped that Kenyatta's government would resettle them back to their ancestral lands. However, Kenyatta's government instituted a land-reconsolidation policy that vexed many of the poor squatters, peasants and working classes.

Kenyatta eventually developed a series of strategies for the continual investment of European interests in Kenya while also brokering a deal for the transfer of land to Native Kenyans. In order to implement this plan, he took a loan from the British government in order to buy back land from the European settlers who chose to leave Kenya. Instead of overhauling the agrarian inequalities that were established during the colonial period and redistributing land among the majority of Africans who were either landless or land poor, Kenyatta's government introduced the infamous land policy known as 'willing buyer, willing seller', which required Africans to buy back their land. However, at independence, the majority of Africans were poor squatters, workers and peasant farmers with very little capital. This postindependence policy was seen by many as a blatant injustice because only those who worked closely with the British and earned an income had the necessary resources to buy land or secure bank loans. Thus the early forms of stratification gave an unfair advantage to those who were on the colonial government's payroll during the Mau Mau struggle. But it also instilled feelings of injustice for many who felt that the terms for buying back land that was initially procured illegally were unjust.

Over time, the formation of landless squatters unravelled and took on an ethnic dimension, especially during the 24-year reign of Daniel arap Moi. Both Kikuyu squatters and those members of the Kikuyu who acquired land in the Rift Valley legally were seen as 'foreigners' who needed to be forcefully evicted. The reality that various members of the Kikuyu elites – who eventually became known as the 'Mount Kenya Mafias' – had acquired immense wealth and power in Kenya's postcolonial period only made matters worse for those deemed to be 'foreigners' in the Rift Valley. To contextualise the violence that erupted following the 30 December 2007 democratic deposal of President Daniel arap Moi, one must consider the events leading up to the elections, which seemingly reveal a nation fractured along ethnic-tribal lines, especially the way that a discourse of evicting the 'foreigners' became a rallying cry for Rift Valley politicians during election time.

Ethnic tensions ostensibly worsened when, amidst accusations of election rigging, competing parties – the Party of National Unity (PNU, led by sitting President Mwai Kibaki) and the Orange Democratic Movement (ODM, led by Raila Odinga) – both claimed electoral victory.[21] When Kenya's Electoral Commission announced that Mwai Kibaki was the winner of Kenya's 2007 elections, a two-month period of violence broke out throughout Kenya, particularly in pro-Odinga areas: the slums of Nairobi, the Rift Valley (Eldoret) and Nyanza (Kisumu).[22] In the end, rioting, excessive use of force (by police and security forces), burning, looting, sexual violence and murder left 1200 people dead and displaced thousands.[23] More than a year later, on 26 November 2009, the prosecutor for the ICC requested authorisation from Pre-Trial Chamber II to investigate Kenya's 2007–2008 post-election violence. The Office of the Prosecutor argued that it had reasonable grounds to believe that 'crimes of murder, rape and other forms of sexual violence, deportation or forcible transfer of population and other inhumane acts' had been committed in Kenya from 2007 to 2008.[24]

On 15 December 2010, the Pre-Trial Chamber granted the relevant permission to indict Ruto and Kenyatta using the conception of superior responsibility. This legal frame involved the doctrine of hierarchical accountability wherein expectations of supervision pertain and a related liability for the failure to act were further established through the doctrine of 'command responsibility'. In the case against Kenyatta, charges were based on his supposed command of murders committed in Naivasha on 27 and 28 January 2008, and in Nakuru on 24 and 27 January.[25] For Ruto, the demarcated period was from 1 to 4 January 2008, and involved violence allegedly committed in the greater Eldoret area.[26]

Admittedly, the ICC's temporal jurisdiction over the case was limited by Article 11 of the Rome Statute (*Jurisdiction ratione temporis*), which indicates that the 'Court has jurisdiction only with respect to crimes committed after the entry into force of this Statute'.[27] The ICC's judges examined its temporal jurisdiction over potential cases against Ruto and Kenyatta when it granted the prosecutor permission to commence an investigation over the situation. These considerations are also apparent in the temporal scope of the asserted crimes in relation to the evidence provided to cover the entire time period included in the prosecutor's initial charges. Expressly, Ruto was alleged to have held a series of meetings in which he distributed money and arms with the goal of commissioning the crimes of murder and displacement of supporters of the PNU (led by sitting president at the time, Mwai Kibaki). Following this logic, these activities correspondingly fomented the violence following the 2007 election. With regard to Kenyatta, the Prosecutor alleged that he organised meetings with various government leaders, the police and the leadership of the outlawed Mungiki sect; it was in those meetings that he supposedly provided funding, uniforms and weapons to various pro-PNU youth to carry out their attacks. The Mungiki, whose name means 'a united people' in the Kenya Kikuyu language, is known as a mafia-oriented organisation in Kenya and is notorious for its participation in the 2007 post-election violence. Kenyatta is said to have mobilised their support for the purposes of 'defending' Kikuyu interests, leading the ICC to consider him criminally responsible for the violence the Mungiki perpetrated.[28]

Citing the gravity of the acts of violence and the absence of national proceedings, the prosecutor argued that the cases originating from the investigation of violence during 2007 and 2008 should be admissible before the ICC.[29] The Kenyan government challenged this. Simultaneously, the African Union (AU), in partnership with the Kenyan National Dialogue and Reconciliation (KNDR) team, under the leadership of former UN Secretary General Kofi Annan, recommended that the government establish a national commission of inquiry to investigate the causes of the post-election violence.[30] Known as The Waki Commission, this Commission of Inquiry into Post-Election Violence (CIPEV) was established and recommended that a Special Tribunal for Kenya be set up within a given time frame to investigate and prosecute suspected perpetrators of crimes committed during the crisis period.[31] The Waki Report (October 2008)[32] indicated that a meeting was held in the statehouse to coordinate revenge on Luos and Kalenjins; it cited then-minister Uhuru Kenyatta as being criminally responsible for financing and mobilising electoral support through the Mungiki. Similarly, the Luos and Kalenjins purportedly mobilised their support to attack the Kikuyus (the ethnic group to which Kenyatta belonged). The African Union-sponsored Waki Commission recommended that if the Kenyan government failed to set up a tribunal to investigate and adjudicate the cases, then the ICC should take over.

In early 2009, amidst increased ethnic party tensions, Kenyan parliamentarians tried to bring forward a bill to establish a Special Tribunal. In the end it received limited support and was defeated on two different occasions.[33] Parliamentarians from across the ODM (Raila Odinga) and PNU (Kenyatta and Kibaki's party) united to defeat it under the slogan: 'Don't be vague; let's go to The Hague.' The public statements made by various ODM and PNU politicians revealed their interest in seeking legal accountability for the other party. The prevailing argument was that no Special Tribunal in Kenya could be trusted to deal independently and impartially with issues that involve legal accountability for the post-election violence. On 8 March 2011, the ICC issued a summons for the suspects to appear before the court.[34] The prosecutor named six persons (known as the Ocampo 6) suspected of bearing the greatest responsibility for crimes committed during Kenya's 2007 post-election period. The six were divided into two sets of cases representing two historically opposed factions divided along ethnic lines.

On one side was Major General Mohammed Hussein Ali, a Somali Kenyan who at the time of the post-election violence had been the commissioner of the Kenyan police; Uhuru Kenyatta (Kikuyu), then the deputy prime minister and minister for finance as well as the chairman of President Kibaki's PNU; and Henry Kiprono Kosgey (Kalenjin in ethnicity), former minister for industrialisation and a member of the National Assembly as well as the chairman of the ODM.[35] The opposing side included Francis Kirimi Muthaura, the Head of Public Service, Cabinet Secretary, and Chairman of the National Security Advisory Committee; William Ruto, the Minister for Higher Education, Science and Technology, and ODM member of the National Assembly for Eldoret North; and Joshua Arap Sang, the head of operations at the Kalenjin-language radio station KASS FM, and a radio presenter at the time of the post-election violence (respectively of the Meru and Kalenjin ethnic groups).[36]

In January 2012, the Pre-Trial Chamber judges confirmed the charges of crimes against humanity against only four of the six indictees for Kenya's 2007–2008 post-election violence. The chamber did not find that the evidence against Mr Kosgey met the necessary evidentiary threshold, so the charges against him were not confirmed. In Mr Ali's case the judges did not find that the evidence provided substantial grounds to believe that the National Police partici-pated in the attacks in Naivasha and Nakuru, so the charges against him were also dropped, leaving Ruto and Sang on that case. By summer 2013, due to various setbacks in the prosecu-tion's evidence such as the loss of key witnesses for the *Muthaura* case, the charges against him were dropped, leaving only three indictees overall and only Kenyatta left in the second case. Though the mode of liability initially confirmed for Kenyatta/Muthaura was indirect co-perpetration, after the charges were dropped against Muthaura, the charge against Kenyatta was connected to him being 'individually responsible' for the violence in Naivasha on 27 and 28 January and in Nakuru on 24 and 27 January 2008.

The case against Ruto and Sang began in September 2013.[37] The case against Uhuru Kenyatta was continually adjourned and was finally dropped by the Office of the Prose-cutor on 5 December 2014.[38] The Ruto and Sang case is beset with controversies and complexities. In a poll conducted by Ipsos Synnovate in February 2014, more Kenyans opposed the ICC process than ever before: 46% of the Kenyan population was opposed to ICC engagement, compared to 29% in 2013.[39] Interestingly, by fall of 2012 the once age-old competing parties/ethic groups came together to create the Jubilee Party, led by indictees Ruto (formerly of the ODM party) and Kenyatta (formerly of the PNU party). Despite the ICC indictment, in March 2013 the Kenyan people supported the Jubilee Party and voted for Uhuru Kenyatta as President of the Republic of Kenya and William Ruto as Deputy President, quickly leading to a drastic shift in public opinion on the ICC engagement, with more than half of the population becoming increasingly dis-mayed with the ICC indictments.[40]

While the question of who is responsible for violence committed against various victims has led to disagreements over the ICC indictments of perpetrators for crimes against human-ity, especially those involving African sitting heads of states, longer histories of violence and questions of proximate violence have gained traction as the basis for the attribution of guilt. According to a report by the International Center for Transitional Justice, though victims understood that in ICC judicial contexts greater responsibility is borne by those who gave orders that led to violent outbreaks, more than half of those who responded to the question, 'Who should be prosecuted?', identified direct perpetrators or 'foot sol-diers' of violence as being directly responsible.[41] Though supportive of the ICC concept, in principle, many victims also felt that instead of pursuing a lengthy ICC process in order to achieve compensation for violence and property loss, local and national mechan-isms were preferable – even given the reality that in many ICC-situation countries many did not feel fully satisfied with the domestic measures taken.[42]

In a 2013 survey that my research team and I conducted with victims of 2007–2008 post-election violence in Nairobi's low-income Kibera neighbourhood,[43] an overwhelming majority of Kibera residents insisted that criminal responsibility needs to be understood clearly through notions of collective guilt as clarified through the *Mungiki* phenomenon, the role of the police in post-election violence, and the way that the British colonial settle-ment of the Rift Valley led to the demise of both the Kikuyu and Kalejin ethnic traditional networks. Despite this perception on the ground, international criminal law prioritises command/superior responsibility rather than holding proximate perpetrators accountable; the expectation is that direct perpetrators will be held accountable under domestic criminal law. Accordingly, for some, the law falls short. This is not only because perpetrators of proximate violence are not being prosecuted in Kenya's national judiciaries; it is also attributable to the reality that international courts cannot situate crimes historically. Thus, as I will show, international legal processes have had the effect of producing images of African perpetrators that on the one hand are being met with unease. And on the other hand are seen for some as the only alternative for ending impunity in postcolonial Kenya. This duality exists both because international law is not seen by large numbers of Kenyans in our study as being capable of addressing the imbrication of continuing crimes and because they see Kenya's postcolonial elite as being structurally culpable. This structural culpability calls for a temporal analysis of modes of legal liability and is connected to a colonial–postcolonial continuum for parsing guilt.

Command responsibility, legal time and the problem of continuing crimes

In the Rome Statute system, those most responsible for the commission of crimes over which the court has jurisdiction can, in accordance with Article 25 of the Rome Statute, be held individually responsible and liable for punishment. This criminal responsibility extends to individuals who commit such a crime jointly; those who order, solicit or induce the commission of a crime; persons who aid, abet or otherwise assist in the crime; and those who provide the means for the crime's commission.[44] Article 28 of the Rome Statute stipulates that a military commander or a person acting as a military commander with effective command and control over his forces shall be individually, criminally liable for the criminal conduct of his or her subordinates, provided he or she knew (or should have known) that the forces were committing or were about to commit such crimes. The article also concerns a commander who fails to take all necessary measures to prevent or suppress the commission of these crimes.[45]

Accordingly, the Rome Statute for the ICC set out substantive laws and procedural rules through which to address violence. It ascribes guilt based on a particular period within the temporal jurisdiction of the court and highlights questions of responsibility in individualist terms. Notwithstanding the stipulations for legal responsibility, many of the very victims on behalf of whom international judicial institutions seek to act protest the designations of criminal responsibility strictly in relation to individual responsibility, especially when there is an understanding that longer histories of imperial land disenfranchisement created (and were not products of) such forms of contemporary violence. Many of my respondents insisted that focusing on 2007–2008 post-election violence failed to attend to deep-rooted historical and political issues. For example, Kiamu – a young Kenyan human rights advocate, maintains:

> One of the biggest weaknesses of Kenyan criminal law, we do not have a scheme for compensating victims of crime and the idea that these people of the 2007 violence are the only victims of crime, they're not the only victims of crime, I'm also a victim of crime I lost ten teeth, I nearly died; the state isn't compensating me. The best the state will do if they find the guys who beat me they might even hang them but they'll never pay me a coin for the injuries I've suffered. We've had victims in this country since the colonial times so if you're going to address the system of victims of political violence in Kenya we do it holistically. We begin with the day the British landed here, the evictions that the settlers did – today the biggest land owners are settlers. All of these issues need to be addressed. We're not going to just come here and create a situation and it becomes an industry for everyone to make money and the reference point becomes 2007. My reference point is in the eighteenth century, and I think something needs to happen. If we're going to address the question of criminal politics of domination, exploitation and impoverishment and eviction then my reference point is not 2007 it goes much [further] back. And the ICC has no capacity to address that, so I'll not waste time on it.

Kiamu has a strong conviction about the limits of culpability in domestic and international criminal law; we also see a critique concerning the inability of law to adequately encompass historical forms of violence. Despite these other conceptualisations of guilt, it is unlikely that the ICC will permit itself to consider activities that occurred prior to its temporal jurisdiction, thereby violating basic principles of legality.[46] Set against this vexed juridical backdrop, who should be held responsible for contemporary crimes of violence?

One of the most challenging examples of how courts wrestle with problems of strict temporality can be seen through attempts to address continuing and composite crimes as they force courts to address conduct that exists over a long time rather than in more familiar crimes such as murder. A continuing or composite crime is one that necessarily occurs over an extended period, such as, for example, the crime of apartheid. Apartheid, unlike murder, does not occur in a single instant.[47] It involves legal policies, state action, social control and prolonged practices of exclusion and separation. Continuing and composite crimes also include specific, discrete acts that, by definition, must occur over a longer time frame. For example, the Rome Statute outlaws murder as a crime against humanity. By definition, to be a crime against humanity, the act of murder must occur as part of a widespread or systematic attack against a civilian population.[48] In contrast, when addressing regular crimes, such as murder, which occur in a discrete temporal instant, courts rarely if ever address the importance of temporal limits. However, with continuing and composite crimes, courts must regularly address the temporal scope of the conduct being prosecuted.[49]

Challenges with continuing crimes: the *Rainbow Warrior* case

The *Rainbow Warrior* is one of the most famous examples in the international case law concerning continuing violations. The case is important for the history of international tribunals recognising continuous crimes. In this case, two French agents were convicted by a New Zealand High Court for assisting in the sinking of the *Rainbow Warrior*, a Greenpeace ship docked off the coast of New Zealand (which was going to protest French nuclear testing in the Pacific Ocean). France refrained from detaining the two agents and returned them to Hao, a French Pacific island, in violation of its agreement with New Zealand. In determining France's culpability for refusing to detain the agents, an international arbitration tribunal measured France's liability not just from the moment the agents were removed. Rather, the misconduct was deemed continuous and ongoing, and it included each day the agents remained outside of New Zealand's control.[50]

British seizure of US slave ships

A handful of cases involving the British seizure of US ships illustrate that courts will rule on the absolute moral wrongness of historical practices – here, slavery – but that courts remain largely unwilling to impose criminal liability except for specific acts and only after the conduct is clearly understood to be against the law. In this case over a few decades the British authorities had seized numerous American ships and freed the slaves that belonged to American nationals who were aboard.[51] The governments referred to the Mixed Arbitration Commission that had the task of determining whether, at the time each incident took place, slavery was 'contrary to the law of nations'. Umpire Bates held that the incidents during the 1830s to the 1840s, when the slave trade was considered lawful under the law of nations, amounted to a breach on the part of the British authorities.[52] But the later incidents occurred when the slave trade had been 'prohibited by all civilized nations' and did not involve the responsibility of Great Britain.[53] Thus, the arbitration tribunal did not determine the timing of the wrongfulness of the acts – slavery was always wrong – but the (formal) illegality of the acts.

In *Prosecutor* v. *Musema*, the International Criminal Tribunal for Rwanda (ICTR) allowed the prosecutor to present pre-1994 evidence in order to establish the *mens rea* needed for genocide. Thus, the ICTR jurisprudence allowed pre-1994 evidence of intent but not of conduct.[54] In this case as well as subsequent ICTR cases, such as *Prosecutor* v. *Nahimana* we see an example where the court allowed the introduction of evidence from outside the jurisdictional temporal window.[55] But this compares with *Prosecutor* v. *Barayagwiza*, in which the court interpreted its jurisdiction restrictively, holding that no facts pre-dating or post-dating 1994 could be used to support a count in the indictment.[56]

Continuing and composite crimes force courts to address conduct that exists over longer time periods than other, more familiar, crimes such as murder. They create legal dilemmas not just for questions of jurisdiction but also around questions of evidence and admissibility. The cases identified here address the limits of legal time and represent compelling examples of how courts have attempted to wrestle with problems of strict temporality. In the ICC cases relating to post-election violence in contemporary Kenya, it is clear that a close reading of the ICC's charges allow us to reflect on the tension between specific instances of criminality (violence), on the one hand, and histories of inequalities and perceived injustices that have occurred over extended periods, on the other hand.

Cross-cultural differences in concepts of time abound in the social science literature. In *The Elementary Forms of the Religious Life*, Émile Durkheim noted that 'time' is socially constructed and the form it takes in each society reflects the activities and rhythms of the society's culture, reinforcing the regularity of those activities and rhythms.[57] E.E. Evans-Pritchard similarly asserted that, '[For the Nuer] time ha[ve] not the same value throughout the year … The Nuer have no expression equivalent to "time" in our language, and they cannot, therefore, speak of time as though it were something actual, which passes, can be wasted, can be saved, and so forth.'[58] And Clifford Geertz, in 'Person, Time, and Conduct in Bali', sustained that a Balinese calendar 'is not used … to measure the rate at which time passes … [I]t is adapted to and used for distinguishing and classifying discrete, self-subsistent particles of time … The cycles and super cycles are endless, unanchored, uncountable, and, as their internal order has no significance, without climax. They do not accumulate, they do not build, and they are not consumed. They do not tell you what time it is; they tell you what kind of time it is.'[59]

Contemporary approaches such as David M. Engel's 'Law, Time, and Community',[60] also examine competing, cyclical or 'iterative' versus linear conceptions of time shared by residents of a rural American town. These different conceptions of time influence the community's responses to litigation and the law. Carol J. Greenhouse examines representations of time within American legal culture and social life. For Greenhouse the relationship between cultural conceptions of time – 'social time' – and the organisation and management of legal institutions' 'temporality and legality' are conceptually fused in the West. As such they produce the terms in which social life acquires meaning.[61] This scholarship on temporality has established the role of time as socially constituted. Let us turn to the Kenyan example with John to demonstrate how temporality and legality played out in the conceptions of my informants. John – a known Kenyan journalist – insisted that in 2007–2008 neither Kenyatta nor Ruto were heads of state, so it is not clear why they, over others, would be seen as bearing the most responsibility.

> Neither of them were running for president. I don't think there was [responsibility] if you look at the violence and protest in ODM strongholds. I think you would see 'no Raila no peace', not 'no Ruto no peace', and especially in Kalenjin stronghold. So how on earth do you then begin to design these cases against the two of them? I think that it is possible to finger Uhuru Kenyatta

for post-election violence in Naivasha and Nakuru, I think that it is possible. It is much more difficult to [connect him] to the North Rift.

By referring to the slogan, 'No Raila, No Peace', John was explaining that those who supported Raila were fighting for his presidency and not for Ruto's (who was in the ODM leadership). After the election results and the announcement that Kibaki had won again, it became clear that Raila, through his ODM supporters, mostly from the Luo ethnic group in the ODM strongholds (like Kibera), refused to accept a situation in which Raila was not going to be in power. Much of this was connected to the problem of the concentration of power among a few families and ethnic groups.

From the time Jomo Kenyatta took office from the colonial Home Guards in 1963 to the last election, power was seen as remaining within a very tightly sealed vacuum in which the Kikuyu and the Kalenjin constituted a small community that governed all others and shielded their political and economic elite from accountability to the people and to the law.[62] The violence of 2007–2008 was, in many ways, seen as a response to the unwillingness of others to concede to the monopolisation of power by particular members of the elite once again. Yet, the media contributed to the production of the concept of the perpetrator by depicting the situation as ultimately being about the ethnic Kalenjin mobilising against the Kikuyu. As Bornu – a Kenyan political analyst – explained,

> Some say the Kalenjin rose up as a community – though it's not true at all! If you just go back to reports of the violence, the violence was up and down the railway line. There was looting and violence in Mombasa, there were Kikuyu and Kisii evictions in Maasai Land; there was no violence in Central Highlands but Nairobi and going all the way to the border! So the idea that the Kalenjin were some ... atavistic, blood thirsty Others just served to demonize them ... The ignorance about the Kalenjin was mind-blowing. I mean the Kalenjin were otherized so effectively ... But when you talk to people in Nakuru or Kikuyus who had family or whatever in Nakuru, there was a point at which the Kalenjin were invading and there was just utter fear. [Because of their fear, people didn't] know what kind of monster [was] coming to attack [them]. But the reality was that the violence was across the board and along party lines and also along a very anti-Kikuyu level. Then you'd have to provoke the question of why is everybody standing up, rising up against the Kikuyu? What is going on? But the Kalenjin were very insistent that that violence was spontaneous, and were very insistent that any form of planning or organization happened after the announcement of the election results, not before.

Bornu's statement highlights that there was not only a sense that the violence was perpetrated across the board by many actors – police, local people, outside forces, militia, gangs – but also that it was inspired by deep-seated histories of disenfranchisement and the monopolisation of power throughout Kenya. In Kiamu, John and Bornu's statements, we can begin to see that at the heart of the impunity gap is the difficulty in ascribing guilt to particular individuals; some feel that the ICC's focus on command responsibility not only overlooks the guilt of those who actually engaged in criminal conduct, but that, in the Kenyan cases, it also produces a framework in which the cases are argued in a way that overlooks the temporality of collective responsibility for age-old political problems.

Understanding the inter-ethnic consolidation of Ruto's United Republican Party (URP) with Kenyatta's Nation Alliance Party (TNA), which came together to produce the Jubilee Party and its victory, is central to grasping the emergence of an impunity gap in the Kenyan national imaginary. It is worth asking how would-be 'perpetrators' of Kenya's 2007 post-election violence, according to the ICC, could facilitate the consolidation of historically opposed ethnic groups, whose candidates then won Kenya's 2013 presidential elections.

On the one hand, the histories of land dispossession during and following British colonialism produced the conditions through which Kenyatta and Ruto's Jubilee coalition could be perceived as settling a more than 50-year-old history of injustice. On the other hand, since Kenya gained independence, political and economic power in government has circulated among the Kikuyu and Kalenjin elite to the exclusion of other groups. The recognition of these two realities suggests that the violence actually attests to the way that histories of dispossession became sedimented along various patronage lines. Thus, the attacks against the Kikuyus represented the mobilisation of particular ethnic patronage networks to try to change the Kikuyu and/or Luo and Kalenjin monopolisation of power in postcolonial Kenya. It is the realisation of the deep-seated complexities of culpability playing out through a sense of communal responsibility to protect that has contributed to the recognition of the centrality of proximity and patronage. This sensibility of collective responsibility – instantiated through oathing, but later sedimented through patronage – informs the production of a popular national imaginary in which Ruto and Kenyatta are not widely seen as 'perpetrators' awaiting indictment of the ICC but as national heroes to be protected and celebrated.

My informant's answer to the related question of who should be held accountable instead highlights the extent to which collective responsibility is relevant. According to Ngogi, a local Kenyan activist,

> The financing of that violence involved the entire Kikuyu diaspora as well as [the] domestic population. People from southeast London to Texas were holding meetings and sending cash to support the cause. They were planning meetings all over this city. There w[as] supposed to be at one point a huge incident in Umoja and Eastlands where especially Luos were going to be flushed out of the houses that they allegedly occupied. Kikuyu shopkeepers in Umoja raised a lot of cash and it just so happened that the peace deal came before they were able to carry out the plan.

Some of the Kenyans that we spoke with during fieldwork in Nairobi[63] alleged that Kenyatta and Ruto actually defended the powerless. From these interviews it became clear that the complexity of financing violence as a part of the co-perpetration of violence was not only central to parsing responsibility. Rather, the act of financing and arming fellow Kenyans was seen as a response to the call to protect the collective whole – the Kikuyu against Raila's supporters, the Luo, for example. Accordingly, what the OTP saw as Kenyatta's legal culpability was actually seen by members of the Kikuyu elders as a necessary act of communal responsibility in which he – as well as others in Kenya and throughout the diaspora – was perceived to be taking critical steps to protect his community from ethnic-inspired violence and to ensure Kikuyu prominence/dominance in Kenyan politics.

Uhuru Kenyatta's rapid rise to power is seen as an indicator of the importance of the notion of collective responsibility, in which it is understood that Kenyatta was obligated to contribute to the financing of the violence in order to protect his community against other ethnic forces set on displacing them from their land. With this rationale, Kenyatta's community saw him as protecting the collective, and thus they do not see him as culpable. The overt problem is that admitting to the existence of Kenyatta's participation and the role of others in actually financing the violence would be seen as a legal admission of guilt during the designated post-election period of violence. Instead, Kikuyus often make vague admissions by describing Kenyatta's actions as collectively appropriate. See statements such as, 'Uhuru stepped in because Mwai Kibaki was asleep.' Or, 'Kibaki was too weak, Mwai Kibaki was useless', and 'Uhuru is our hero because he took responsibility when it really mattered'.[64] These claims – with their legal implications – speak to the affective sentiments of solidarity and alliance through which contemporary Kenyans are asserting a new narrative about political violence in their country. According to interview participants, because of reprisal violence on the part of Luos against any ethnic group they felt had supported the Kibaki victory, the Kikuyus in coordination with Kikuyu elders mobilised forces to protect themselves in various places; hence the mobilisation of the Mungiki forces. Actions taken in the Ruto camp, and by extension the Kalenjins (and Kenyatta through his Kikuyu networks) in terms of mobilisation – i.e. financing and executing violent acts – were ultimately seen by participants as being in support of two principal players: Kibaki and Raila. The compromise related to this standoff eventually resulted in the creation of a new position, prime minister, as part of the power-sharing agreement in which historically opposed parties came together.[65] Thus, among a particular contingent, Kibaki and Raila were seen by many as the most invested parties in the post-election violence, and, therefore, though not seen as those engaged in proximate violence, when respondents were pressed to parse responsibility according to principles of international law, many argued that Kibaki and Raila should have been the ones seen as bearing the greatest responsibility and not Kenyatta and Ruto.

Proximity, intimacy and redirecting the culpability of the perpetrator

When we asked Marcus, a villager from Kibera, – whether he thought Kenyatta was the most responsible, he, like many, responded by insisting that many Kenyans believed that Prosecutor Moreno Ocampo was interested in prosecuting those listed on the Waki Commission's list because the OTP was outsourcing a significant amount of its investigations to non-governmental organisations and others, who many discredited as being incompetent and far from thorough. As Marcus elaborates:

> So, how do these guys end up at the ICC? If not through a process of kind of political roulette, how does he end up there? That is completely arbitrary; you have twenty people or twenty plus people fingered for the violence by Waki, he narrowed it down too. I think a lot of people will be asking questions about why isn't so and so and why isn't so and so on the list, but I don't know by what logic somebody like John Michuki could have escaped? He was Internal Security Minister, the one who directly banned any type of street demonstrations. He was very much involved at the National Security, NSAC, and on top of that Michuki had said on multiple occasions he was directly ordering the police to shoot to kill Mungiki. But if you are not going to touch Mungiki, I don't how then you are going to deal with reprisal violence in the North. The other person who should be at the ICC, I mean one would think, would be Maina Njenga [the head of the Mungiki] himself.

By referring to the perception that the OTP accepted the names outlined in the Waki Commission report, Marcus suggests that the logic was political and, in some cases, arbitrary. He continued,

> If you are talking about the criteria for these kinds of charges to warrant a case at the ICC, I think one of the things that Luis Moreno Ocampo has been at pains to show is that there was a structured violence, that there was an organization with a hierarchy and so on. It is called Mungiki and his head is Miana Njenga. In many ways one can then begin to understand that there is something legitimate about the angle of Uhuru Kenyatta and William Ruto.

Yet, despite this concession about the plausibility of guilt, a range of actors, such as the police chief, members of the police force, and Mungiki gangs were also seen as contributors to violence but were actually dropped from the list. Also part of the story, and as my informant explained, was that the police were part of this process. The existence of the police also raises questions about why the ICC's prosecution did not pursue the head of the Kenyan police force. Here the presumption was that the violence should not be attributed to one or two commanders. The planning for the violence was said to precede the elections and was mobilised as part of the defense of the Kikuyu. The reality is that there is not only a sense that the violence was perpetrated across the board by many actors – police, local people, outside forces, militia, gangs – but also that the violence was inspired by deep-seated histories of disenfranchisement in which various persons saw themselves as carrying out their obligations to protect their community. But despite the recognition of the responsibility to protect, the point, ultimately, is that they, and not Kenyatta and Ruto, were the ones who were seen as being engaged in inflicting proximate violence. Here Marcus maps out the forms of proximate violence relevant to the Mungiki phenomenon:

> There are a number of men that were targeted because of their ethnic leanings, and the link between those ethnic groups to certain political leanings. And because of that they were attacked in certain sex-selective ways. You know having their penises amputated, or having them sodomized, and because then when you think about them from the political reasons why it happened then they qualify as gender crimes ... Sexual and gender-based crimes post-election have been downplayed. They're taken as serious crimes related to the election violence. The police have been implicated and other security agents that some victims have described in detail, that it is for sure the people that raped them were security agents that had been deployed to that area or to those places during the period of the chaos.
>
> So, for instance, in Kibera a number of victims have described the attire that the men that raped them were in and for some of them they describe it in detail; they talk about the way the teargas canisters were dangling and making noises, those are some of the noises they remember. So we were concerned that our own security agents have been implicated and that the government has not done anything.

As we see, the realities of intimate violence – rape, castration, sodomy – remain part of the ways that victims of violence are also conceptualising guilt. Those responsible for violence against their bodies are those who actually committed the crimes: the man who raped, the boy next door who killed his neighbour, and the foot soldiers of the security forces who maimed. Yet, the problem for many is that because of the ICC indictment it is the Kenyan government through the figure of Kenyatta and Ruto that is being held responsible for those alleged perpetrators of violence in the police and security forces.

In response to our question about whether Kenyatta and Ruto should assume responsibility for the 2007–2008 post-election violence, the journalist Ngugi turns around the question and asks us:

> Responsibility for what? Some of the worst violence happened in Western Kenya and, yes, it is often mentioned that Kisumu [is] burning, but it's actually not considered a media epicenter of the violence. And in both cases [they] let the state security forces off the hook. In Kakamega, Bungoma, in Kitale, the vast majority of people that were killed were killed by police bullets usually found in [their] back; they were running away. If you omit that, then all the violence becomes is a long-held ethnic dispute. You know all the rhetoric that influenced – is it called Agenda Four items?[66] – it is absolute *bullshit*.

Here by referring to *Agenda Four* items Ngugi is referring to part of the national dialogue and reconciliation efforts that took place after the 2007–2008 violence. Four agendas were proposed to address the way forward for Kenya. The fourth and final agenda item was to address 'long-term issues and solutions' and include items such as land reform, national unity, etc. The Agenda Four items were the last items agreed to in the Annan-brokered peace agreement. They had to do with further long-term peace-building concerns. But Ngugi's point is that the issue is a lot more complex than simply ethnicity and land. The issues are also about the perceptions of narrative erasures – the production of false narratives that are seen as being part of the maintenance of state power. He suggests that the violence was not simply 'routine' ethnic violence, as it was often framed. He insists that the security forces – those in proximate relations to daily citizens – were actively involved, and people from Western region were being targeted.

> I spent a lot of time, January and part of February, in the North Rift, in places like Kiptere, just around Eldoret town in the outskirts of Eldoret. I was scooping spent cartridges, G3 cartridges. I mean the ops had gone completely amuck … because even the security forces … were divided along party and ethnic lines.

He emphasises how ethnically segmented the divisions became:

> If you went to the police station in Eldoret town, I remember the first time I went there on a Sunday and a policeman comes striding out. I am coming into the compound and she is coming out and she is loudly announcing, 'This is an ODM zone, so understand where you're coming.' I needed security to go into a place called Munyaka, which was a Kikuyu settlement, and she told me, 'Eh listen my friend this not the place, and now you have to make special arrangements, you are not going to find people here that are going to go in there.' The cops, General Service Unit, Administrative Police, and so on who were shooting up the place in Kiptere and so on were imported and it was very specific because they were Kenyan police and, again according to locals, again another narrative that's never discussed, Ugandans. But if you went to Moi referral hospitals and you found anyone who was working at Moi referral hospital in January/February 2008, [they say] there was an invasion by Administration Police-looking types of the hospital at one point, and they said these people could not speak Kiswahili. That is one of the stories you will also here in Kisumu.

In this passage Ngugi counters what he sees as false narratives – or massive omissions of facts – in which the proximate role of the police, the security forces and the use of foreign forces like the Ugandans were underplayed. He insists, rather, that the state security machine played a major role in the violence and were in fact the largest perpetrators. He argues that when you remove these major players from the story, the violence begins to look like a long-standing ethnic dispute. It involved a range of actors engaged in intimate killing whose affiliations were conveniently segmented along ethnicity and party alliances; but some of the worst forms of violence involved the police and security forces from nearby states who were imported to perpetrate violence. The implications debunk Kenyatta and Ruto's criminal responsibility for the perpetration of violence by suggesting that Kibaki had requested assistance from Museveni, who responded by sending security forces from Uganda to parts of the Rift and Western Kenya. The report that the 'police-looking types' did not speak Kiswahili was taken as further evidence that they were not Kenyan and had been 'imported'. He also seems to suggest that even Kenyan security forces were stationed in different areas, or at least 'imported' into certain hot spots like Eldoret, based on ethnicity/political affiliation. Given the way the security forces are 'divided along party and ethnic lines', the Kibaki government was calculating in its deployment of the forces. Thus Ngugi suggests that there was more at play than different ethnic communities fighting each other. The key point is that the violence was based on much more than ethnic patronage. It was about the fight to overtake government – at all costs – or for the Kibaki government to maintain power within it.

Of the most pronounced redirections of culpability – from Ruto and Kenyatta to the police, security services or neighbours accused of stealing – was those accused of perpetrating the most intimate forms of violence: sexual violence ranging from rape to castration and sodomy. Proximity mattered in those contexts and notions of culpability were directly tied not to individual commanders who directed and enabled violence but to those who were themselves engaged in proximate violence.

Conclusion

Articulating guilt through narrow terms like superior responsibility limits the representational life of those deemed most responsible for violence. International criminal legal concepts of culpability rely not only on rational reasoning for clarifying the line of command, but they also depend on a particular production of the guilty perpetrator without whom violence would not be possible. Thus far we have seen that the different levels of perpetration – senior level and the execution level of proximate violence – are not separate but are interconnected. How one may attribute guilt, and by extension how the perpetrator of violence is conceived, becomes difficult when questions of historical collective responsibility are introduced. This is especially a challenge because international crimes normally involve a plurality of individuals acting within the framework of a common plan. In this context, the direct perpetrators or proximate actors who physically commit the criminal acts – typically occupying low-ranking positions – are set alongside those who orchestrate systematic commission and execution of violence. These notions of culpability and the related liability understood in legal circles are often argued in relation to strict temporal designations. And this is where the problem lies.

New international-law assertions of culpability are not enough to make sense of the deep roots of violence. There is an affective dimension, an emotional indignance about colonial injustices and their arbitrary power proximate actors that remains part of the postcolonial condition. But large numbers of the Kenyan public see the postcolonial complexities that have taken shape as being misdirected by the ICC indictments. Ultimately this has had implications for the construction of the African perpetrator as the Kenyan prime minister or the deputy president and the limits of the law in attributing histories of violence according to contemporary approaches to command responsibility.

The construction of international criminal law has involved the production of strict understandings and demarcations in time through which to attribute guilt. Rather than reflecting on historical developments or broader root causes, ICC jurisprudence has adopted a relatively strict view of temporality with the recognition that non-retroactivity or the principle of *nullum crimen sine lege* – no crime except what is proscribed by law – is one of the central principles of law. The criminalisation of acts occurring over long periods of time is seen as potentially threatening this principle because it is hard to define what precisely is being punished and when exactly the conduct becomes criminal. But this is where the problem lies.

The impunity gap represents an abyss between legal presumptions of temporally relevant responsibility, and the growing grass-roots conception of who is actually criminally responsible for acts of violence – including historically relevant institutions such as colonial agents and discriminatory segregation politics. I have shown how – in relation to these historical realities – the impunity gap highlights a hierarchical/vertical disjuncture due to the limitations of attributing conduct from one person to the other – distinguishing between foot soldiers and 'those most responsible – and the problem of legal time as it relates to strict applications of the temporality of violence. What the ICL impunity gap reveals is the difference between social and legal justice and the varying understandings of guilt and responsibility. It highlights the afterlife of a failure to balance power historically in postcolonial Kenya, set alongside the use of the law to rectify histories of dispossession manifest in acts of violence. We also see how fraught with meaning the assignment of culpability to one perpetrator really is – especially in contexts in which the state has failed to adequately address the needs of those victimised by violence.

Whether the disjuncture occurs because of a difference with attribution based on proximate violence, or because of the inability to reconcile contemporary violence in relation to guilt attributed within a strictly narrow temporal period in 2007–2008, the reality is that this impunity gap exists in the Kenyan political landscape because people recognise that legal time and the individualisation of criminal responsibility do not account for the deep histories that produced the conditions under which police violence, ethnic rivalries and land dispossession were made possible.[67] Rather, there is a realisation that inscriptions of power in colonial Kenya were central to the play of power in post-independence Kenya. And since independence, power has never been balanced or distributed beyond those ethnic groups – the Kikuyu and Kalenjins – that inherited power. Yet, the other reality is that in postcolonial Africa, the afterlife of imperialism, colonialism and the violence of dispossession persist deeply in the psychic life of social justice. And alongside ethnic divisions, there is also an awareness of the ways that imperial injustices remain part of the postcolonial reality – a continuity of structures of economic, legal and political power. And while the image of the African perpetrator as warlord and killer has been constructed through the law to produce a narrative of the merciless mercenary, the African head of state as perpetrator has been subject to another moral imaginary that represents a new shift.

The Kenyan cases being pursued by the ICC demonstrate an alternate conceptualisation of culpability. What they show us is that the impunity gap can actually be explained through affective sentiments of historical solidarity that suggest that not only do most Africans want to end violence, impunity and the abuses of the postcolonial elite, but they also want to reassert a new narrative imaginary about the political nature of contemporary violence in Kenya.

The new imaginary of collective crimes understood through a colonial–postcolonial continuum competes with the ICC perpetrator figure. It represents a new socio-cultural realisation tied to particular historical attachments that reflect the reality that we live in a world where meanings of justice extend beyond the law. What we see is that the colonial–postcolonial continuum is complexly interconnected. Senses of the continuity with the past and present are tied to an emotional afterlife that shapes the subordination of liberal legalism to the realities of postcoloniality. These notions of continuity show how people understand collective responsibility in relation to affective and historically influenced domains. These affective forms structure engagements with justice and reproduce forms of desire, freedom and ways of rejecting hegemony in daily life. In that process they produce an affective continuity in which agents struggle for the power to articulate meaning and produce relevance. Seen as thus, exploring the work of the temporal imagination in legal practice can be enriched through bringing it into dialogue with transnational fields of power, such as international law – historically situated subjects who imagine transformative possibilities in contemporary democracy. The Jubilee Party victory of 2013 demonstrates how social justice can exceed the juridical. On the one hand, the political elite was able to implement an UhuRuto promotional strategy and politicise ethnicity, leading to a merger and consolidation of the Jubilee Party and its deployment of a strategic narrative of colonial victimhood. On the other hand, we are seeing the emergence of a renewed sense of ethnic solidarity based on a different 'moral imaginary' within their respective to the culpability for violence in postcolonial Africa. The contemporary period is characterised by a rupture with the past in which the imagination and the imaginary is constructed within a landscape of social practices and relations of power. Thus, when set alongside a broader temporal continuum, how one imagines culpability of a perpetrator involves the new negotiations between individual agency in the reading of colonial and postcolonial history in relation to globally defined fields of possibility in which social knowledge contributes to the production of new meanings of justice.

To understand the play of the imagination and the conditions of possibility through which legal logic is reconceptualised, the interrogation of the figure of the perpetrator calls for new theoretical models for explaining how through conceptions of continuing crimes new global imaginaries of conflict and violence are being deployed to address histories of protest against liberal legal forms and their institutions. They are being deployed to rethink continuing challenges of violence and their impact on proximate social worlds and are providing the vocabulary for managing the globalisation of the rule of law and the discourses of justice in terms that are contextually meaningful.

Ultimately, the competing discourses that are embedded in conceptions of culpability are actually reflective of a turn in the modernity of international justice and its reassertion as an ontological problem – that of the existence of temporal continuities that have traditionally been written out of modern legality. The insistence of temporal linkages through colonial–postcolonial continuums call on us to rethink how articulations of temporal jurisdiction presumed to be 'natural' and rational are just as shaped by ideologies of constructing rationality as they are by actual connections. With this insight, the attribution of the perpetrator figure is a question of how temporal continuity as an ontological question is negotiated in complex sites of international meaning making.

Acknowledgements

The author thanks the following research assistants and colleagues for their input to this article: Sarah-Jane Koulen, Thomas Saunders, Ifrah Abdillihi, Brenda Kombo, Muoki Mubunga, Luladay Berhanu, Ahadu Yeshitela, Tewodros Dawit, Bethel Genene, Sara Kendall, Ronald Jennings, Adam Branch and Charles Jalloh.

Disclosure statement

No potential conflict of interest was reported by the author.

Notes

1. Hannah Arendt, *Responsibility and Judgment* (New York: Schocken, 2003).
2. H.M. Hart, 'The Aims of the Criminal Law', *Law and Contemporary Problems* 23, no. 3 (1958): 401–41.

3. Elies van Sliedregt, *Individual Criminal Responsibility in International Law*. Oxford Monographs in International Law (Oxford: Oxford University Press, 2012).

4. Chrisje Brants, 'Guilty Landscapes: Collective guilt and international criminal law', in *Cosmopolitan Justice and its Discontents*, ed. Cecilia Bailliet and Katja Frank Aas (London: Routledge, 2011), 53–68.

5. A. Cassese, *International Criminal Law* (Oxford: Oxford University Press, 2003), 7.

6. Cassese 2003.

7. Brants, 'Guilty Landscapes', 60.

8. Gerry J. Simpson, *Law, War & Crime: War Crimes, Trials and the Reinvention of International Law* (Cambridge: Polity Press, 2007).

9. Ibid.

10. Brants, 'Guilty Landscapes', 61.

11. Justice Robert H. Jackson, Opening Statement Before the International Military Tribunal, 21 November 1945, http://www.roberthjackson.org/the-man/speeches-articles/speeches/speeches-by-robert-h-jackson/opening-statement-before-the-international-military-tribunal/.

12. Simpson, *Law, War & Crime*, 62.

13. Rome Statute of the International Criminal Court, Article 8.

14. Mark A. Drumbl, *Atrocity, Punishment and International Law* (New York: Cambridge University Press, 2007).

15. Simpson, *Law, War & Crime*.

16. van Sliedregt, *Individual Criminal Responsibility in International Law*.

17. Simpson, *Law, War & Crime*, 59.

18. Bethwell Ogot, ed., *Zamani: A Survey of East African History* (Nairobi: East African Publishing House and Longman Group Ltd, 1974), 249.

19. Maina wa Kinyatti, *History of Resistance in Kenya: 1884–2002* (Nairobi: Mau Mau Research Centre, 2009), 144–50. The question of ethnicity in the Mau Mau struggle is one of the most controversial in the historiography. The debate revolves around whether the struggle was of a nationalist nature or just a Kikuyu affair. For details of this debate please see: Maina wa Kinyatti, 'Mau Mau: The Peak of African Political Organization in Colonial Kenya', *Kenya Historical Review* 5, no. 2 (1977): 287–311; and E.S. Atieno-Odhiambo, 'The Production of History in Kenya: The Mau Mau Debate', *Canadian Journal of African Studies* 25, no. 2 (1991): 300–7.

20. It is worth noting here that Kenyatta denied his involvement with the Mau Mau during the Kapenguria trial.

21. Nic Cheeseman, 'The Kenyan Elections of 2007: An Introduction', *Journal of Eastern African Studies* 2, no. 2 (2008): 166–84.

22. Human Rights Watch, *High Stakes: Political Violence and the 2013 Elections in Kenya*, February 2013, http://www.hrw.org/sites/default/files/reports/kenya0213webwcover.pdf (accessed 15 July 2013).

23. Ibid.; See also Peter Kagwanja and Roger Southall, 'Introduction: Kenya – A Democracy in Retreat?', *Journal of Contemporary African Studies* 27, no. 3 (2009): 259–77.

24. ICC Pre-Trial Chamber II, 'Situation in the Republic of Kenya, Request for Authorization of an Investigation Pursuant to Article 15', http://www.icc-cpi.int/iccdocs/doc/doc785972.pdf (accessed 15 July 2013), 3.

25. *The Prosecutor* v. *Uhuru Muigai Kenyatta*, ICC-PIDS-KEN-02-010/14 [2014].

26. *The Prosecutor* v. *William Samoei Ruto and Joshua Arap Sang*, ICC-01/09-01/11-859 16-08-[2013]; the prosecutor did seek permission to amend the charges against Ruto/Sang to include events on 30 and 31 December 2007, but the judges deemed this request inadmissible at the time it was made, as it was after the confirmation of charges hearing and no postponement was requested in order to amend the charges.

27. Rome Statute of the International Criminal Court, Article 11.

28. Interview 0037, Kamari Clarke, 18 July 2013.

29. ICC Pre-Trail Chamber II , 'Situation in the Republic of Kenya, Decision on the Prosecutor's Appeal against the Decision on the Request to Amend the Updated Document Containing the Charges Pursuant to Article 61(9) of the Statue', http://www.icc-cpi.int/iccdocs/doc/doc1699466.pdf (accessed 28 April 2014).

30. Monica Kathina Juma, 'African Mediation of the Kenyan Post-2007 Election Crisis', *Journal of Contemporary African Studies* 27, no. 3 (2009): 407–30.

31. Kagwanja and Southall, 'Introduction'.
32. *The Waki Commission Report*, Commission of Inquiry into Post-Election Violence (CIPEV), 2008.
33. The first defeat was in 2009 when the government failed to obtain enough support in parliament to pass the relevant laws to set up the tribunal.
34. The Kenyan National Dialogue and Reconciliation (KNDR) Monitoring Project, 'Progress in Implementation of the Constitution and Other Reforms', October 2011, Review Report (Funded by the Open Society Institute), 45.
35. Susanne D. Mueller, 'Kenya and the International Criminal Court (ICC): Politics, Election and the Law', *Journal of Eastern African Studies* 8, no. 1 (2014): 25–42.
36. Ibid.
37. On 23 January 2012, the Pre-Trial Chamber II decided to move cases against Ruto, Sang, Muthaura and Kenyatta to trial. Judges declined to confirm charges against Henry Kiprono Kosgey and Mohammed Hussein Ali. The recent decision to move the majority of the Kenyan cases to trial is bound to provide a window into another set of international juridical processes on the world stage and assessments on the extent to which the ICC has the potential to produce justice.
38. On 31 March 2014, Trial Chamber V(b) of the ICC adjourned the commencement date of the trial in the case against Uhuru Kenyatta to 7 October 2014. The purpose of the adjournment being to provide the government of Kenya with a further, time-limited opportunity to provide certain records, which the prosecution had previously requested on the basis that the records are relevant to a central allegation to the case. Press Release: 31/03/2014 Kenyatta case: 'Trial Adjourned until 7 October 2014', ICC-CPI-20140331-PR991, http://www.icc-cpi.int/en_menus/icc/press%20and%20media/press%20releases/Pages/pr991.aspx (accessed 28 April 2014).
39. Ipsos-Synovate, 'One Year into the Jubilee Government: A Reality-Check by Kenyans', 14 March 2014, https://www.google.com/search?q=One+Year+into+the+Jubilee+Government%3A+A+Reality-Check+by+Kenyans&ie=utf-8&oe=utf-8 (accessed 28 April 2014).
40. Ibid.
41. Simon Robins, '"To Live as Other Kenyans Do": A Study of the Reparative Demands of Kenyan Victims of Human Rights Violations', *International Center for Transitional Justice* 52 (2011), http://ictj.org/sites/default/files/ICTJ-Kenya-Reparations-Demands-2011-English.pdf (accessed 28 July 2013).
42. Ibid.
43. The survey was conducted during Author's fieldwork in Nairobi with research team from September to December 2013.
44. Chantale Meloni, 'Command Responsibility. Mode of Liability for the Crimes of Subordinates or Separate Offence of the Superior?', *Journal of International Criminal Justice* 5, no. 3 (2009): 619–37.
45. The requisite threshold requires that the material elements of the crimes occur within the temporal jurisdiction of the court (from 1 July 2002 onward); it also obliges that the crimes be committed with knowledge and intent. This doctrine of hierarchical criminal or command responsibility – established by The Hague Conventions (IV) and (X) of 1907 and first applied during the Leipzig War Crimes Trials after World War I – involves the reassignment of the guilt of thousands who committed violent acts to a single chief commander and a few top aides.
46. See Alan Nissel, 'Continuing Crimes in the Rome Statute', *Michigan Journal of International Law* 25 (2004): 681.
47. Rome Statute of the International Criminal Court, Art. 7(2)(h).
48. Ibid., Art. 7(1)(a) .
49. See also Alan Nissel, 'Continuing Crimes in the Rome Statute', *Michigan Journal of International Law* 25 (2004): 653, 665.
50. See Case Concerning the Difference Between New Zealand and France Concerning the Interpretation or Application of Two Agreements, Concluded on 9 July 1986 Between the Two States and which Related to the Problems Arising from the Rainbow Warrior Affair (N. Z./Fr.), 20 R.I.A.A. 217 (1990).
51. John Bassett Moore, IV *History and Digest of the International Arbitrations To Which The United States Has Been A Party* 4372-75 (1898); see James Crawford, *The International*

Law Commission's Articles on State Responsibility: Introduction, Text and Commentaries 131, P2 (2001).
52. Ibid., 4349, 4375.
53. Ibid., 2824 .
54. Citing *Prosecutor* v. *Musema*, ICTR Case No. ICTR-96-13-A, P164 (ICTR Trial Chamber 27 January 2000) (Judgment and Sentence).
55. ICTR Case No. ICTR-99-52-T, P103 (ICTR Trial Chamber, 3 December 2003).
56. ICTR Case No. ICTR-97-19-AR72 (ICTR Appeals Chamber, 12 September 2000).
57. Emile Durkheim, *Elementary Forms of Religious Life* (London: Hollen Street Press, 1915).
58. E.E. Evans-Pritchard, *The Nuer: A Description of the Modes of Livelihood and Political Institutions of a Nilotic People* (London: University Press, 1940), 102–3.
59. Clifford Geertz, *The Interpretation of Cultures* (New York: Basic Books, 1973), 393.
60. David M. Engel, 'Law, Time, and Community', *Law & Society Review* 21, no. 4 (1987): 605–38.
61. Carol J. Greenhouse, 'Just in Time: Temporality and the Cultural Legitimation of Law', *Yale L. J.* 98 (June 1989): 1631.
62. Home Guards were African village policemen who were working for the British colonial government in Kenya to quash the Mau Mau struggle. They had a reputation of being extremely vicious in their anti-Mau Mau campaigns.
63. Concentrated ethnographic fieldwork and survey data collection for this project was funded by the National Science Foundation and conducted by the author and three researchers during May to December 2013 and then again in summer 2014. Surveys were disseminated in Kibera and Nashava, Kenya and focus groups were conducted in various sites throughout Western and Southern Kenya.
64. Interview data collected in Nairobi during May to December 2013.
65. A. Nicoll and J. Delaney, eds, 'Kenya's Election: Risk of Renewed Violence', *The International Institute for Strategic Studies* 19, no. 1 (2013): vii–ix.
66. Following the violence over Kenya's disputed 2007 general elections the Kenyan Dialogue and Reconciliation forum was created to facilitate mediation among the various parties. As part of this process four agendas were identified as areas of focus for national dialogue and reconciliation. Agenda Four focused on long-term issues and solutions such as land reform, legal and institutional reform, unemployment and several more.
67. The Truth, Justice, and Reconciliation Commission (TJRC) report tried to address these very questions, but the process was significantly delayed and marked with internal wrangling, which served to discredit the process significantly.

False promise and new hope: dead perpetrators, imagined documents and emergent archival evidence

Michelle Caswell and Anne Gilliland

Department of Information Studies, University of California, Los Angeles, USA

When those accused of being high-level perpetrators of human rights abuse die before publicly yielding their secrets in legal and archival arenas, victims may simultaneously express relief about the perpetrator's demise and grief that, along with it, possible crucial information about the past is lost forever. Although the accused do not usually directly admit their actions and the teasing out of what actually happened is dependent upon the complex processes of cross-examination of their testimony and of records and other forms of evidence, victims project such moments of revelation onto the public act of holding accused perpetrators to account. In their deaths, the accused become forever-from-now-on unavailable and thus unassailable evidence – in essence; they are transformed into imagined documents that can never be cross-examined. In this construction, the would-be testimony of perpetrators is given epistemological validity over that of victims, offering up the false and unfulfillable promise of establishing a singular truth. Complicating this scenario, however, is the increasingly open-ended hope offered to victims, judicial processes and historians alike by the application of new forensic methods, for example, in the examination of gravesites and human remains, and by satellite footage, that are generating additional categories of evidence. Using the juridical and archival legacies of the Khmer Rouge in Cambodia and the Yugoslav Wars as case studies, this article argues that when perpetrators die before giving legal testimony, survivors and victims' families construct them as unavailable documents with imaginary agency to settle competing versions of history. Such imagined documents enter into a complex landscape of human rights archives that has heretofore been exclusively focused on tangible evidence. *First*, this article frames the case of Khmer Rouge leader Ieng Sary, charged with crimes against humanity and war crimes, who died before giving his testimony in a hybrid tribunal. In the face of diverse archival documentary evidence capable of presenting a more complete and complex picture of atrocities, it contemplates why survivors and victims' family members placed high hopes on his potential testimony, essentially constructing him as a now-dead living document. *Second*, it explores a parallel case, that of the death of Slobodan Milošević while being tried by the International Criminal Tribunal for the Former Yugoslavia (ICTY), and argues that the notion of a dead perpetrator as imagined document has less sway when the public has the opportunity to hear the perpetrator defend himself, regardless of the perpetrator's own admission (or denial) of culpability. *Third*, it proposes the notion of imaginary documents. It argues that such imaginary documents challenge dominant conceptions of the evidentiary qualities of tangible records and the archival legacies of trauma by insisting on a more dynamic and holistic view of records that takes the affect of survivors and victims' family members into account.

Introduction

The legal and political instrumentalism of the latter twentieth-century phenomena of inter-national criminal tribunals (ICTs), special courts and truth or truth and reconciliation com-missions (TRCs) – as well as the extent to which they are ever able to establish an unassailable singular 'truth' about the horrendous acts that defendants are charged with per-petrating – has been extensively discussed in the media and in relevant scholarly literature.[1] The precedent for using international law to prosecute those who violated 'the laws of humanity' and the establishment of such legal bodies was established earlier in the twenti-eth century, first with the Commission to Consider the Responsibility of the Authors of the War that was set up as a component of the Versailles Peace Conference following World War I, and then with the International Military Tribunal (IMT) and subsequent tribunals held in Nuremberg after the end of World War II to prosecute crimes against peace, war crimes, and crimes against humanity.[2] Notably, in both cases, the bodies were established by the victorious sides. More specifically, in the case of the IMT, such trials, marked by new legal precedents, had to simultaneously prevent those on trial from being able to claim that they were being tried *ex post facto* (i.e., under a law that did not exist when the alleged crimes were committed), or to argue *tu quoque* (i.e., that 'you also did it'). TRCs, on the other hand, may have various mandates, and may not always result in the punishment of perpetrators.

The notion that a singular 'truth' can be elicited by such official means is considered essential to the prevailing of justice and the processes of forgiveness, reconciliation and healing. Such an idea – in theory – subsequently allows affected individuals to move on with their lives and communities and nations to move forward with their recovery.[3] Even so, a singular truth is at best transitory, and misleading. As important, this is likely an impossible objective, given each party's selective memories, the often-integral relation-ship of those memories with identity, and the high degree of affect that those memories invoke. Within the scope of the legal proceedings, the dimensions, dynamics and perform-ance of those memories have also been extensively examined; different narratives have accordingly been juxtaposed or correlated with various forms of documentary evidence. The volume of evidence introduced in some of the proceedings has proven to be unprece-dented, even overwhelming. It can include not only personal testimony, photographs and news recordings, and physical and digital records of political and military decisions and actions, but also recordings of telephone conversations and footage collected through sat-ellite and drone surveillance and local security cameras. In some cases, this documentation continues to be supplemented on an almost daily basis by emergent evidence, particularly the results of DNA matching performed on recovered human remains; increasingly, further insights have been 'mined' from existing documentation using new technologies for searching and analysing data. To this we might add the release by individuals of photo-graphs and videos recorded using personal cellphones and digital cameras by soldiers and private citizens who were first-hand witnesses. New forms of post hoc documentation are also being created, including oral and video history projects and ethnographic research being conducted in post-conflict regions and with diasporic community members around the world. Both because and in spite of this dynamic unfolding of documentation, the understandings and perceptions of 'truths' and the associated emotions can shift consider-ably in and across time and arguably may never truly be resolved.[4] Understandings and perceptions are also highly subject to influence from contemporary political ideology, social change, the effects of time, and generational transitions on what is remembered, how and why.

Despite the wealth of documentary evidence in many post-conflict and transitional justice contexts and the near-universal unwillingness of high-level perpetrators to discuss the details of their crimes, admit culpability or express remorse, survivors of atrocities, the families of victims and their advocates may still place much faith on perpetrators testifying before a tribunal or commission to the point where they may invest high-level defendants with unparalleled power to establish the truth about past horrors. Consequently, when those accused of being high-level perpetrators die before publicly yielding their secrets in legal and archival arenas (and given the length of time it may take before perpetrators are put on trial this has proven to be quite a likely outcome), such individuals may simultaneously express relief about the perpetrator's demise and grief that, along with it, possible crucial information about the past is lost forever. In their deaths, the accused may become forever-from-now-on unavailable and thus (in essence) unassailable evidence; they are transformed into imagined documents that can never be cross-examined. Despite the fact that most high-level defendants have remained defiant in the face of tribunals and have refused to admit any culpability, in this construction, the would-be testimony of perpetrators is given epistemological validity over that of victims and over documentary evidence, offering up the false and unfulfillable promise of establishing a singular truth.

Such phenomena precipitate more nuanced and expansive discussions about the evolving nature of both tangible and intangible documents as archival records and as evidence. This in turn opens the door for a more sophisticated contemplation of the roles archives might play with regard to understanding 'perpetration' and 'perpetrators', as well as recovery from human rights atrocities. Using the juridical and archival legacies of the Khmer Rouge in Cambodia and the Yugoslav Wars as case studies, this article argues that when perpetrators die before giving legal testimony, survivors and victims' families construct them as unavailable documents with imaginary agency to settle competing versions of history. These imagined documents enter into a complex landscape of human rights archives that has heretofore been exclusively focused on tangible evidence in a quest to identify statements made by perpetrators of their intent to commit genocide or other war crimes. *First*, this article frames the case of Khmer Rouge leader Ieng Sary, charged with crimes against humanity and war crimes, who died before giving his testimony in a hybrid tribunal. In the face of diverse archival documentary evidence capable of presenting a more complete and complex picture of atrocities, it contemplates why survivors and victims' family members placed high hopes on his potential testimony, essentially constructing him as a now-dead living document. *Second*, it explores a parallel case – that of Slobodan Milošević, who passed away while being tried by the ICTY – and argues that the notion of a dead perpetrator as imagined document has less sway when the public has the opportunity to hear the perpetrator defend himself, regardless of the perpetrator's own admission (or denial) of culpability. *Third*, it proposes the notion of imaginary documents. It argues that such imaginary documents challenge dominant conceptions of the evidentiary qualities of tangible records and the archival legacies of trauma by insisting on a more dynamic and holistic view of records that takes the affect of survivors and victims' family members into account.

Dead perpetrators as living documents

The Case of Ieng Sary

In March 2013, Ieng Sary died of a heart attack at the age of 87. As former deputy prime minister and foreign minister for the Khmer Rouge, Sary personally oversaw the transfer of many Foreign Ministry staff to the notorious Tuol Sleng (aka S-21 prison), where they were tortured and then sent to the Choeung Ek Killing Fields to be executed.[5] As the Khmer Rouge's third in command, Sary was aware of and played an active role in enacting the regime's plans to evacuate Phnom Penh, which placed millions of Cambodians on communal farms as slave labourers. He was also intimately involved in military actions against neighbouring Vietnam. At the time of his death, Sary had been standing trial for the international crimes of genocide, crimes against humanity, and war crimes, as well as homicide, torture and religious persecution under Cambodian law at the Extraordinary Chambers at the Courts of Cambodia (ECCC). The ECCC, which has been in operation since 2006, is a joint effort between the Royal Government of Cambodia and the United Nations, and has, at the time of writing, issued only three verdicts at the cost of more than $150 million of international funding. Once thought to be a significant milestone for justice in Cambodia, the tribunal has been plagued by financial setbacks, corruption allegations, charges of political interference and strikes by unpaid translators, and, as such, has come under fire by an ever-increasing number of survivors of the regime, international legal experts and human rights advocates. Sary's death underscored the failure of the tribunal to administer justice in a timely and effective manner and highlighted the possibility that the other two defendants in the case might also die before the court reaches final verdicts (Sary's wife, Ieng Thirith, once a fourth defendant in the case and former Khmer Rouge social affairs minister, was ruled unfit to stand trial in 2010 due to an Alzheimer's diagnosis.) Despite Sary's role in the death of approximately 1.7 million Cambodians from starvation, execution and untreated disease, hundreds of Khmer Rouge loyalists and family members attended his weeklong funeral, which was capped by fond reminiscences, Buddhist chants and evening fireworks.[6]

During his time at the tribunal, Sary invoked his right to remain silent and refused to give testimony. This noncooperation was due, in part, to claims that a 1996 royal pardon protected him from a conviction by the ECCC (the ECCC deemed the royal pardon invalid). Sary was often absent from the proceedings, watching via closed circuit television from his holding cell, allegedly due to health issues. In 2011, before the start of the trial, his lawyers issued a failed motion for his release on house arrest. Even prior to the tribunal, Sary never discussed the details of his involvement, nor did he admit guilt for his actions, deflecting all blame to Pol Pot and Nuon Chea (the Khmer Rouge's second in command). At the time of his royal pardon and return to Cambodia in 1996, he was estranged from the Khmer Rouge leadership and claimed that Pol Pot 'was the sole and supreme architect of the party's line, strategy and tactics' and that 'Nuon Chea implemented all Pol Pot's decisions to torture and execute those who expressed opposite opinions and those they hated'.[7] We can reasonably assume that, even had Sary lived to see his own conviction, he would not have yielded any information about his involvement with the regime, nor accepted any responsibility for his actions.

In the face of Sary's deafening silence in life, survivors of the regime, victims' families, and their advocates still lamented what they saw as the irrevocable loss of key evidence in his death. In this regard, key stakeholders placed a disproportionate faith in the hypothetical, nonexistent (and forever-from-now-on impossible) oral testimony of a dead perpetrator in establishing legal and historical facts. Cambodian responses to Sary's death reveal this paradox. For example, Vannarith Chheang, Executive Director of the Cambodian Institute for Cooperation and Peace told a reporter from the *Los Angeles Times*, 'We've lost another living document … Thirty-five years after committing such heinous crimes, they're still getting away with it'.[8] In this conception, Sary was himself a form of evidence that was necessary to establish legal accountability. This sentiment was echoed repeatedly in interviews with members of the Cambodian public taken by staff at the Documentation Center of Cambodia (DC-Cam). One elderly man, Chen Mut, said,

> When I heard about the death of Ieng Sary, I felt only regret that the country had lost an individual who could provide answers to the questions many have about the Khmer Rouge period. With his death I have lost the opportunity to hear his explanation about the atrocities and violence committed by so many. I am still hopeful that the senior leaders who are still alive will provide some answers. I want the tribunals to come to a conclusion about who was responsible ... [9]

As this quote reveals, some Cambodians linked the existence of testimonial evidence from the perpetrator to the establishment of legal justice, despite both the noncooperation of the perpetrator while alive in establishing such evidence and the ongoing impossibility of creating such evidence anew after the perpetrator's death.

Furthermore, many of those interviewed by DC-Cam conflated legally admissible evidence and historical evidence (i.e., proof that might establish the facts about a past event), positing that without Sary's testimony, legal truth could not be established, and without legal truth, historical truth could not be established. For example, Sambo Manara, a professor in the Department of Media and Communication at the Royal University of Phnom Penh, told DC-Cam staff, 'With Ieng Sary's death, the case has been closed. An important document on the Khmer Rouge period has been lost forever. I pity the victims who thought that they would receive answers about the violence and suffering during the Khmer Rouge years ... As a historian and researcher, I cannot comment upon whether Ieng Sary committed crimes because the court has not concluded its working'.[10] Legal evidence, conflated with evidence in the archival sense, is intermixed with the court's ruling with the truth about the past. Yet, the truth of Sary's guilt is independent of Sary's conviction; even if Sary had lived to see a verdict, and even if the court had ruled Sary not guilty, Sary stills bears culpability in the death of 1.7 million people, as ample textual, photographic and verbal evidence from victims and witnesses attests (as will soon be addressed). Here, we see false hopes pinned on the ability of the judicial process to induce testimony from a heretofore silent perpetrator and on the ability of a perpetrator to provide indisputable truth about the past. In this construction, Sary's hypothetical (and now impossible) testimony trumps all other forms of evidence presented to the court and widely available in other arenas. Manara, like many of the Cambodians interviewed by DC-Cam in response to Sary's death, gives the perpetrator a disproportionate, undeserving and paradoxical evidentiary power, re-inscribing Sary's potency even in death.

Several of the interviews conducted by DC-Cam in the wake of Sary's death reveal how, like Manara, many Cambodian stakeholders have impossibly high and unrealistic expectations, both for the court to establish historic truth and for the perpetrators to detail their actions and motivations. One interviewee, Abdugani Pin Musa, told DC-Cam staff, 'The death of Ieng Sary has left behind uncertainty about the perpetrators of the cruelties committed during the Khmer Rouge regime. The question remains of whether Ieng Sary was a killer during the Khmer Rouge, or if he was just a subordinate. Therefore the history of the Khmer Rouge period remains unclear.[11] In this vein, some Cambodians have broadened their expectations for the tribunal, expecting it not only to convict a few top leaders of the regime but also to induce noncompliant perpetrators to speak, and in so doing, to reveal the truth about the past.

Although some of those Cambodians interviewed by DC-Cam did acknowledge that, while alive, Sary was silent about his role, most still pinned hopes on the future possibility of his testimony, hopes which had to be abandoned in his death. 'Due to his old age and illness, Ieng Sary talked very little during his trial and from an academic standpoint with his death we have lost a source of potential information on the Khmer Rouge', said interviewee Cheng Hong.[12] Similarly, Am Sophal said, 'I feel only regret at his death as he has not provided any information or answers yet … His death means that the young generation will not receive proper answers. With his death the court has lost a source and the judicial process has become even harder'.[13] Yet, it is not Sary's death that caused this perceived gap in information, it was his silence in life. Had Sary survived until the end of the trial, it is highly unlikely he would have reversed his previous 25 years of silence; even if he had testified, such testimony would not have provided victims with any satisfactory answers. In death, Sary becomes a forever-from-now-on unavailable piece of evidence, an eternally 'potential source of information' that can never be decoded.

Notwithstanding this overwhelming faith placed on Sary's nonexistent testimony, more than enough documentary evidence exists to establish Sary's role in the regime. Prior to the tribunal, historians Stephen Heder and Brian D. Tittemore made the case for Sary's indictment in their book *Seven Candidates for Prosecution*. Accordingly, Heder and Tittemore describe the text of numerous speeches, radio addresses and statements made by Ieng Sary during the Khmer Rouge period that reveal his knowledge, support of, and participation in the regime's policies to 'smash' all alleged enemies.[14] Heder and Tittemore also show how Sary was copied on several confession statements extracted under torture, and that he was the recipient of numerous telegrams and internal memos reporting the 'smashing' of 'enemies' in the field.[15] Heder and Tittemore conclude that such documentary evidence 'suggests that Sary knowingly contributed directly and substantially as an aider and abettor to the commission of crimes throughout the country'.[16] Heder later recounted and showed such evidence in detail as he testified in the tribunal.

Contributing to this list of incriminating evidence, the ECCC's office of the prosecution presented a multitude of additional records establishing Sary's involvement in Khmer Rouge crimes. These included: minutes from 19 Standing Committee meetings that clearly indicate Sary as third in command (after Pol Pot and Nuon Chea); more than 100 telegrams sent to Sary which reported how internal enemies were identified and 'swept clean'; communications Sary had with the United Nations wherein he warns foreign countries to stay out of Cambodian internal affairs; a diary spanning 1976–1979 that detailed the actions of the Foreign Ministry and Sary's role in enacting them; and a 1977 letter in which an S-21 detainee describes his torture and pleads with Sary to release him, suggesting that Sary had authority over who was detained and tortured at S-21.[17] Video represented a key medium of evidence, including: footage from 1975–1979 in which Sary is seen shaking hands with Pol Pot, addressing crowds of cadres and welcoming a Vietnamese delegation; a 1975 interview Sary gave with a French journalist in which he justified the evacuation of Phnom Penh; and an interview with Khmer Rouge military commander Ta Mok naming Sary as third in command.[18] Throughout the trial, dozens of civil parties testified to the horrific conditions they endured under the regime, including forced labour, torture and the execution of family members and friends. Thus before Sary's death, the trial both established Sary's role in the regime and the regime's role in the death of millions of Cambodians, despite the absence of a formal conviction.

Given the wealth of documentary evidence collected by DC-Cam, interpreted by historians and presented as legal evidence in the tribunal, why are Cambodians lamenting the loss of the imagined testimony of a now-dead perpetrator? Why give epistemological validity to the nonexistent statement of a mass murderer? Is documentary evidence alone not enough to establish the facts about the past? An essay by DC-Cam legal advisor John D. Ciorciari hints at an answer.[19] He writes, 'In thousands of interviews with DC-Cam, victims often show more interest in seeking an explanation than in seeking revenge. To cope with the past, those who bear the scars of Khmer Rouge rule and lost loved ones want to know why'.[20] Perhaps it is not the facts of the past that Cambodians need Sary to establish (as those facts are overwhelmingly established by documentary evidence), but a justification for why so many people died, an account of the reasoning behind such unreasonable acts, a way to make sense out of the nonsensical. With Sary's death, such answers will remain perpetually elusive.

Worsening the impact of such unanswerable questions in the minds of many survivors, Sary left behind the equivalent of $20 million in a Hong Kong bank account. Sary accrued the fortune through the Chinese government's funding of the Khmer Rouge and the regime's lucrative gemstone and timber trade after its toppling in 1979. In embezzling these funds from the official Khmer Rouge coffers, Sary later invoked the ire of Khmer Rouge leadership, who pushed him out of the party. Victims' advocacy groups and civil parties to the tribunal called for Sary's wealth to be investigated in 2009, but the ECCC refused. After Sary's death, they called once again for the funds to be seized by the Cambodian government and redistributed to victims as reparations. Youk Chhang, DC-Cam's Director, urged that Sary's wealth be used to create a national mental health care system, which would provide therapy to survivors of the regime. Despite such demands, government seizure of Sary's accounts remains highly unlikely given the absence of a formal conviction. In his death, Sary's family reaps the benefits of his wealth, even while his motivations remain a tortuous mystery to the regime's victims.

The case of Ieng Sary begs some important questions about whether the presence and power of imagined as opposed to tangible documents is a phenomenon distinctive to the Cambodian context or is one that might be anticipated and accounted for in other cases with similar circumstances. Furthermore, if there are multiple cases in which a dead perpetrator is imbued with the power to establish 'truth', is the imagined forever-unassailable living document just one of several possible constructions of an imaginary document that might be at work in the aftermath of traumatic events? If so, what other kinds of constructions might be anticipated and how might such notions of intangible or imagined documents interplay or hold sway in the face of tangible documents?

The case of Slobodan Milošević

> People can always say it didn't happen but now there are documents (Zdravko Grebo, Director, Center for Interdisciplinary Postgraduate Studies, University of Sarajevo).[21]

One place to begin to explore these questions is to consider a situation where there are some parallels. Slobodan Milošević was the first head of state ever to be brought before an international criminal tribunal. In 2006, he died in the Hague, before the ICTY rendered its judgment. Unlike Ieng Sary, he had ample opportunity to give testimony before his death. Milošević's trial was supposed to 'shape all future efforts at punishing the world's bloodiest war criminals', but as a result of his death he was never found guilty of the crimes with which he was charged.[22] Despite the length of the work of the ICTY (established by the United Nations in 1993 and projected to conclude appeals by 2015), the ongoing trials of other recently captured key figures, Radovan Karadžić and Ratko Mladić, and the millions of documents introduced as evidence, the death of Milošević and the later overturning upon appeal of the convictions of both Serbian and Croatian generals for war crimes left victims from Bosnia, Croatia and Kosovo without seeing justice served. It also left Serbia, as *The Guardian* put it in June 2012, 'A nation still wavering between guilt and victimhood'.[23]

Indicted in 1999 by the ICTY for war crimes and crimes against humanity in Kosovo, Croatia and Bosnia and Hercegovina,[24] Milošević was arrested on charges of corruption and abuse of power in Belgrade by Serbian authorities in April 2001 following his 2000 first round loss in the presidential elections and subsequent mass protests on the streets of Belgrade at his refusal to accept that loss. He was transferred to the ICTY on 29 June 2001 by Zoran Djindjic, the new (and subsequently assassinated) reformist and pro-Western Serbian prime minister just in time to meet a US deadline for handing over Milošević or face losing US and international economic aid. By the time his trial began in February 2002, several lesser figures had already been tried and convicted, and other individuals who had played key roles in the Yugoslavian Wars had passed away or been killed. The trial was drawn out on account of Milošević's health and because he insisted, as a trained lawyer, on serving as his own counsel. He suffered from high blood pressure and a heart condition and the stress of the trial likely exacerbated these conditions. To provide him with time to prepare as well as to accommodate his poor health, the tribunal only met three days a week. He requested permission to go to Russia for medical treatment but his request was turned down by the tribunal on the grounds that good medical care was available in the Netherlands. Milošević was found dead in his United Nations prison cell in Scheveningen on 11 March 2006 before the ICTY rendered its judgment (expected to be in May 2006). He was 62. The proceedings against him ended on 14 March 2006.

Diane Orentlicher, principal author of the Open Society Justice Initiative's 2010 report on the impact of the ICTY on Bosnia, cites an almost universal sentiment about the ICTY expressed in extensive qualitative interviews she conducted of a cross-section of individuals from different ethnic groups in Bosnia and Herzegovina between June 2006 and July 2009. The sentiment was that the creation of the ICTY had offered the only possibility for justice during and after the violent inter-ethnic conflict that took place in Bosnia between 1992 and 1995,[25] even though its creation in 1993 did not halt atrocities and the proceedings of the ICTY have been criticised as ineffective, overly lenient, costly and politically biased. She quotes, for example, Kada Hotić, whose husband and brother were among those murdered in Srebrenica, recalling that:

> … when the Hague Tribunal was established it gave us a big hope, not only to convict criminals … but we expected to have the truth in this country revealed and proved, because we have a big problem here regarding acknowledgement of the truth. But in the absence of such acknowledgment, many Bosniaks believe it matters enormously that the ICTY has at least produced 'the evidence and proof that will someday make [Bosnian Serbs] understand they lied to themselves'.[26]

Human Rights Watch researcher and Serbian human rights lawyer Bogdan Ivanisevic presents another view of the impact of the ICTY, this time contemplating the impact of the tribunal on Serbians:

> Even though they have resistance to hearing non-Serb witnesses, people do take into consideration what they hear. The trial has caused reduced myth-making in Serbia. You don't hear, as you did prior to the trial … that Srebrenica didn't happen or that the Muslims killed themselves. I wouldn't minimize this reduced space for rewriting history. As for acknowledgment of our side's crimes, it's a psychological barrier too difficult [to cross – admitting] that the policy we supported was criminal. It will take time. It may take a new generation that was not implicated.[27]

The ICTY itself makes the following claim: 'The Tribunal has contributed to an indisputable historical record, combating denial and helping communities come to terms with their recent history. Crimes across the region can no longer be denied.'[28] As for the death of

Milošević, it produced deep disappointment among his victims that he had not lived long enough to be sentenced for his crimes, and little public sorrow in Serbia or among Bosnian Serbs.

In this context, then, it would seem like the death of Milošević resulted less in dashed expectations about what he might have revealed because there were copious other living and documentary sources of 'truth' as well as indictments of many other figures that were deeply associated with the genocides that took place in Bosnia. Instead it further diminished expectations about what the tribunal might actually achieve. Rather than Milošević becoming an imaginary document to survivors, the trial process actually assisted in debunking myths that had been used by some Serbians to deny or at least protect themselves from the realities of the crimes committed. In Ieng Sary's case, however, the context was very different; the conflict was more than 30 years in the past, there were fewer accused high-level perpetrators still alive who might still provide the longed-for 'truth', and none of the new 'hope' offered to survivors by wide-scale DNA matching. Most important, Ieng Sary had not taken the stand, which operates in contrast to Milošević. Milošević's arrogant, bullying and unrepentant conduct as a defendant and, as his own counsel clearly demonstrated, no truth would be forthcoming. As the long drawn-out trial progressed, expectations about what it could accomplish changed and were also influenced by surrounding circumstances, including the escalating ongoing conflict in Bosnia and Kosovo. To surmise and summarise, the notion of an unassailable living or imaginary document in the minds of victims is something that might arise under certain, but not all, circumstances where an accused perpetrator dies before being convicted. The imaginary document construct most likely arises when the public does not have the opportunity to hear the perpetrator defend himself or watch how he comports himself in trial, and when an unrealistic amount of hope has been pinned on the testimony of a single individual in what is often a much wider web of complicity. In this way, the conception of dead perpetrator as imaginary document loses its sway when the perpetrator testifies before his death, regardless of the quality of the testimony given.

It should also be noted that the notion discussed here of an imaginary document is an archival and not a legal one, just as archival notions of evidence are not coterminous with those in legal theory. For example, in writing about how Milošević's trial ended without judgment, legal scholar Timothy William Waters discusses a legal version of an imaginary document in the form of the Trial Chamber's ruling on Decision on a Motion for Acquittal brought under the tribunal's Rule 98bis halfway through the trial.[29] The chamber ruled that the trial could proceed because the prosecution had presented enough evidence that a court might find Milošević guilty. Waters argues that in the absence of a verdict, 'the prosecution, defense, chambers, and outsiders deployed the Rule 98bis Decision to tell a story about Milošević's guilt or innocence and craft a final judgment in the eyes of the world, if not in the law'.[30]

Emergent archival evidence and the imaginary

What are we to make of these paradoxical constructions of the evidentiary value of the imagined testimony of dead perpetrators from an archival studies perspective? Scholarship within the field of archival studies, in part reacting to technological and media developments over recent decades, and in part to the so-called archival turn in the humanities and social sciences, has considerably expanded upon traditional constructions of documentation, records and evidence. While some archivists might be keenly aware of legal definitions of evidence and the intricate rules of what counts as admissible evidence in various legal settings, archivists generally employ the term 'evidence' in a more general sense as 'that which we consider or interpret in order to draw or infer a conclusion about some aspect of the world'.[31] In this regard, evidence does not exist in and of itself: it is 'relational' and contingent.[32] It exists in support of a particular argument; it is a building block in making a larger case. In this regard, the documentation does not 'speak for itself', nor does it necessarily 'speak truth', despite ample claims to the contrary; it must be activated by users in support of a particular claim. This evidentiary quality is what distinguishes records from other forms of documentation; records may serve as evidence of activity in addition to their capacity to relay information. In its invocation as evidence in support of a claim, veracity may be less important in ascertaining the weight of a document than its emotive or affective capacity to effect particular understandings and outcomes.

In this light, this article advocates for taking the affective dimensions of records – tangible or intangible, real or imagined – seriously in our considerations of the human rights impact of archives. While hypothetical documents will never help convict a perpetrator, they nevertheless are powerful forces in the imaginary of survivors of human rights abuse and victims' families, and as such, are crucial to dealing with the aftermath of mass murder in the communities most impacted. As such, these imaginary documents help expand our conceptions of records and their evidentiary qualities beyond narrow legalistic frameworks to more fully engage the emotional and psychological dimensions of archives in the wake of trauma. Considering imaginary documents reminds us that, for many survivors of human rights abuse, 'truth' will always be forthcoming, justice will always be unattainable, and closure is not an option.

Furthermore, the timing with which such evidence emerges is key to understanding its invocation in support or against particular claims. Not all documentation of human rights abuse is created contemporaneously to the abuse itself, nor does documentation created at the time of abuse always or completely come to the fore as soon as the abuse is over. Rather, there is a complicated cycle during which particular types of documentation emerge or are excavated and are put to use as evidence in support of particular truth claims. Tangible documentation of human rights abuse could be loosely assigned into several categories – those generated through routine bureaucratic and media processes that are later introduced as evidence of abuse and complicity; those created by the perpetrators (and sometimes victims) at the time of the abuse as part of the abuse itself; those created by observers such as the world media, peacekeeping forces and other nations' surveillance activities; those created after the abuse by witnesses and survivors with the express purpose of documenting the abuse; and those created by truth commissions and tribunals in the process of exposing the abuse. Within this multi-format, multi-source and multiply-motivated documentary landscape, the testimony of alleged perpetrators is but one piece of a complex moving puzzle of evidence invoked to establish facts about the past.

Some of this documentation will subsequently be placed in an archive for long-term access and preservation, where some of it will be discovered by future users over time. Throughout each of the categories of human rights documentation, evidence is created, incorporated into archives and brought to the attention of interested parties over the course of years; the accumulation of evidence happens over large swathes of time and is dependent on the distribution of resources, the political agendas of those with the power to pursue such evidentiary investigations, and cultural contexts that impact what gets remembered and what gets forgotten. What all of these forms of documentation that usually end up in archives have in common, however, is that they are tangible and able to withstand intellectual cross-examination as evidence of decisions made, actions carried out and human motivation and complicity. This is not the case for an imagined document.

In this archival milieu, the construction of dead perpetrator as imaginary document arises at a particular moment in time – after the juridical process has begun, after the death of the perpetrator, but before the perpetrator gives testimony and before a legal verdict has been issued. This new imagined form of human rights documentation has the power to effect action, be exhibited as 'proof', and shape collective memory, despite its inadmissibility as legal evidence. These dispositive and probative capabilities are also key characteristics of tangible 'real' records. If they are at work also in the form of intangible 'imaginary' documents, then an important augmentation to classic archival and records theory is required.

These records – imagined rather than tangible – nonetheless become important source materials for the ongoing process of shaping collective memory of past atrocities. Collective memory has come to denote the ways in which everyday people socially construct the past through shared forms of remembrance and forgetting, as distinguished from history as the official story that is told about the past by a guild of trained historians.[33] As this article has demonstrated, paying attention to records and archives as a genre enables us to see how communities of survivors imbue records with the power to conceptualise, re-envision and make meaning of the past. The power of records to shape collective memory remains constant, regardless of the tangible or imaginary nature of the records in question. Furthermore, as imaginary records get reimagined with time, so to does collective memory of the past, opening up the records for infinite reinterpretation and reuse by subsequent generations.

In light of these newly imagined documents, we argue that human rights and social justice concerns – and particularly the prosecution of and recovery from war crimes and crimes against humanity – have surfaced additional conceptions of evidence that are fundamentally different from those based around commonly understood traditional legal, bureaucratic and historical premises. The notion of the record as evidence of human activity has become far less physically bounded, allowing not only for constructions that are premised in virtuality, but also in affect and effect. Such constructions draw the realm of the record away from the tangible and into that of the imaginary. Conjured by the unattainable hopes for closure by survivors and victims' families, such imaginary documents are bound by their impossibility; they are always out of grasp, falsely promising to make sense of the nonsensical, always emerging on an intangible horizon. They will never serve as legal evidence, nor provide answers about past atrocities. Yet, despite these limitations, imaginary documents help us to both broaden our definition of human rights documentation to include the affective needs of survivors and victims' families and to reconceptualise archives as institutions that can make meaning out of past atrocity when legal systems are unable to or are perceived to fail to administer justice.

Disclosure statement

No potential conflict of interest was reported by the authors.

Notes

1. Verne Harris, *Archives and Justice: A South African Perspective* (Chicago: Society of American Archivists, 2007); Michelle Caswell, 'Khmer Rouge Archives: Accountability, Truth, and Memory in Cambodia', *Archival Science* 10, no. 1–2 (2010): 25–44.
2. Benjamin B. Ferencz, 'International Criminal Courts: The Legacy of Nuremberg', Paper 122. *Pace International Law Review* (1998): 202–35, http://www.issafrica.org/anicj/uploads/Ferencz_International_Criminal_Courts.pdf.
3. Hamdi Muluk, 'Memory for Sale: How Groups "Distort" Their Collective Memory for Reconciliation Purposes and Building Peace', in *Peace Psychology in Asia*, ed. C.J. Montiel and N.M. Noor (New York: Springer Science+Business Media, Peace Psychology Book Series, 2009), 105–22; A. Nadler and N. Shnabel, 'A Needs-based Model of Reconciliation: Satisfying the Differential Emotional Needs of Victim and Perpetrator as a Key to Promoting Reconciliation', *Journal of Personality and Social Psychology* 94 (2008): 116–32.
4. The authors wish to note that they do not intend to convey that there is a hard-and-fast dichotomy between perpetrators and victims. They recognise that while there are many individuals who fall into one category or the other – in the case of victims, often thousands or even millions – there are also unwilling perpetrators and those who at different moments or in different contexts or from different perspectives might be viewed as a victim, a perpetrator or even both.
5. Jaya Ramji-Nogales and Anne Heindel, *Genocide: Who Are the Senior Khmer Rouge Leaders to Be Judged?: The Importance of Case 002* (Phnom Penh: Documentation Center of Cambodia, 2010).
6. Sebastian Strangio, 'How a Brutal Khmer Rouge Leader Died "Not Guilty"', *The Atlantic*, 1 April 2013.
7. Associated Press/National Public Radio, 'Khmer Rouge Co-founder Ieng Sary Dies at 87' (2013), http://www.cambodiatribunal.org/2013/03/14/khmer-rouge-co-founder-ieng-sary-dies-at-87/.
8. Mark Magnier, 'Khmer Rouge Leader Dies, Eluding War Crimes Verdict', *Los Angeles Times*, 14 March 2013.
9. Sok-Kheang Ly, 'Cambodian Survivors Want the Khmer Rouge Tribunal to Speed up Proceeding', in *Searching for the Truth* (Phnom Penh: Documentation Center of Cambodia, 2013), 45–8, 45.
10. Ibid., 45.
11. Ibid., 47.
12. Ibid., 45.
13. Ibid., 46.
14. Stephen Heder and Brian D. Tittemore, *Seven Candidates for Prosecution: Accountability for the Crimes of the Khmer Rouge* (Phnom Penh: Documentation Center of Cambodia, 2004).
15. Ibid.
16. Ibid., 90.
17. Doreen Chen, 'Documents Reveal Khmer Rouge-Era Roles of Ieng Sary and Khieu Samphan', *The Trial Observer*, 30 January 2013, http://www.cambodiatribunal.org/_archived-site/blog/2013/01/documents-reveal-khmer-rouge-era-roles-ieng-sary-and-khieu-samphan.
18. Ibid.
19. John D. Ciorciari, 'Introduction', in *On Trial: The Khmer Rouge Accountability Process*, ed. John D. Ciorciari and Anne Heindel (Phnom Penh: Documentation Center of Cambodia, 2009), 13–29.
20. Ibid.
21. As quoted in Diane F. Orentlicher, *That Someone Guilty Be Punished: The Impact of the ICTY in Bosnia* (Open Society Justice Initiative; International Centre for Transitional Justice, 2010), 19, http://www.ictj.org/sites/default/files/ICTJ-FormerYugoslavia-Someone-Guilty-2010-English.pdf.

22. Gary J. Bass, 'Milosevic in the Hague', *Foreign Affairs* (May/June 2003), http://www.foreignaffairs.com/articles/58976/gary-j-bass/milosevic-in-the-hague.

23. Julian Borger, 'Serb Elite Face Exposure over Aid to War Crimes Suspects Karadzic and Mladic', *The Guardian*, 21 June 2012.

24. The indictments were 'for genocide; complicity in genocide; deportation; murder; persecutions on political, racial or religious grounds; inhumane acts/forcible transfer; extermination; imprisonment; torture; wilful killing; unlawful confinement; wilfully causing great suffering; unlawful deportation or transfer; extensive destruction and appropriation of property, not justified by military necessity and carried out unlawfully and wantonly; cruel treatment; plunder of public or private property; attacks on civilians; destruction or wilful damage done to historic monuments and institutions dedicated to education or religion; unlawful attacks on civilian objects', http://www.icty.org/x/cases/slobodan_milosevic/cis/en/cis_milosevic_slobodan_en.pdf.

25. Orentlicher, *That Someone Guilty Be Punished*, 35–6.

26. Ibid., 43.

27. Bass, 'Milosevic in the Hague'.

28. ICTY, 'About the ICTY', http://www.icty.org/sections/AbouttheICTY.

29. Timothy William Waters, 'A Kind of Judgment: Searching for Judicial Narratives After Death', *The George Washington International Law Review* 42 (2010): 279–348, http://docs.law.gwu.edu/stdg/gwilr/PDFs/42-2/2-%20Waters.pdf.

30. Ibid., 279.

31. Jonathan Furner, 'Conceptual Analysis: A Method for Understanding Information as Evidence and Evidence as Information', *Archival Science* 4 (2004): 233–65, 247.

32. Ibid., 247.

33. This construction can also be noted as a false dichotomy in the sense that history and collective memory are often entangled in complex and multidirectional ways. Michel-Rolph Trouillot, *Silencing the Past: Power and the Production of History* (Boston, MA: Beacon Press, 1995).

The space of sorrow: a historic video dialogue between survivors and perpetrators of the Cambodian killing fields

Susan Needham[a], Karen Quintiliani[b] and Robert Lemkin[c]

[a]Department of Anthropology, California State University, Dominguez Hills, USA; [b]Department of Anthropology, California State University Long Beach, USA; [c]Old Street Films, Oxford, England

In this article filmmaker and anthropologists collaborate to explore an alternative Cambodian strategy for truth seeking that grew out of the making and release of the documentary film, *Enemies of the People*, and culminated in a historic videoconference between former Khmer Rouge soldiers in Bangkok and killing fields survivors in Long Beach, California. Along the way the figures of 'victim' and 'perpetrator' were transformed becoming more nuanced and complex. Because Khmer Rouge soldiers and their victims have been represented in many genre – written, spoken, and filmic – we examine this transformation through the conceptual lens of *chronotope*, the 'essential ground' of time-space created within a literary work to represent events. At its core is dialogue, through which new interpretations of the self and others beyond a victim-perpetrator narrative can be constituted.

If we had a keen vision and feeling of all ordinary human life, it would be like hearing the grass grow and the squirrel's heartbeat, and we should die of that roar which lies on the other side of silence.– George Eliot (*Middlemarch*)

Between April 1975 and January 1979, an estimated 1.7 million Cambodians died from starvation, overwork, disease, or execution during the rule of the Communist Party of Kampuchea, known to the outside world as the Khmer Rouge. Although the Vietnamese overthrew the Khmer Rouge central government in early 1979, civil war between these and other contending groups continued until 1991, when the Paris Peace Accords were signed and the United Nations began helping the country prepare for national elections held in 1993. As political and military groups vied for control of the country, thousands of displaced Cambodians – victims and perpetrators alike – slowly resumed daily village life, living side by side in virtual silence. No programme of reconciliation or national dialogue was established and public discussion of what had happened was, and continues to be, actively discouraged by the government. Afraid of being implicated in crimes against humanity and of possible widespread violent retaliations, Cambodia's leaders told the citizens they should put what happened behind them and 'bury the past'.[1] It has been 35 years since the Khmer Rouge were driven from power and Cambodians scattered throughout the world. To make sense of the enormity of the trauma and loss, for the sake of those who died, and to prevent such atrocities from happening again, many Cambodians continue to ask why this tragedy happened and who is responsible; they continue to ask for the truth.

In this article, filmmaker, Lemkin, and anthropologists, Needham and Quintiliani, explore an alternative Cambodian strategy for truth seeking that grew out of a project spanning more than a decade and leading to a historic videoconference between three former Khmer Rouge soldiers in Bangkok and survivors in Long Beach, California. The videoconference was conceived and organised by the authors and members of the Cambodian American Community in Long Beach, California. It was inspired by the work of Thet Sambath, a Cambodian journalist and genocide survivor, who set out on a ten-year journey to discover the truth of why the Khmer Rouge killed. Along the way the figures of 'victim' and 'perpetrator' became more nuanced and complex. In 2006, Thet met filmmaker Lemkin, whose documentary, *Enemies of the People*[2] (hereafter referred to as EOTP), chronicles Thet's work. Although not the first post-Khmer Rouge era project to document the stories of former Khmer Rouge soldiers,[3] EOTP provides a model for dialogue and transformation that Cambodian American audiences responded to with interest. Part of what makes the documentary compelling for them is the way former Khmer Rouge talk about themselves and what they did. For Cambodian American survivors of genocide the process of 'working out' and 'working through' the past has been an ongoing feature of their social-psychological experience of being refugees.[4] Far less has been understood – at least publically – about what perpetrators think about their actions or how they have dealt with the reality of being killers until the release of EOTP.

Because Khmer Rouge soldiers and their victims have been represented in many genres – written, spoken, and filmic – we examine this transformation through the conceptual lens of *chronotope*, the 'essential ground' of time-space created within a literary work to represent events.[5] At its core is dialogue, through which new interpretations of the self and others beyond a victim-perpetrator narrative can be constituted. Bakhtin's literary poetics of inquiry provide a textured means of understanding social-psychological relations and the interweaving of history, dialogue, morality, and identity.

We begin this article by introducing the concept of chronotope and its application to understanding how victims and perpetrators are portrayed in each medium. This is followed by an examination of how victims and perpetrators have been characterised in survivor narratives written since 1975. We then describe Thet's goal and research process, identifying various elements of his personal quest which contributed to his success. In this section we also discuss the narrative form of the documentary film portraying his work. Next we introduce the videoconference during which survivors of the Khmer Rouge in Long Beach, California spoke with Thet, the two former Khmer Rouge soldiers featured in the film, Suon and Khoun, and a third former soldier, Choeun, who assisted Thet with research and was present during filming, but was not shown in the film. In this section we describe the planning process and steps the authors and Cambodian planning team took to create a Cambodian social and moral space for the videoconference. Drawing on post-videoconference interviews, we conclude by exploring the role of EOTP in providing a shared discourse that participants used to co-construct a new chronotope in which victims and perpetrators engaged in dialogue.

Chronotope: creating meaning across time and space through dialogue

In the Cambodian case under examination here we are interested in how the figures of 'victim' and 'killer' are formulated and transformed across encounters in two distinctly different formats: a documentary film and videoconference. To structure our analysis we have turned to discourse analysis and Bakhtin's chronotope.[6] Bakhtin pointed out that in literature, time and space are not a physical reality, but are a semiotic production expressed and recognised through established literary techniques and linguistic forms. Bakhtin argued that all written texts contain references to previous texts as well as real historical time and space as a way to establish literary reality and that literary genres reflect the diversity of social groups, points of view, and experiences found in human societies. The literary chronotope takes shape through the development of motifs or narrative expressions that reflect concerns for the development and transformation of human identity and help to produce qualitatively and ideologically distinct relationships between characters and their social worlds. As a story unfolds, 'time, as it were thickens, takes on flesh, becomes artistically visible; likewise, space becomes charged and responsive to the movements of time, plot, and history'.[7]

The same can be said for interactions between persons in the lived social world. All interactions are chronotopic in that people make use of established discourses and symbols which can be shown to 'circulate' or move through and across the time and space of social organisation.[8] A novel, a documentary film, and, as in this case, a videoconference, all demonstrate qualities of what Silverstein calls 'interdiscursivity' as they express related, but varied interpretations of self and the other in dialogues which draw on and reference back to a variety of times and places creating within them 'dialogic reverberations'.[9] In this manner, people create a 'figured world' which is a 'socially and culturally constructed realm of interpretation in which particular characters and actors are recognized, significance is assigned to certain acts, and particular outcomes are valued over others'.[10] The figured world is a projected imagined space that people use to construct meaning; a story enacted in real time with a level of organisation that allows social actors to establish social conditions using shared symbols. Most important, the interdiscursive nature of chronotope helps focus attention not only on social processes and cultural symbols (linguistic and non-linguistic) used to create particular bounded chronotopic settings but also helps us understand how these events are interconnected with multiple past encounters and project possible or anticipated future encounters.

It is at the intersection of time, space, history, identity, and morality that our analysis of the videoconference illustrates how persons are historically produced during talk[11] and take up particular stances based on cultural values and resources important to making the dialogue possible.[12] This production is not a linear or mechanical process, but rather a selective, creative, and strategic practice of identity. It is within this dynamic dialogical process in the form of the videoconference that Cambodian victims and former executioners constructed a social space in which to represent and interrogate the past, reformulate the present, and project a possible future.

Configuring the perpetrator: a Cambodian chronotope for representing the Khmer Rouge period

To understand how the victim and perpetrator have been re-configured through EOTP and the videoconference, it is helpful to consider how the perpetrator has been portrayed in English-language Cambodian literature and filmmaking since the 1970s. In the wake of the genocide, Cambodian refugees and westerners created a genre for representing the Khmer Rouge cadre and the atrocities that occurred between 17 April 1975 and January 1979 within a framework which to some extent has been influenced by Western sensibilities of storytelling, especially stories of trauma.[13] Teri Shaffer Yamada describes Cambodian

American refugee accounts as 'testimonial autobiography' representing the 'collective cultural identity caused by a horrific, shared experience'.[14] In the over 23 autobiographies produced since 1980, Yamada identifies a common temporal-spatial frame for representing the Khmer Rouge period that is divided into three parts: (1) a description of urban life in Phnom Penh before 1975 leading up to 17 April 1975 when the Khmer Rouge take control of the city; (2) the author's personal experience with death, forced labour, starvation, and torture at the hands of Khmer Rouge until the regime's defeat by the Vietnamese in January 1979; and, (3) the author's dramatic escape to a refugee camp and eventual arrival as a refugee in a third country. The typical conclusion includes a statement about the impunity of the Khmer Rouge leadership and a call for justice, advocating a tribunal or criminal prosecution of the Khmer Rouge for crimes against humanity.[15] The prototype for this genre of Cambodian survival narrative, according to Yamada, is Sydney Schanberg's 1980 *New York Times Magazine* article, 'The Death and Life of Dith Pran', upon which the 1984 film, *The Killing Fields*, is based. It is unlikely that many Cambodians have read Schanberg's article, but almost all Cambodian Americans have seen the film. Being among the first of the survivor narratives available to the general public, *The Killing Fields* became infused with shared meanings and affected the configuring of events, people, and identity in Cambodian literature and film.

For the most part, Khmer Rouge soldiers are depicted in testimonial autobiographies in one-dimensional terms as cogs in a 'killing machine'. Individuals are barely distinguishable, differing only in gender or their degree of cruelty. Some authors were fortunate to have encountered a soldier who took pity on them and in some small way helped them to survive, but this is rare. The uniformity described by authors was purposefully constructed by the Khmer Rouge regime. A hyper-secretive group, the identities of the leadership were concealed from the Cambodian people for nearly two years. Cadre referred to the new government only as Angkar Lieu, which means 'high organisation'. To erase individuality Khmer Rouge all wore black pants and shirts with black tire-soled sandals and the traditional Cambodian red and white checked scarf, known as a *krama*. Schanberg, who was in Phnom Penh on 17 April 1975 when the city fell, described the Khmer Rouge this way: 'Most of the soldiers are teenagers, which is startling. They are universally grim, robotlike, brutal. Weapons drip from them like fruit from trees – grenades, pistols, rifles, rockets.'[16]

Another early influence that provides vivid examples of the cruelty of the frontline soldiers is Haing S. Ngor's *A Cambodian Odyssey*. In one particularly graphic example, Ngor describes witnessing Khmer Rouge soldiers cut open a pregnant woman, remove the fetus, and hang it from the eaves with other dried fetuses.[17] Through acts such as these the Khmer Rouge were clearly merciless, depraved monsters who were beyond redemption and who formed a singular, ever-present deadly backdrop to the daily ordeal of life during that time.

Narratives told from the point of view of former Khmer Rouge soldiers are uncommon. To confess to having been a Khmer Rouge soldier is not only dangerous, it is difficult for an otherwise ordinary human being to admit to the terrible things they did. The documentary film, *S-21: The Khmer Rouge Killing Machine*, directed by Cambodian filmmaker Rithy Panh, is the first to have victims confront their torturers.[18] In the film, former S-21 guards, who were teenagers during the Khmer Rouge, appear to be intimidated by their accusers and unwilling to show remorse. Their minimal, forced responses serve to reinforce the characterisation of the Khmer Rouge as mechanical and inhuman. However, with time and distance, these images are beginning to break down. In a recent book, *Never Fall Down*, by Patricia McCormick, Arn Chorn Pond has found the courage to confess what happened to him as an orphaned Khmer Rouge child-soldier.[19] His story provides firsthand accounts of the horrifying conditions of daily life for Khmer Rouge soldiers and the trauma and crushing remorse he felt when it was all over.

The point in analysing how the Khmer Rouge period has been represented in artistic forms is not to dispute the author's experience or question the depravity of the acts; this is understood. But in the lived social world it is extremely difficult to reconcile with people who are deemed to be monsters. Looking beyond the violations of the self, as Thet Sambath did, to larger questions of how and why such events as the Cambodian genocide occurred can provide new interpretations and a new chronotope within which dialogue can occur.

Documenting the truth of what happened: Thet Sambath and *Enemies of the People*

Like thousands of others of his generation, Thet Sambeth was orphaned during the Khmer Rouge. Growing up in a refugee camp in Thailand, he never stopped asking himself why his parents had died, 'not the details of their individual deaths but why they were among 1.7 million people who lost their lives during the Khmer Rouge years'.[20] In 1999, after returning to Cambodia and while working as a journalist for the *Phnom Penh Post*, he began going to the countryside on weekends to see if he could find and persuade former Khmer Rouge to talk about what had happened. Because village-level cadre had no knowledge of the workings of the regime beyond their immediate superiors, Thet's plan was to begin with these men and women and after gaining their trust see if they would introduce him to their supervisors. In this way he hoped to work his way up the chain of command. To assuage fears that he may be trying to avenge the deaths of family members, he did not tell people he had lost his parents during the Khmer Rouge. As he went through the countryside, he explained he was a private researcher seeking the truth of what happened for the sake of the historical record and the next generation.

Thet also took his time talking with former soldiers, listening to their stories, and returning each weekend until he had gained their trust. At first most denied any involvement in the executions; but, as time passed, people came to trust Thet, and their stories began to change. Former soldiers admitted to having killed maybe only one or two people. Eventually, some confessed to having executed hundreds by hand and showed him how they had done it. Others took him to meet their superiors, who after getting to know him, took Thet to meet those who had given them orders. His patience, sincere interest in learning the truth, and unthreatening manner paid off and he was eventually introduced to Nuon Chea, the man who had been second only to Pol Pot during the Khmer Rouge period and knew the truth of why so many Khmer were killed. Thet spent the next several years visiting Nuon on the weekends recording his story. Nuon Chea became one of the central figures in EOTP and was filmed until his arrest in September 2007.

A few years after first meeting Nuon, Thet met documentary filmmaker, Lemkin, and the two began working together on what would become EOTP. To tell this story Lemkin chose to use the Western definition of tragedy informed by George Eliot's epigraphical dictum: that the greatest catharsis is produced when the main character experiences first a Recognition (in ancient Greek *anagnorisis*) followed swiftly by a Reversal of fortune (*peripeteia*).[21] EOTP begins by introducing the main characters: Thet and his quest for the truth, former soldier Suon and his recurring nightmare that the killing is still going on, and Nuon Chea and his recurring dream of seeing Pol Pot alone at a meeting in the jungle. After many years of visiting Nuon and building a relationship with him, Thet felt he should be honest about his own past and he reveals that he was orphaned as a result of Khmer Rouge policies and actions. This put a whole new perspective on the nature of the inquiry he had been undertaking throughout the film. Nuon Chea, to his credit, was magnanimous and sympathetic in his response. But in the film the scene is soon followed by Nuon Chea's *peripeteia* – his arrest on charges of genocide, war crimes and crimes against humanity by the United Nations-backed court trying the crimes of the Democratic Kampuchea state.

In the same tragic vein, Lemkin was concerned to present the other two main characters, executioners Khoun and Suon, as stuck in a destiny from which they might never emerge. In their last scene (actually interspersed between Nuon Chea's Recognition and Reversal) they admit to cannibalism and more murder in a nighttime field lit only by the resin torches they used to carry out their killings in the 1970s. The filmmaker felt it was symbolically appropriate for Khoun and Suon to exit the film via the flames of hell, as it were. However, Lemkin also took pains to give Khoun and Suon a humanity that reflected their own spiritual journey. Consequently, in their last scene, both recount how they received the order to stop the killing. They did so immediately. Khoun makes the point that he was very relieved and he could spend more time with his family. So in one sense, Khoun and Suon are locked in a world that has come to an end; in another sense, they are able to re-join humanity and get back to the business of living.

Although the story arc of EOTP was based on the Western notion of tragedy, Cambodian audiences responded strongly to its content. The discourse and perilinguistic semiotics of the documentary film were immediately recognisable to Cambodian audiences, but at the same time, strikingly different because for the first time former Khmer Rouge were making un-coerced and remorseful confessions. Witnessing Thet's success at getting the truth, some audience members expressed a desire to talk with the former killers themselves. Based upon these types of responses to EOTP, the authors conceived the videoconference as a way to give victims in Long Beach, where the largest community of Cambodian Americans in the US reside, the opportunity to have a conversation with perpetrators. Despite the limitations of having a conversation via video link, EOTP provided an opportunity to begin talking directly to former Khmer Rouge in a way not previously possible.

Creating the conditions for dialogue

The goal of the videoconference was to replicate Thet's example of how to engage in peaceful, non-judgemental dialogue, but some gaps in time and space posed concerns for the planners. First, the interaction would not be face-to-face in the traditional sense, but mediated via satellite and recorded by a number of non-Cambodians with notebooks and cameras crowded together with the survivors into a small conference room. How would the distance and additional people impact the dialogue? Second, even though the former soldiers and survivors would not be together in the same room, the videoconference would occur in real-time and be co-constructed by participants in the moment through the narrative/dialogical process. Given the novelty and uncertainty of the setting and the risk of emotional strain for all involved, the event needed to be carefully planned to ensure the physical and emotional safety and wellbeing of those who would participate. To be successful, the videoconference would have to 'fuse and consolidate' personal narratives and historical time and space in a way that allowed participants to take up social positions and interact in meaningful ways.[22] The planning stages for the videoconference have been described elsewhere.[23] In this section we want to draw attention to how the Cambodian team members and the authors adapted an existing mediation model to fit a Cambodian social and moral order for the videoconference setting.

Before forming the Cambodian team, Needham and Quintiliani consulted with A. Marco Turk, a Professor of Negotiation, Conflict Resolution and Peace Building at California State University, Dominguez Hills and specialist in the areas of restorative justice and implementing victim-offender mediation (VOM) in an international context.[24] Turk recommended a model based on Umbreit[25] used in the criminal justice systems in the United States and Canada to bring offenders face to face with their victims to seek avenues for forgiveness and healing through dialogue.[26] Needham and Quintiliani then asked Mr Sakphan Keam, a Khmer-English court translator and former Los Angeles County Human Relations Commissioner, to serve as mediator. In consultation with Keam, a team of cultural experts, including the anthropologists, was formed to plan and guide the process. The team was ultimately composed of a diverse group of nine Cambodian Americans: three women and six men, aged 25–60, self-identifying as Buddhist or Christian, one of whom was a licensed Cambodian mental health professional. The planning team members had different experiences of the Khmer Rouge period and included individuals who fled Cambodia before 1975, individuals who were adults during the Khmer Rouge, individuals who had been children during that time, and individuals born in the United States to survivors of the Khmer Rouge. All members of the team, including Needham and Quintiliani, were actively involved in different segments of the Long Beach community. All had seen the film and most were known to each other and had worked together on other projects.

Over the next three months, the team met to adapt VOM core values and practices to the Cambodian experience and to the unconventional format. Modifications made by the planning team resulted in the creation of a Khmer moral and social order supportive of the dialogue. Among these were thoughtful accommodations for Cambodian social and spiritual order. In Cambodian society, all persons are ranked relative to each other primarily by age, but also by gender, occupation, title and so on. This social order is maintained in part through the use of special linguistic forms and appropriate behaviour within social roles.[27] Because of this, a mismatch in social status and/or age between the perpetrators and survivors during the videoconference could impede dialogue. Those who would talk with Suon, Khoun, and Choeun (who, as noted above assisted in the filming, but was not shown in the film) during the event would have to come from the same socio-economic background: rural famers with no formal education. The Seniors Nutrition Program in Long Beach serves Cambodian Americans of this same background so we invited this group to work with us. Another concern was accommodating family members of those who would participate. The basic social structure of Cambodian society is the extended family and family members often accompany each other in their daily activities. Because of this all videoconference activities were open to family members.

Our facilitator, Keam, took the lead in incorporating Khmer symbols and rituals which would further help create a Khmer social order conducive to dialogue. To introduce the seniors to the project we scheduled a screening of EOTP at a local community centre. Keam arranged for a blessing ceremony to be performed by monks from a local Buddhist temple before the film started. The blessing ceremony honours the Buddha and requests protection, and is a regular part of Cambodian Theravada Buddhist observances and life passage ceremonies. Prior to the Khmer Rouge period, it was routine to request blessings from monks before beginning a journey or a new project. The blessing ceremony symbolically expanded the time and space of the community centre to include everyone and anyone who had been in some way affected by the Khmer Rouge and who might be touched in any way by the project, including the planning team, all victims and all perpetrators, all survivors and all those who died, and all who were known and unknown to us.

Of the over 60 people who attended the screening, 18 participated in a preparation meeting the following week, at which the planning team explained the videoconference ground rules. Individuals would be able to tell their story to or ask a question of the men in Bangkok. At each stage the team asked people to evaluate whether they felt the process would benefit them and they were reminded that if they felt it would not be of benefit or they felt it would be too disturbing or painful they were free to stop participation. The team's Cambodian therapist was present for all the discussions and offered advice and her assistance at that time and into the future. Of those who came to the preparation meeting, eight chose to participate in the videoconference scheduled for the next day. While all this was going on in Long Beach, Thet was working out logistics in Cambodia. Because having this conversation in Cambodia would be dangerous for the men, it was decided they would travel to a videoconference center in Bangkok, Thailand.

It is important to note that the VOM format was appropriate in this case not because it might lead to 'forgiveness and healing' as the authors initially thought, but because of the principles it is based upon which resonated with the Cambodian planning team. Among these were the expansion of the definition of 'victim' from those who are directly affected by the offence to include family and community members of both victims and offenders as well as witnesses and members of the community. Cambodians see reintegration as an all-inclusive practice, as evidenced by the blessing ceremony described above. The VOM process also respects the victim, empowering them to speak for themselves to determine need and to shape outcomes. Perhaps most important to both victims and former Khmer Rouge soldiers was that the videoconference would be conducted by the affected individuals within a supportive community without interference from the state, which neither group trusted.[28]

Additionally, as will be seen below, there are generational and cultural differences in what 'forgiveness and healing' mean and their importance in this context for these individuals. We take up the issue of forgiveness below, but wish to note here that at no time during this project did older Cambodian Americans or the former soldiers in Cambodia express a desire to 'heal' in the Western sense.[29] It was only the authors and younger members of the Cambodian American team who thought participating in the videoconference might result in some relief or 'healing'. Older Cambodian Americans tend to refer to the Khmer Rouge experience as a wound that has covered over, but remains raw underneath and can never heal. Talking about what happened has the effect of re-opening rather than healing the wound, bringing painful memories to the surface where they are experienced with full force once again. Instead, the victims wanted the former killers to do the talking, explaining what they did and why.

Dialogue and transformation

In this section we present an analysis of segments of the dialogue that occurred between the former Khmer Rouge in Bangkok and survivors in Long Beach during the videoconference. We explore how participants made use of established cultural symbols (including linguistic) to create a Cambodian chronotope – a Khmer moral social order – in which victims and killers could meaningfully and peacefully interact. We also consider how participants made use of and built on EOTP to seek truth, and in what ways this affected the reconfiguring of 'victims' and 'killers'. While there are many topics and aspects of the videoconference worthy of in-depth analysis, we look closely at three themes: (1) discerning the perpetrators' intention; (2) motivating other killers to tell the truth; and (3) recognising common experiences and shared pain.[30]

The videoconference was held in a small conference room in downtown Long Beach. Nine survivors and the facilitator sat at one end of a large table so they could all be seen by the men in Bangkok. Off camera were the authors, members of the planning team, a camera crew, and a *Los Angeles Times* reporter. The facilitator, Keam, brought artifacts symbolic of Cambodian culture and Angkorean history to create a Khmer space, including an oil painting of Angkor Wat, a red and white checked *krama* (Cambodian traditional cotton scarf), two five-headed bronze naga (Cambodian guardian serpents), a bronze conch shell and bronze bowl with water, flowers, candles, and incense. Keam wore a white shirt and *krama* to indicate his ritual status and round glasses to appear like an elder. He had prepared the space so those in attendance would 'know we are Cambodian'. In symbolising Cambodian history and culture, the artifacts helped to establish a Cambodian social and moral structure within which the talk would proceed. The objects reminded those present they are Khmer and demonstrated to the men in Bangkok that the people in Long Beach knew how to treat others with the proper respect of Khmer.

The videoconference began with Lemkin greeting Thet and the men in Bangkok. Lemkin introduced Keam, who after saying a few words of welcome, asked those who could be seen on camera to introduce themselves, giving their names and something about their family. With hands pressed together in front of their chest just below their chin, each person greeted the men across from them on the screen, addressing them as older or younger brother depending on the perceived age difference between them. Using kinship terms in this manner indicated 'cordiality, respect (especially toward older people), and a tacit acknowledgement of being on the same social level'.[31] Thet and the other men smiled and returned the greeting after each introduction, enthusiastically expressing thanks and raising their hands higher towards their foreheads to show their utmost gratitude and respect. A couple of people on the Long Beach side drew laughter as they jokingly introduced themselves. One of the middle-aged men joked 'I'm an old bachelor and a rusty one. I still can't find a wife', after which someone on the Long Beach side teased that the men in Cambodia should 'help find a wife for him'. The teasing foregrounded the spatial distance between them and at the same time made a surprisingly close social connection very early in the encounter. This was not something they would have suggested of anyone they had just met, let alone former Khmer Rouge executioners. Not all of the Cambodian Americans were comfortable with the level of familiarity or the light tone and said quietly to Keam that those men are killers and, 'you should not bow to them and call them *bong* (older brother)'. Despite these complaints, Cambodian rules for polite social engagement were held in place as the remaining participants used kin terms to greet the men.

The first question we will look at was the initial question of the evening asked by Som, a man in his 60s, and who, as the oldest male present was given the right to be first. In his question he clearly referenced the film to establish its relevance and focus on a topic that was revisited in many different forms that night: the problem of discerning the intention of the men.

Segment #1: 'we are all victims'

Som began by asking for forgiveness if his questions caused the men in Bangkok 'any great emotional discomfort'. In so doing, he acknowledged that the topic and directness of the questions broke powerful social rules to avoid direct confrontation. Som went on to explain that he took particular interest in the claim the men made in the film that 'whatever they did was done at Angkar's orders'.[32] He stated he personally witnessed throats being slit as the men described in EOTP and that he lost 20 of his immediate family members: his father, mother, his younger siblings and their families, and his uncle's entire family. Following this introduction Som asked the men, 'If Angkar ordered you to kill your own fathers and mothers, your own siblings, and your own children; would you dare to do it?' Khoun answered:

> For me personally, I had no intention of doing it. If Angkar ordered me to do it, and if I disobeyed, I would also be killed. What if they ordered you to kill your mother, your father, your siblings, and your relatives, you had to do it. If you disobeyed, they would kill you. They would kill everyone. Not only my family members; they would kill me as well.

Som thanked the men and asked more directly, 'Older brother Suon and older brother Khoun, how many members of your own families did you kill?' Both Khoun and Suon responded that during that time they had lived in provinces far away from their families. Suon explained, 'Because of that, I do not know if I would have touched my own relatives or family members. But, when I returned to my village, a large number of them were gone also.' More quietly, Som concluded, 'Yes. Yes. We are all victims.'

The importance of EOTP as a foundation for the dialogue and how strongly some Cambodians identified with it is clear from the first question. As he framed this question, Som referred to the film three times and introduced himself as a witness to the crimes described in it. In so doing, he acknowledged both the film's authority and the truth of the men's testimony. The film also provided a common reference point for questioning the killers and advancing the participants' understanding of events and intention, which Som identified as his central concern. As Som noted, the men addressed the question of motivation in the film, but being able to ask them directly underscores the difficulty we all have in coming to terms with how such heinous crimes could occur. Were these men really hapless victims of the Khmer Rouge or had they been dedicated soldiers who believed those people must die and now they were trying to appear blameless? Khoun repeated what was said in the film: they were following orders; it was kill or be killed. But Som challenged the legitimacy of the answer and wanted to know if in the course of 'taking orders' any of these men had in fact killed their own family members. Suon's answer is perhaps the most frighteningly honest: he was away from his family and because of that he does not know if he would have harmed them. When he did return many had been killed. What is not said but can be understood is that his family members were likely killed by someone just like him. With this last revelation, Som's tone changes and he responds in a lowered voice: 'Yes. Yes. We are all victims.'

When it is revealed that the killers lost family members at the hands of other Khmer Rouge assigned to those areas, it brings into focus the chaos and widespread terror of the regime. It also makes relevant an important strategy of the Khmer Rouge to prevent organised uprising: the scattering of family members. In pre-Khmer Rouge Cambodia, the family was the basic unit of society.[33] Most of what was needed for daily life was produced and consumed within nuclear and extended family units. The family provided physical, emotional, and economic support, so breaking up families would effectively disorient and immobilise the entire population. People were moved out of the cities into the countryside where males and females were given different jobs and placed in separate work groups. Children were grouped by age and gender and older ones were sent to segregated work camps in other parts of the country. There was no, or only sporadic, contact between family members. Everyone lived among strangers with whom they had no ties and no trust. Suon and Khoun were in the same situation. Separated from their families, the fear was great and the choices few.

However, these men did more than just execute the people brought to them and as will be discussed further, the 'killer as victim' narrative is contested terrain for the videoconference participants.

Segment #2: challenging Angkar's 'absolute authority'

In a question related to the one above, Kea, also a man in his 60s, asked why the men did not think about 'confronting or rebelling against the insane Angkar'. Khoun responded they did think of rebelling, but Angkar's 'absolute authority held a firm grip on us. If I refused to follow their plan, they would take me out and kill me. Rebellion was impossible.'

Giving way to some emotional expression, Kea raised his voice slightly while voicing disbelief, 'I disagree that you did it without intention. If you had no intention at least you would have let the people know one by one to revolt and get free from the killings … '[34] He seemed to have more to say, but instead turned his head away from the men, waving his hand towards the screen indicating he was finished. Suon wanted to make sure the Cambodians in Long Beach understood the impossibility of their situation and began his explanation by questioning the premise of Kea's accusation,

> So you would like me to protest as an individual and the people in general to rebel. Rebel against what, great-uncle? All our people, how do we rebel if we are barehanded? They had weapons. That's my first point. Secondly, as you saw, they took victims from here and there. When we got to the killing field, they ordered us. See? Sorry, I would like to say it more loudly aunts and uncles, [raising his voice, arms and hands] if I revolted I would be killed, my family would end up in one ditch. To revolt, you needed weapons to confront them with up to fifty people from each village. They would just wipe you out.

Again, EOTP plays an important role in the videoconference as a common and legitimate resource for dialogue and addressing the question of who had intention, who had power, and why someone did not act. Suon became increasingly agitated as he worked to convince the survivors in Long Beach of the reality of the regime from his position at the bottom of the chain of command. Not only did he speak more loudly, he also raised his shoulders, arms, and hands, taking up more space and becoming more emphatic in his speech. He invoked EOTP to support his argument, reminding those in Long Beach that they saw for themselves how it was. Certainly he killed as he was told, but he killed with his bare hands. He was not a soldier with a gun. What chance did he and others like him have against the weapons of the Khmer Rouge that could quickly and easily wipe out large numbers of people? Even though the men killed for Angkar, they did so against their will and with the intention only of protecting their families. Because the family formed the foundation of Cambodian social activity, an individual family member's behaviour was accepted as evidence of how the entire family would behave. In keeping with Cambodian culture, Angkar did not treat anyone as an individual. If someone proved themselves to be an enemy of the regime then it was axiomatic that their immediate families would be executed along with them. This policy was supported by the communist saying often used by the Khmer Rouge regime, 'If you pull out the grass, pull it out by the roots.' Although Suon and Khoun lived far from their families and had rare if any contact with them, the Khmer Rouge upper cadre knew who their families were. The men were aware of the consequences of disobedience and lived with that constant fear. In this way they too were victims of the regime.

This segment also highlights another way Angkar circumvented any chance for rebellion. As Suon attests, people marked for execution were mixed with people they did not know and moved to unfamiliar areas where they would be killed. Suon did not know the people brought to him, where they came from, or what they were guilty of. He only knew what he was told, which was they were 'enemies of the people', and must be eliminated. As shown by Hinton[35] these men and women often had trouble seeing the difference between themselves and those brought for them to kill, increasing their fear that they would also be killed. They experienced a 'psychosocial dissonance', not wanting to kill, but knowing that by refusing to kill they would be identified as an enemy of the people and subjected to torture and death.[36]

Segment #3: facing the truth of the unthinkable

Uce, a man in his early 40s, was one of the participants assigned to help with translation during the videoconference, but he also wanted to speak with the men. He was orphaned during the war like Thet and had become quite emotional during the community screening of the film. Like Som and Kea, Uce was concerned with intention, but he confronted the men with the most depraved acts they performed: eating the livers and drinking the bile of their victims as traditional medicine. He wanted to know, 'Did your superiors order that too or was that your own will?' Khoun repeated what he had said in the film, that he saw others drinking the bile and he was curious about how it tasted, so he tried it. However, he found it disgusting and did not drink any more than the one sip. Suon, who in the film admits to drinking human gall often and even carrying a bladder with him to sip, did not answer. He remained silent.

Uce thanked the men and added: 'I already forgive you. I know who the top murderers are – devious, conniving. I don't speak out his name. You, older brothers were given orders that had to be obeyed.'

Two of the most disturbing admissions recorded in the film are the act of cannibalism and the execution of young children. Cannibalism was particularly troubling because the men admitted to trying it out of curiosity. This action provided strong evidence that the men had some degree of free will and chose to not only participate in the plans of the 'insane Angkar' but also indulge their own depraved interest. Asking the men directly about these horrific acts could have led to emotional outbursts or accusations, but did not. As we learned in follow-up interviews, some of the survivors, Uce among them, made use of cultural conventions of kin address, apology, and forgiveness to mollify the situation and sustain the space in which to ask such difficult questions. The planning and preparation for the videoconference specifically aimed to allow for difficult questions to be asked while still allowing discussion to move forward.

Uce's final statement reveals he is prepared to forgive the men for their most heinous crimes and accept that they had no choice. It also reveals a conflict many Cambodians face between seeking the truth and seeking justice for individual crimes. On the one hand, the men candidly admitted to terrible acts for which they could be prosecuted. On the other hand, these men are seen as pawns in the geopolitics of the time. They are guilty by their own admission, but do they deserve to be prosecuted or vilified like the upper echelons of the regime? One aspect in their favour and confirmed in follow-up interviews with the participants was that they stopped killing when the Khmer Rouge ended. Others in the government continue such behaviours and they remain guilty. The fact that these men stopped can be accepted as evidence they would not have perpetrated these crimes if not for Angkar.

Uce's concluding comment also references an alternative narrative of blame circulating among Cambodians in Long Beach, which posits that other, more powerful forces outside Cambodia had a hand in directing the killings and are the ones truly responsible for the deaths of so many Khmer. This suspicion is made more explicit in the question we take up next.

Segment #4: beyond the videoconference

In this segment, Cham, a Cambodian woman in her 40s, acknowledges how important the men's confessions are. Through their involvement with Thet and the EOTP documentary they have helped provide proof that the Khmer Rouge had a programme for execution and that all those people did not die of natural causes as the former leaders claim. Cham then asserts a strongly held belief among many Cambodians that Khmer are blameless victims of the sinister plans of another nation that wishes to exterminate all ethnic Khmer. She asks the men for their suggestions for how to encourage former killers to come forward in order to gather evidence for this theory:

> It's fair to say the main aim was to permanently wipe out the Khmer race. The Khmer weren't at fault. Because of that, I'd like to ask you, uncles, what you think of urging the Khmer who were once the murderers to voluntarily come forward and admit their crimes for more documentary evidence and information. It does not mean the Khmers living here want to take revenge or kill you. But for the victims, if we forgive the killers, we'd like to know the truth ... the truth for our history like you come out and to speak the truth.

Thet, who has spent the last ten years of his life seeking answers to this very question, repeated what Cham asked, encouraging the men to respond. Suon spoke first:

> Auntie, if you want to persuade others like me where I live to come out and speak the truth, no real killers would show up. You could only find them through further research and thorough investigation. If you want to do that, we need to rethink, auntie. We need to continue to do more research to know who's who.

Khoun agreed with Suon that it will take time. Suon adds that forgiveness is important, but emphasises the enormity of such a project, 'We are talking about people throughout the whole country. It's extremely difficult.'

Choeun volunteers to help in the effort and reveals his personal perspective on what it has meant to be a part of EOTP:

> I'll help with research and to enlighten them to give them the courage to come forward, just like us three. Because this is a very high honor, I'm very glad to have that honor today. Once they're enlightened, they'll have the courage to step forward like us in order to speak the truth. All of us will help and talk to enlighten them so they have the courage to speak because they hide themselves.

For many Cambodians in Long Beach, the truth of who was behind the killing of so many Khmer is the most relevant and pressing question. Many suspect it is the Vietnamese who are responsible for the genocide and, although Cham did not state this in her question, Vietnam is specifically named in several of the post-videoconference interviews we conducted with the participants. This is an alternative chronotope in which all Khmer, including the men in Bangkok, are victims and therefore blameless. The men become 'Khmer who were once murderers', but are no longer. Having come forward with the truth Cham restores their status as fellow Khmer and casts them as experts and potential collaborators who can encourage others to do the same, helping document the truth for the greater good, for the sake of what can once again be 'our history'.

It is not clear from Suon's response if he recognises or accepts Cham's premise that Khmer are not to blame for what happened. These men had no knowledge of the inner workings of the Khmer Rouge and were unaware of the larger geopolitical forces at play during the 1970s. They cannot provide information beyond what they were told by their immediate superiors. Instead Suon's response addressed Cham's request for assistance and spoke to what he knows – other killers like him. Thet's approach worked with them and will likely work with others, but its success is based on Cambodian values of one-to-one personal communication and allowing sufficient time to build trust.[37] The entire country in a sense is filled with perpetrators who, like them, have hidden their past. Former killers need time to feel safe to admit what they did. He rightly points out this is an enormous undertaking that will require time and patience. Forgiveness will help, but former killers have to be told they have been forgiven and this will take time.

Choeun, who played an active role in locating important places for the film and helping research new sources, wants to continue this work and help with the project Cham proposes. His remarks offered insights into how the men now think of themselves and how this has shifted over time. He took up a new trope, to 'enlighten' others so they will 'have the courage to step forward like us ... to tell the true story'. For Choeun the entire project, from conducting research for the film, to this conversation with Cambodian Americans in Long Beach, to extending the project to the whole country, is a 'very high honour'. To imagine the self as honourable in any way did not seem possible for these men prior to meeting Thet. The larger goal of recording history for the next generation situates the perpetrators very differently in the discussion. Cham sets up the possibility of this conclusion by expressing her gratitude and assuring them the victims do not want revenge; they want the truth, which only these men can begin to provide.

Segment #5: the space of sorrow

Most of the questions asked during the videoconference focused on the intention and responsibility of the executioners. Towards the end of the videoconference, Meng and Ung, both of whom worked at a mental health agency serving Cambodians in the Long Beach area, shifted the perspective towards the former killers' feelings of remorse. Meng had already asked the men a question about killing children. Now, standing with Ung, the youngest of the Cambodian participants and a licensed clinical social worker, they represented the generation these men hoped to reach with their story. Since Ung did not feel as comfortable speaking Khmer in public, Meng, who is a caseworker at the same agency, spoke for them. He explained that they work with Cambodians who lived through those traumatic times and who, after 30 years, continue to have nightmares of that time. He asks if these men also have nightmares.

Khoun answers that during the 1980s he would dream about what happened often and 'wake up totally anxious, thinking to myself, "you shouldn't have done what you did"'. Now his nightmares are infrequent and occur every few years.

Suon, however, explains that he cannot escape the memories of what he did. As he describes his current condition there appears to be no separation between his waking life and his dreams:

As time passes, it seems that strange feelings keep carrying me off away and away. I'm not even fully thinking about our past deeds. I feel our minds have been blinded by what we've done. This strange feeling keeps waking me up. And I'm always kicking. It's been like that up to the present day.

Awake, I find myself walking in a graveyard and I think I should never have done what I did. Every day is the same; I walk by the Buddhist pagoda and after time, I keep going around [moving his hands/arms in a circular motion]. I go this way; the story goes the other way. Then I see the path and I think about things deeply.

I cremate people at the mortuary nowadays. I help at burials. When I see the dead I sit and shed tears. People say, 'They're not related to him. He sits and cries, for what?' Some get curious and they come to see me crying. Yes, I help with seven or eight cremations a day for the purpose of collecting good dharma and giving alms to others. I help out with many cremations, whether or not I'm related to the dead. Even now, I can barely rest, they call out to help so often. Whenever an incident happens, they call me out. At the cremation, I sit, lost with my head between my knees and shed tears, all alone, unaware that I am weeping. And I think about what I've done in the past. It's not the right thing to do great-uncle.

Suon's response reveals a deep and unrelenting remorse that he carries with him every day. Circumambulating the temple is part of many Buddhist ceremonies, including funerals. In what appears to be an endless loop, Suon cannot lay his deeds to rest; they circle around the other way to meet him. In the film, Suon talked about his concern for the afterlife, acknowledging it will take him an unimaginably long time to be reborn a human after what he has done. Here we learned what action he now takes to begin again to create good merit; following Buddhist precepts, he helps with cremations. His words also speak to the victims in Long Beach on a very personal level. They too continue to have nightmares; they too feel like it was only yesterday.

The last question of the videoconference came from Thet, who asked those in Long Beach for a show of compassion and advice for the men, 'I'd like your advice. They have great remorse about killing human beings. You are the victims. How do you think they can achieve peace of mind?'

Keam translated the question into English and invited Ung, as a mental health specialist, to answer. Ung answers in Khmer, 'Uncles, all of you should tell your family members to make you feel better.' Meng also makes a recommendation,

… whatever happened was 30 years ago, now please only speak the truth. When you say it out loud, it can help ease your pain and our anger and frustration will subside bit by bit. You won't be healed right away. It's not like that. It will take a long time. But by speaking the truth, it will make us as human beings understand and find solution to the problems we face.

Ung added, 'And afterwards, uncles, forgive yourselves and move on in life.'

The videoconference ended with Ung, the child of genocide survivors, giving these men a distinctly Western view of forgiveness and responsibility that involves telling one's family the truth and then forgiving oneself. It also underscores the central theme of the encounter: the truth trumps everything and transforms everything; the truth has the power to turn monsters into human beings. But how the truth accomplishes this transformation is different for older Cambodian Americans than it is for Meng and Ung, who grew up in the United States and have been trained in Western cultural approaches to trauma and mental health.

The men looked jubilant mainly to hear someone of the younger generation speak to them in Khmer and to acknowledge them. This is one reason why they came forward, for the younger generation to know and understand what they had done so that history will not be repeated. Everyone raised their hands in *sompeah* and thanked each other with wishes for a happy life.

Discussion

This article has presented a process through which Cambodian survivors of the Khmer Rouge – victims and perpetrators alike – may successfully move from separation and silence towards reconciliation and action. From Thet's personal quest (truth seeking) to documentary film to videoconference, a new chronotope emerged: a chronotope in which dialogue became the basis of transforming or reconfiguring the meaning of Khmer Rouge perpetrators from killers to knowledgeable collaborators and potential partners in documenting and telling the truth. A critical step in this process was the documentary film, *Enemies of the People*, which provided an introduction to the former executioners, the model for interacting with them, and a shared experience between the men in the film and audiences. With this introduction, an awkward and potentially threatening first meeting between victims and perpetrators was accomplished at a safe distance, allowing time for reflection and analysis of one's feelings and possible next steps. After viewing the film, Cambodian Americans felt they had met and knew Suon and Khoun to some extent. Hearing and seeing the confessions in EOTP and judging them to be genuine, some Cambodian Americans felt compelled to follow Thet's lead and talk with these men themselves. Thet's example showed one way to bridge the space of sorrow, providing an approach that could peacefully reunite victims and former soldiers of the Khmer Rouge in a single positive purpose: working together to document the truth of what happened. The videoconference confirmed this work is possible.

In post-videoconference interviews, participants and members of the planning team overwhelmingly expressed gratitude for Thet's efforts to seek the truth and for the courage of the former Khmer Rouge involved in EOTP for coming forward for the sake of the next generation. One of the women expressed the overall feeling of the group, 'I really appreciate them because they have courage. They are brave. I can see [that]. Before they decided to come to that videoconference, I thought about how many days they had nightmares before coming to confront [us].'

The videoconference participants, however, stopped short of saying they fully forgave these men or that they believed the men felt enough remorse for their horrendous actions. As one of the men remarked emphatically during a post-videoconference interview, 'Who can forgive them? Not me. I'm not [their] direct victim … Honestly, I think they are sorry, but not fully sorry … I'm trying to find a way to forgive them, but simultaneously I would like them to get justice done.'

The tension between justice and forgiveness is an ongoing issue for Cambodian Americans. Many do not feel the tribunal, which recently sentenced Nuon Chea and Khieu Samphan, the former president of Democratic Kampuchea, to life in prison, is an effective way to attain justice. Many feel these men should have been executed for their crimes. But while many want the leaders put to death, they do not seek harsh punishment for soldiers at the lowest levels, like Suon, Khoun, and Choeun, who were made to carry out the executions and who can be seen, to a limited extent, as victims. These men have value, if only as fellow humans and survivors. One of the videoconference participants reasoned, 'Of course I really want to have a trial. But a trial that finds justice for the victims, not a trial to put the killers to death. Half the country did it, right? How can we kill half the country again? No.' Others have told us that no amount of punishment will bring back their families.

They feel the killers will receive their punishment in another life, 'It is not for me to punish them. I want to calm my heart.'

In keeping with what we learned throughout this project, what many victims of the Khmer Rouge have said they wanted and expected from the trials – but have not gotten – was to hear former Khmer Rouge admit to killing and to express remorse. EOTP is unique in having provided that: Former Khmer Rouge frontline cadre recreating the events of that time in a way that matches the experience of those who lived it. For the first time perpetrators acknowledge and substantiate what the victims know to be true, but has been denied. The film succeeded in bringing the past into the present, allowing audiences to see what has become of two Khmer Rouge soldiers and executioners. It is clear to the victims that Suon and Khoun did not prosper after the end of the regime. In fact, they have lost much and are living in poverty and ill health. Facing possible threats from both their victims and the government, these men could lose what little they have left. Through their admissions, they demonstrate they know what they did was wrong and that they suffer for it. EOTP offers a new chronotope for discussing the Cambodian genocide that affords the possibility for un-coerced admissions of guilt.

But the film by itself is not enough to reconfigure the victims and perpetrators. The film is an imagined, constructed chronotope in a literary space, a suggestion of what is possible, but it is not the real thing. This article suggests that it is possible to bring the people and acts portrayed in EOTP into the lived world, where they can interact directly with those who were harmed. A structure that allows individuals, families, and communities the opportunity to talk or simply be present as observers is needed, but difficult to achieve. The video-conference provided the social and moral space for victims to speak directly to former killers, to question them about the past and to assess for themselves that these men are not killers in the present time. As noted earlier in this article, to be successful, the video-conference would have to provide a chronotope in which personal stories and historical time and space would come together in such a way that it would be possible for participants to take up social positions and interact in meaningful ways. Evidence that the videoconference would fulfil this potential came an hour into the event, when the Long Beach side had to take a break for technical reasons. The previous hour had been tense with tears and very little laughter. When they returned, the moderator, Keam, greeted the men in Bangkok,

> We meet again. It helps ease our feelings a lot … If we don't spill it out, we won't know. We won't know until we speak it out and then we know. If we see you in the film, we're afraid. But when we see you today, it seems like a different story. We get more acquainted.

Suon agrees that some of the scenes in the film are frightening, but says there is no need to be afraid anymore and that he is no longer afraid, 'If I had money, I'd personally fly over to see you, show you my face, and if you great-aunts and great-uncles chop me up then let it be. I won't say a word.' By making this statement, Suon shows he is willing to give his life as proof of his desire to be open and honest. While still not complete, the reconfiguration and transformation of the former killers is clear in Keam and Suon's exchange. 'Spilling it out', speaking the truth, has 'eased feelings' and contributed to the knowledge of some – but not all – of those present.

The videoconference chronotope provided the space and opportunity in which perpetrators could be seen as humans, as Khmer, and as individuals with families and a history. Occurring in the aftermath of the Khmer Rouge era, they can now co-construct new historical identities as potential knowledgeable collaborators who can encourage others to come forward and contribute to documenting the truth. To paraphrase Bakhtin, these men are no longer uniform, machine-like executioners; they have thickened and taken on flesh, becoming 'visible and responsive to the movements of time, plot, and history'.[38]

The victims have also been reconfigured vis-à-vis the perpetrators. The reversal of fortune for both is clear. The Cambodian Americans, no longer at the mercy of the Khmer Rouge, are now in the position of authority and control. In Cambodian culture, the Cambodian Americans are potential patrons with the power to positively (or negatively) impact the lives of the former soldiers. As Suon stated, it is now within the power of the Cambodian Americans to kill him if they wish. The honorifics the men added to the kinship terms, addressing the Cambodian Americans as 'great' uncles and aunts, marks the distinction in their social positions. But those in Long Beach seek accountability with compassion. It is the Cambodian Americans who, through their effort and interest, bestow the honour Choeun feels for having been part of this project. It is those in Long Beach who suggest a possible future that includes the men working with them to document the truth. Both victims and perpetrators have a restored sense of agency and self-direction predicated on working together – even if only possible during the videoconference.

Following the success of the videoconference, there was serious discussion among the members of the planning team to develop a programme using EOTP to promote dialogue between perpetrators and victims in Cambodia. Unfortunately, no one on the team had the time or resources to devote to directing such an undertaking. The film has been shown in Cambodia, but due to its content, filmmakers could not get a permit from government officials to show it in theatres. Instead, it premiered at Meta House, a non-governmental organisation in Phnom Penh, the capital, with fewer Cambodians able to attend than the filmmakers had hoped.

The videoconference illustrates that within a Cambodian context perpetrators coming forward to tell the truth for the sake of their collective history has the potential to transform the sorrow and shame into achievement by providing a course of action – working together to regain personal and collective agency. The crimes of the past cannot be undone, nor can those who died be brought back. Nevertheless, there is a process through which those survivors who wish to can ensure that the truth of what happened is recorded and remembered.

Acknowledgements

We wish to thank all the Cambodians who participated in this project and their families who supported them. We are deeply moved by your courage and are forever changed as a result of having worked together. We also wish to thank our journal editors and reviewers for valuable comments.

Disclosure statement

No potential conflict of interest was reported by the authors.

Notes

1. Seth Mydans, 'Cambodian Leader Resists Punishing Top Khmer Rouge', *New York Times*, 29 December 1998.
2. *Enemies of the People*. Directed by Rob Lemkin and Thet Sambath. London: Old Street Films, 2010.
3. Works of note that include testimony of former Khmer Rouge soldiers are, Alexander Laban Hinton, *Why Did They Kill?: Cambodia in the Shadow of Genocide* (Berkeley: University of California Press, 2004); Meng-Try Ea and Sorya Sim, *Victims and Perpetrators?: Testimony of Young Khmer Rouge Comrades* (Phnom Penh: Documentation Center of Cambodia, 2001).
4. Dorothy Holland et al., *Identity and Agency in Cultural Worlds* (Cambridge, MA: Harvard University Press, 1998).
5. Mikhail Bakhtin, *The Dialogic Imagination: Four Essays*, trans. Michael Holquist (Texas: University of Texas Press, 1981), 250.
6. Ibid.
7. Ibid., 84.
8. Michael Silverstein, 'Axes of Evals: Token versus Type Interdiscursivity', *Journal of Linguistic Anthropology* 15 (2005): 6–22.
9. Bakhtin, *The Dialogic Imagination*, 94. For a discussion of chronotope and interdiscursivity in documentary film, see Michael Chanan, 'The Documentary Chronotope', *Jump Cut: A Review of Contemporary Media* 43 (July 2000): 56–61, http://www.ejumpcut.org/archive/onlinessays/JC43folder/DocyChronotope.html.
10. Holland et al., *Identity and Agency*, 52.
11. Dorothy Holland and Jean Lave, *History in Person: Enduring Struggles, Contentious Practice, Intimate Identities* (Santa Fe, NM: School of American Research Advanced Seminar Series, 2001).
12. See Alexandra Jaffe, 'Introduction', in *Stance: Sociolinguistic Perspectives*, ed. Alexandra Jaffe (New York: Oxford University Press, 2009), 1–28.
13. For a discussion of the role of trauma narratives in the context of psychotherapy with survivors of political violence, see Kelly McKinney, 'Breaking the Conspiracy of Silence: Testimony, Traumatic Memory, and Psychotherapy with Survivors of Political Violence', *Ethos* 35 (2007): 265–99.
14. Terri Shaffer Yamada, 'Trauma and Transformation: The Autobiographies of Cambodian Americans (1980–2010)', in *Cambodian American Experiences: Histories, Communities, Cultures and Identities*, ed. Jonathan H.X. Lee (Dubuque, IA: Kendall Hunt Publishing, 2010), 218–46.
15. Ibid., 220–1.
16. Sydney Schanberg, *The Death and Life of Dith Pran* (New York: Penguin Books, 1985), 18.
17. Haing Ngor and Roger Warner, *A Cambodian Odyssey* (London: Macmillan, 1988), 223.
18. *S-21: The Khmer Rouge Killing Machine*. Directed by Rithy Panh. New York: First Run Features, 2003.
19. Patricia McCormick, *Never Fall Down* (New York: Balzer + Bray, 2012).
20. Sambath Thet, 'Perpetrator's Perspective: Befriending the Khmer Rouge', *BBC News Online*, 12 December 2010, http://www.bbc.co.uk/news/world-asia-pacific-11968144.
21. George Eliot, 'Notes on Form in Art (1868)', in *George Eliot: Selected Essays, Poems and Other Writings*, ed. A.S. Byatt and Nicholas Warren (New York: Penguin Books, 1990), 231–40.

22. Bakhtin, *The Dialogic Imagination*, 89.
23. Karen Quintiliani et al., 'Facilitating Dialogue between Cambodian American Survivors and Khmer Rouge Perpetrators', *Peace Review: A Journal of Social Justice* 23 (2011): 506–13.
24. A. Marco Turk, 'Cyprus Reunification is Long Overdue: The Time is Right for Track III Diplomacy as the Best Approach for Successful Negotiation of this Ethnic Conflict', *Loyola of Los Angeles International and Comparative Law Review* 28 (2006): 205–55.
25. Mark S. Umbreit, *The Handbook of Victim Offender Mediation* (San Francisco: Jossey-Bass, 2001).
26. Rachel MacNair, *The Psychology of Peace: An Introduction* (Westport, CN: Praeger, 2003).
27. David Chandler, *A History of Cambodia* (Boulder, CO: Westview Press, 1992), 90.
28. For an overview of the principles of restorative justice, see Howard Zehr and Harry Mika, 'Fundamental Principles of Restorative Justice', *The Contemporary Justice Review* 1, no. 1 (1998): 47–55.
29. For a discussion of how 'healing' is not a universal goal for individuals in post-conflict societies, see Rosalind Shaw, 'Memory Frictions: Localizing the Truth and Reconciliation Commission in Sierra Leone', *The International Journal of Transitional Justice* 1 (2007): 183–207.
30. The videoconference was conducted in Khmer and transcribed and translated into English by a certified Cambodian American court translator. The authors worked primarily from the English translation, however key terms and phrases were double checked with our facilitator, Keam, often resulting in lengthy and valuable discussions about subtle cultural practices and meanings. Space limitations prevent us from including full transcripts of the talk. What is presented here is therefore selective and reflects the particular question under examination in this article. For more on transcribing, see Elinor Ochs, 'Transcription as Theory', in *The Discourse Reader*, ed. A. Jaworski and N. Coupland (London; New York: Routledge, 1999), 167–82. For a transcript of the videoconference, see 'Videoconference: Victims, Perpetrators: Survivors', *Enemies of the People*, Special Edition, DVD, Disc 2. Directed by Rob Lemkin and Sambeth Thet. London: Old Street Films, 2011.
31. May Ebihara, 'Svay, A Khmer Village in Cambodia' (PhD diss., Columbia University, 1968), 668.
32. Angkar (pronounced Angka) means 'organisation' and is what the Khmer Rouge called themselves. 'Khmer Rouge' (Red Khmer) was the name given to the group by Norodom Sihanouk, who was king and later prime minister of Cambodia from 1941 until 1970 and became king once again from 1993 to 2004.
33. Ebihara, 'Svay, A Khmer Village'.
34. The Khmer word is *chaetanaa* ᩮᨧᨲᨶᩣ meaning intention, will, volition, design, inclination, purpose; determination; end or aim in any plan, measure or exertion. From R.K. Headley, *Cambodian-English Dictionary* (Washington, DC: The Catholic University of America Press, 1977), 186.
35. Hinton, *Why Did They Kill?*
36. Ibid., 236.
37. Taking time to build trust is a salient feature of Cambodian culture and has been advocated by others working in this area. See for example, Meas Nee, *Towards Restoring Life: Cambodian Villages*, 3rd ed. (Phnom Penh: JSRC, 1999). Also relevant is Alexandra Kent's discussion of the role of Buddhist practices in rebuilding trust among Cambodian villagers, in 'Recovery of the Collective Spirit: The Role of the Revival of Buddhism in Cambodia', http://gup.ub.gu.se/publication/71410-recovery-of-the-collective-spirit-the-role-of-the-revival-of-buddhism-in-cambodia.
38. Bakhtin, *The Dialogic Imagination*, 84.

Perpetrating ourselves: reading human rights and responsibility otherwise

Crystal Parikh

Department of English and the Department of Social and Cultural Analysis, New York University, USA

This article argues for an expanded and more nuanced conception of the figure of the 'perpetrator' than currently exists with respect to human rights. It examines the poetry of the diasporic Chinese-Indonesian writer Li-Young Lee and the postwar history of political violence in postcolonial Indonesia, in relation to the ethical theory of Emmanuel Levinas. By considering how relations of responsibility extend beyond individual agents of violence, to a multitude of beneficiaries, the article provides a model for how diasporic acts of literary imagination grapple with past violence, loss and repression that often remain unaddressed in more official state venues of law and politics.

And I never believed that the multitude
of dreams and many words were in vain.
Li-Young Lee, 'The City in Which I Love You'[1]

If in its English-language denotation to 'perpetrate' relays the sense of committing an illegal or criminal act, the word itself derives from the Latin verb, 'perpatrare': 'per' (to complete) and 'patrare' ('to bring about'). Keeping this etymological shift in mind, in which the commission of an act comes to be understood as the execution of a necessarily *illicit* or *immoral* act, we might ask how we are ourselves perpetrated in the offing. In this article I would have us ask how an ethics of responsibility to others challenges us to 'perpetrate ourselves', thus rethinking clear-cut demarcations of perpetrator and victim, quotidian and spectacular violences, innocence and guilt.[2] How does our being 'committed' to the names and identities we inhabit necessarily involve us in relations of responsibility to those others whom we deem the victims of violence perpetrated by other others and, indeed, what are our relations of responsibility to the perpetrators as well? How, in other words, are we the beneficiaries, unwitting or otherwise, of precisely those very acts of violence that we disavow and from which we seek to distance ourselves?

I consider these questions through the ethical poetics of writer Li-Young Lee, in particular his 1990 collection of poetry, *The City in Which I Love You*, as it addresses the specific history of post-independence Indonesia, from which Lee and his family fled as exiles. Born in Jakarta in 1957 to ethnic Chinese parents, Lee left there in 1959 with his family, eventually to immigrate to the United States in 1964, when his father, a political dissident, escaped the Sukarno regime. In turn, Sukarno's rise to and fall from power proves one example of the extremely complex and violent dynamics by which anti- and postcolonial nationalisms across the globe were swept up into the bipolar logics of the Cold War after 1945. Successfully countering Dutch imperial rule to secure Indonesian independence in 1949 and establishing himself as the nation's first president, by the end of the following decade Sukarno had dismantled the parliamentary government and ruled in partnership with the country's military and the Communist Party of Indonesia (Partai Komunis Indonesia, or PKI) under the guise of what he termed 'guided democracy'.[3] In 1963, Sukarno declared himself president for life and established alliances with the Soviet Union and the People's Republic of China.

However, in 1965, after a coup attempt against the Indonesian army resulted in the death of six leading generals, military leaders accused the PKI of instigating what has since come to be known as the 30th September Movement (a claim historians have found unconvincing, given that the PKI consisted almost entirely of civilians).[4] The army leadership launched a retaliatory counterinsurgency against communists and suspected communists that resulted in the deaths of an estimated 300,000–500,000 people (some scholars have placed the count even higher, to upwards of one million dead) and that eradicated the PKI. It also established a military dictatorship headed by Major General Suharto and placed Sukarno under house arrest, where he remained until his death in 1970 (even as Suharto initially characterised his own actions as a defense of Sukarno's government).

For his part, Sukarno mostly cooperated with the army, to ward off any incursions from former imperial and neocolonial powers (i.e., the United States, Great Britain and the Netherlands): 'Obsessed with the unity of the country, Sukarno seems to have believed that a bloodletting, no matter how loathsome, was preferable to the dissolution of Indonesia as a nation-state and the return to foreign rule'.[5] From the 1940s to the 1960s, the United States alternated between supporting Sukarno's independence movement and later providing aid to the military for the overthrow of the autocratic leader. Nevertheless, as Bradley R. Simpson argues, the United States, consistently upheld a policy of 'military modernization' for developing the Indonesian economy and opening it to United States investment and trade.[6] In Indonesia and throughout the Third World, with its unyielding commitment to such military modernisation yoked to fervent anti-communism, the United States 'stopped promoting democracy in the Third World and allowed local armed forces to crush political opponents, even on such an extreme scale as the mass killings in Indonesia'.[7]

With the release of the award-winning documentary film *The Act of Killing* by director Joshua Oppenheimer in 2012, the ethics of representing human rights atrocities in Indonesia has been a particular topic of renewed critical attention in film, media and cultural studies. In fact, Oppenheimer has become the target of disapproval for collaborating with perpetrators of the massacre, because he interviews and, some argue, elicits sympathy for 'retired gangster qua paramilitary executioner[s]' (although it was only through such collaboration that the filmmaker was permitted to investigate the genocide at all, and the Indonesian government has since protested that the film is misleading in its portrait of the nation's history).[8] My attention to Lee's work means to contribute to this discussion about the representation of political violence in Indonesia, although Lee's own concerns predate the mass killings on which Oppenheimer's film focuses. Nevertheless, in what follows, I construe *The City in Which I Love You* as a material artifact in a transnational archive assembled to remember originary violences that have been otherwise disappeared in state-sponsored history and official speech. In so doing, I am also interested in how, as Cathy J. Schlund-Vials has observed, diasporic cultural productions 'articulate a collected historical truth through narratives involving familial stories of war, genocide, and relocation', a truth that might in turn 'destabilize essentializing narratives of refugee victimhood and engender an alternative mode of politicized selfhood'.[9]

Moreover, beyond deriding individual artists (such as Oppenheimer) for their ambivalent constructions of individual perpetrators, Lee's ethical poetics recasts the line between perpetrator and beneficiary to expand the terms and modes by which we assign responsibility. As Kay Schaffer and Sidonie Smith (building on the work of Mahmood Mamdani) contend, deliberative proceedings, even ones less formally bound to legal protocols such as truth and reconciliation commissions, interpellate persons into the binary positions of the victim and perpetrator, 'often in stereotypical ways that [sentimentalize] the former and [sensationalize] the latter' and remain unable to account for how '[t]hose positioned neither as victims nor as perpetrators' nonetheless accrue the benefits of structural violence and the uneven distribution of privilege and vulnerability.[10] Schaffer and Smith convincingly argue that life writing, authored not only by victims, but by those who enjoy at least some power, provides an alternative arena in which testimony might be performed and ethical responsibility exacted from beneficiaries. While I too am concerned here with the ethics of literary practice, I am especially attentive to how we should think about such local and national instances, so often marked as exceptional and spectacular (e.g., the Shoah, apartheid in South Africa, or, in this case, mass political exterminations in Indonesia) in relation to a much broader, perhaps even planetary, conception of quotidian human life.[11] In what follows, I consider Lee's poetic practice, which draws on his and his family's biography of exile and loss as *topoi* for enacting a phenomenological ethics that holds *us* responsible, at every turn, to and for the cataclysmic past so that we might live our present otherwise.[12]

Versions of the human

In his poem 'Furious Versions', Lee writes,

> ... I own a human story,
> whose very telling remarks loss.
> the characters survive through the telling,
> the teller survives by his telling; by his voice
> brinking silence does he survive.
> But, no one
> can tell without cease
> our human story, and so we
> lose, lose.
>
> ...
>
> But I'll not widow the world.
> I'll tell my human
> tale, tell it against
> the current of that vaster, that
> inhuman telling ... [13]

On first glance, the poem seems to thematise a conventional understanding of how names grant recognition, in particular, the human and the inhuman, and that it is precisely the naming of the human that renders the speaker himself human. To own a human story, in other words, is to know oneself as human and to be recognised by others as such. On the other hand, to lose that story is to slip into the inhuman condition where one's very being is lost. Being human, that is, enjoying the status of human being and the protections, rights and privileges accorded therein, is founded upon a kind of paradoxical and performative 'self-evidence', where the name calls into existence that which it purports to find already constituted and self-apparent in the world.[14]

And of course, naming names is not only a crucial component in narrative acts of literature. It is also the fundamental performance in juridical acts of accusation, testimony and sentencing. In fact, legal historians like Samera Esmeir have argued that modern law aspires to 'transform humanity into a juridical status, which precedes, rather than follows and describes, all humans'.[15] Rooted in late nineteenth-century colonial conceptions, modern legal and judicial discourses determine who has the capacity for 'good governance' and law-based social orders – and thus who enjoys humanity – and who, conversely, continues to 'await' it.[16] The legal and juridical discourses of *human rights* have been especially keen on discovering and reconciling those names in relation to conditions of political and social violence that devastate human life. As such, contemporary human rights discourses constitute dichotomies between the human person, who also is (or has the facility to be) the humanist intellectual, and the humanist's 'suffering, dehumanized other'.[17]

Unsurprisingly, Esmeir observes, in the geopolitics of human rights campaigns on the ground, postcolonial nations in the global south come to represent the latter, and rarely are Western European nations or the United States the *objects* of international human rights politics and critique.[18] Such conventional accounts of human rights violations and other traumatic experiences tend to draw firm lines between perpetrators and other subjects, especially victims, but also bystanders, witnesses and beneficiaries. Trials, tribunals and truth commissions exist to determine whether the defendant is the perpetrator and who are his victims as well as the character of the injuries they have borne.[19] As the law constitutes human persons as a class of recognisable subjects, it puts under erasure other forms of (human) being and enacts 'closures in thinking the parameters of the human'.[20]

In contrast, significant ambiguities mark the passage of 'Furious Versions' cited above, and, indeed, Lee embeds his theme of performative story-telling within the estranging form of poetry to *de*familiarise the seemingly natural character of humanity, to which the law lays claim. In particular, the inevitable defeat augured by the critical truth that 'no one can tell without cease our human story, and so we lose, lose' complicates any apparently straightforward construction of the human. The seemingly heroic effort in refusing to 'widow the world' is, to be sure, an effort circumscribed by the inevitable limits of time and being – this story too will come to an end with the death of its narrator. But 'brinking the silence' and the 'vaster ... inhuman telling', also suggest a displacement of some *other* story, some other possibility of being that the human tale evacuates. After all, 'Furious Versions' begins with the speaker's 'discovery' that 'the birds have stripped my various names of meaning entire', so that 'I lie/dismantled'.[21] As the first section continues, the speaker attempts to recount his family's departure from Indonesia and arrival in the United States, only to have his perspective and memories merge with his father's, so he must ask 'what name do I answer to?' (a point to which I return below).[22] This first section of the long poem ends with the speaker waiting as ' ... on a page a poem begun, something/about to be dispersed,/something about to come into being'.[23]

If it is thus an 'inhuman telling' that counters his own 'human story', Lee nevertheless ascribes to that inhuman other the possibility of existence (like the living presence of the birds that dismantle him), which must be acknowledged; he names it as an-other verging on being that not only undoes him, but, perhaps, makes him 'lie', that is, dissimulate, about the names he claims for himself. Our lies – namely, the fiction that our humanity is essentially distinct from dehumanised victims *and* monstrous perpetrators and that we bear no responsibility to these others – might temporarily enable our heroic projections of self. But Lee's insights about the disturbing, disrupting, inhuman other suggest that we *will* be undone, brought face to face with our own complicity in the loss of those others from whom we withhold recognition. The inhuman other hence demands a justice in which our responsibility must be thought 'otherwise'.

Responsibility, or being in the world

How might the encounter with the 'inhuman telling' allow us to think legal and philosophical attributions of the human 'otherwise'? The ethical theory of Emmanuel Levinas offers an apposite provocation for 'interrogating the perpetrator', such that the figure of the perpetrator can be made to represent a more diffuse set of relations between subjects and others and the grounds upon which they are justified. Developing a phenomenological line of inquiry in continental philosophy, Levinas described ethics as a 'first philosophy' and a 'non-ontological philosophy', that refuses to accord priority to self-present Being or to reduce the Other to the Same. As it considers the 'givenness' of corporeal existence and construes consciousness itself as an external condition in which conscious beings take (a) place, phenomenology undoes the division between interiority and exteriority. The particular phenomena it investigates register as manifestations of being, as 'corporeal gestures' cast against the givenness of existence. 'Existence' (what Levinas figured in the phrase 'there is') always precedes existents and proves the condition of the possibility of being.[24] Phenomenological givenness extends to material culture, and language comprises perhaps the most significant of cultural components, by which conscious being comes into existence.[25] For Levinas, the Other, whose phenomenological appearance he designates as 'the face', materialises the alterity of existence against which subjective beings emerge, an alterity that always encroaches upon the self-presence that idealist philosophy prizes.

In construing the scene of existence and being in this way, Levinas describes the self as one who only comes into existence by the displacement of the Other, that is to say, the displacement of other possibilities of existence. As such, the subject is thoroughly marked by responsibility, called into question and called on to provide an account for the violence that this dislocation entails. The Other is not an abstraction, and Levinas' emphasis on the 'face to face' encounter with the Other intends to register how our concrete and everyday experiences are shot through with responsibility to the Other. The encounter with alterity is at once the very scene of sociality *and* a disturbing trace of that which cannot be contained within the present order of the world, but always disturbs it.[26] The response that the Other demands is a sacrifice or substitution of the self for the other, a one-for-the-other that is like 'being held hostage' by the Other.[27] Even when one has refused the call of the Other, one has not escaped responsibility, but has made a particular kind of response to it. The type of existence enabled by such a refusal will also be subject to accounting. We are and will continue to be held responsible for being in the world.

Nevertheless, we should not mistake ethical responsibility as naming a relation of negativity that amounts to a pure cancellation of the subject. Instead, Levinas contends that, while responsibility certainly demands a ceaseless emptying out of the subject, it also founds a sociality that supplies 'ever new resources' for being.[28] The surplus of existence, the 'there is', fills the void left by the emptying of the subject of his one-self with 'the mute anonymous rustling of the there is … '.[29] As Jacques Derrida writes of Levinas' ethical philosophy, responsibility involves us in a mode of thought that is radically passive in a hospitable sense; one awaits and receives the arrival of the Other.[30] And when that arrival takes place, we are not returned or recollected to ourselves, but rather encounter new dwellings, new forms of being and thinking that are the trace of the encounter with the face. Even where the encounter *is* marked by violence and negative repression, Derrida insists, it attests to a pre-ontological hospitality; every being's exposure to the Other precedes and is the condition of possibility for the violent response and the self in whose name that response is made.[31]

Levinas' work has been crucial to what has been called the 'ethical turn' in critical theory, and its implications for political theory, and, in particular, political theory's approach to human rights, have been promising. But the possibility of 'perpetrating ourselves' is also extremely difficult to maintain in juridical and legal discourses, especially where liberal perspectives insist on individuated personhood and responsibility. Instead, I suggest, *The City in Which I Love You* proposes an ethic of hospitality that risks such legible categories of personhood in its commitment to justice for those subjects rendered otherwise impossible.

Cities and citizens

'Furious Versions' recalls the personal and familial upheaval wreaked as the speaker's father is arrested, interrogated, threatened with summary execution, and detained as a political prisoner before their departure from Indonesia. It is, the speaker observes:

> one year of fire
> out of the world's diary of fires
> flesh-laced, mid-century fire,
> teeth and hair infested,
> napalm-dressed and skull-hung fire,
> and imminent fire ... [32]

The 'world's diary of fire' indexes the sweeping historical changes of the postwar era, as colonised peoples, including Indonesians, demanded freedom and self-determination from imperial rule, demanding, that is, other ways of being on a global terrain. But the poem also embeds within it a recognition of how those demands for freedom took their toll upon other others, the many holocausts fuelled by body parts, made illegibly inhuman as they are violently torn asunder, especially in postcolonial states subject to authoritarian rule.

Most of the poems in Lee's collection are characterised by abstract and figural language such as what I have been citing heretofore. Not only do the speaker's voice, memory and identity intertwine with those of other persons throughout, but symbols and metaphors slide with respect to their referents and sometimes slide *into* their literal referents, becoming synecdoches and metonymies from literal scenes of physical loss and violence.[33] In the midst of so much indeterminacy, however, the poem 'For a New Citizen of These United States', which appears midway through the collection, stands out in part for its specification of quotidian aspects in his family's life as new arrivals in the United States: families waiting on a train platform, mothers singing a particular tune, a 'day-book bound by a rubber band'.[34] At the same time, this poem apostrophises an addressee who, as a child along with his or her family, has fled a homeland shared with the speaker. But the addressee seems not to recall the details of that escape, and the speaker assures the addressee that he will not mar that amnesia with recollections from the past ('so I won't mention'), even as he proceeds in the succeeding stanzas to do exactly that.[35] The poem concludes, 'After all, it was only our/life, our life and its forgetting'.[36]

Against the broader configuration of subjectivity and alterity in terms that are at once elusive and universalising – that is, *all* subjects are vulnerable in their exposure and responsibility to the Other – 'For a New Citizen of These United States' grounds ethical responsibility in the given material and historical conditions that render lived experience of such vulnerability and exposure uneven and unpredictable.[37] The 'new citizen' to whom the poem is addressed is one who necessarily forgets previous lives and beings, in order to enjoy a present-day good life in 'these United States'. In ascertaining what has been disavowed to inhabit American citizenship, the speaker does not level a self-righteous accusation of moral judgement against 'you'. Rather, as it is a shared 'our life', that once existed and is now being forgotten, the speaker's 'I' splits between the addressee's presence and the ineluctable otherness of the past that has nevertheless defined and enabled the living presence and their living in the present. As the poem conjures fragments of that lost past, however, the appearance of the speaker and addressee in the United States figures as both *remnants from that past* that they in themselves embody and, as new Americans, *beneficiaries of that violence*. The nation, in turn, at once contributes to the violent losses of the past *and* distances itself from this history, claiming for itself instead an idealised ethos that incorporates these exiles as citizens (a point to which I return below).

The phenomenological division of the subject continues in the collection's title poem, 'The City in Which I Love You'. There, the speaker describes his search for the beloved other, addressing the 'rough sister' he desires, who will never appear to him but whom he pursues through an unnamed city of 'guarded schoolyards, the boarded-up churches, swastikaed/synagogues', a 'storied, buttressed, scavenged, policed/city I call home, in which I am a guest'.[38] Desire for the Other also leads the speaker into the memories of another, unnamed city, recalling a woman squatting over the corpse of a man shot by a soldier. In this case, the speaker knows that the woman, the corpse and the soldier are all 'not me'; as the poem continues to catalogue victims of violence, he repeats this recognition that they are 'not me forever'.[39] 'The City in Which I Love You' accordingly lays out an ethic of hospitality, by which anyone comes to live at peace with themselves. The speaker can be at home or, more precisely, call 'home' the city in which he is a 'guest', only because some Other has allowed him to take a place in it.

He further experiences that Other as desire within himself, driving him through the streets in search of a reckoning with the beloved who makes his being possible. But, in his search for the Other, Lee also evokes the figure of what, according to Derrida, is the 'problem of the third', posed in Levinas' thought. Those others are 'not me', but rather 'other others' whose lives and deaths enable and constrain the subject's existence, also demanding responses from him. The third, then, as Derrida intimates, intervenes in the immediacy of the face to face relation and interjects other others to whom one is also responsible. The third thus defines the 'passage from ethical responsibility to juridical, political – and philosophical – responsibility', as we are compelled to deliberate and respond to the ongoing but multiple, and often conflictive, demands of others.[40] Throughout the collection, Lee's specific historical and political references are brief and fleeting, a mention of a nation here, a date there. But we should not therefore mistake the ethical project of 'perpetrating ourselves' that *The City in Which I Love You* delineates to be ahistorical and apolitical. Rather, it discloses how every transformation in the conditions of human existence opens on to new and singular relations of responsibility to the Other that faces the newly formulated subject – the subject who enjoys a right to be, and be recognised as, human.

In this case, the 'no one' from the observation in 'Furious Versions' that 'no one can tell without cease our human story', evokes not only the negation of the individual, whose death will terminate the telling of his story. Rather, it also suggests a multiplicity or multitude, *beyond* the one, such that it is only by way of a collective effort that *any* human – and human story – is sustained over time and space. This 'multitude of dreams and many words', which I cite in my epigraph, are then certainly not 'in vain', whether by 'vain' we mean futile or we mean self-absorbed. Instead, they are vital to the social institutions, traditions, rites and rights that exist to nurture and protect human existence. But such conventions are precarious, especially as the traditional arrangements that offered some protection to human life have become denaturalised and deinstitutionalised. As a result, the conditions that make 'embodiment, enselfment, and emplacement' possible have become less reliable, and the exposure of the Other to the violent response urgently demands our recognition of *her* right to be, and to be otherwise.[41] As such, the multiplicity of beings who might keep alive the human story can only do so justly if they recognise themselves in a relation of responsibility, seeking to account for the perpetration of violence they engender and those others who, even in this scene of plenitude, remain yet to come.

Writing otherwise

The formulation of the perpetrator that I am drawing from Levinas and that is put into practice in Lee's work is not meant to relieve individuals of their own responsibility towards and for others, but rather to guard against too easy assignations of guilt and blame as well as the moral self-righteousness that names culprits. Hence, the collection's final poem, 'The Cleaving', traces the speaker's possible affiliation with a Chinese butcher, whom he encounters in an American Chinatown and who in appearance, the speaker notes, 'could be my brother' or 'could be my grandfather'.[42] As the man's chopping of his meats ('the cleaving' to which the title initially refers) triggers in the speaker a meditation on the affinities between human and animal flesh, Lee likens his own reading and writing with daily types of bodily existence, which always depend upon the sacrifice and consumption of others. He is, namely, a necessary perpetrator and beneficiary of others' losses.

Ultimately, the final stanza of this final poem concludes, 'No easy thing, violence./One of its names? Change … ' and

> The terror the butcher
> scripts in the unhealed
> air, the sorrow of his Shang
> dynasty face,
> African face with slit eyes. He is
> my sister, this
> beautiful Bedouin, this Shulamite,
> keeper of Sabbaths, diviner
> of holy texts, this dark
> dancer, this Jew, this Asian, this one
> with the Cambodian face, Vietnamese face, this Chinese
> I daily face,
> this immigrant,
> this man with my own face.[43]

Lee installs the butcher's terrorising and simultaneously necessary violence against the vulnerable body at the heart of what could otherwise be a quiescent portrait of the 'nation of immigrants', as the United States is so often characterised. In so doing, he counts his own family's expulsion from Indonesia as one of the many immigrant stories that constitute the nation. But he also insists upon reckoning with the conditions of loss and violence by which that immigrant face of the nation comes into positive relief, the deadly turmoil that, we should also recall, the United States stoked and fomented for its own interests, even as it maintained that it was engaged in a 'cold' war for freedom across the globe.[44] The soldier in 'The City in Which I Love You' above is assuredly 'not me forever', and he must bear responsibility for the deaths he executes in that other city. Yet the affiliation Lee draws in 'The Cleaving' between himself, the butcher and the other, presumably innocent immigrant faces he encounters, nevertheless inserts the nation of immigrants back into the 'world's diary of fire'.

To be clear, *The City in Which I Love You* does not construe the flight from the homeland as an abdication of responsibility on the part of past selves, whose very survival depended upon such escape. Instead, the collection as a whole suggests that the survivor's account implicates those who otherwise see themselves as innocent humanists and humanitarians, observing inhuman others from a distance, in relations of responsibility by which their own being ought to be transformed. In the articulation of his own tale (as I note above), the speaker blends his memories with those of his father's, borrowing the names (' ... *Professor, Capitalist, Husband, Father*') by which his father was once hailed. The speaker's own future perfect presence (his 'will have been') has always been contingent upon his father's future conditional presence (his 'will be'). If it is ' ... on my father's back, in borrowed clothes/[that] I came to America', the speaker's arrival is shot through with the brutal threats and expulsions and the hospitable reception, in which 'America' has been equal parts embroiled.[45] But, as I have indicated above, it is not only the border between himself and his father that the articulation of the poem renders unfixed and fluid. Rather, in continually adjoining his own presence to human and inhuman others, Lee poses throughout *The City in Which I Love You* an alternative methodological approach to the cultural politics of human rights.

International human rights law has certainly been limited in its ability to prosecute, much less prevent, human rights violations. Nevertheless, in making his own existence dependent upon but also a displacement of others, Lee refuses the clean binaries of villainous perpetrator and pitiful victims. Instead, he demonstrates that a *literary* imagination might commit itself to those subjects to whom human rights are addressed and who have been rendered impossible elsewhere. Acts of literature can thus illuminate how such others impinge upon our present, demanding protection and cultivation of that which is not immediately visible in our present order of things. The final stanza of 'Furious Versions' accordingly describes an insomniac 'someone', who

> ... unable
> to see in one darkness,
> has shut his eyes
> to see into another.[46]

The memory of personal and political upheaval inspires what earlier have been noted as the 'drafts' of the 'poem begun'. No longer rendered in the first-person, the poem concludes with the speaker instead depicted as a synecdoche and metonymy of the poem, at once the instrument that writes and the text being written:

> Know him by his noise.
> Hear the nervous

scratching of his pencil,
sound of a rasping
file, a small
restless percussion, a soul's
minute chewing,
the old poem
birthing itself
into the new and murderous century.[47]

Characterised by and as the pencil as well as the rhythm, meter and material of the poem, the speaker is undone *and* newly authored by the act of writing itself. Literary creation is here both an act and event; writing appears at once as a form of revelation of that which already exists, 'out there', and simultaneously, a radically new break with the existing order of the world.[48] The act and event of the poem thus confronts us with the limits of our commitment to that which we (think we) already know, altering the material, biological, genealogical and cultural terms by which we name ourselves. In short, the literary imagination takes us to task for (thinking we know) the measures by which we write (of) ourselves and challenges us to read and write otherwise, at the limits of intelligibility.

Accordingly, the 'drafts' of the 'poem begun' also refer to spirits and ghost-memories littered throughout 'Furious Versions' and that haunt the speaker at other moments in the poem:

these are not drafts
towards a future form,
but furious versions
of the here and now ... [49]

As 'furious versions/of the here and now', Lee gestures once again to the inhuman others who encroach upon the present order and upon self-presence, demanding their own freedom from the subject. Thematised even more explicitly in 'This Hour and What Is Dead' – where the ghost of the speaker's brother treads heavily on the upper floors of the house, 'opening and closing doors' – 'what is dead is restless' and 'what is living is burning'.[50]

Targeted by the Sukarno regime as an enemy of the state, the speaker's father survives repression, enabling the passage of the speaker into his own American present. But as a diasporic artifact of Indonesian postcoloniality, the speaker-*cum*-poem also carries with him haunting traces of that history into his present to re-member it in ways unavailable in state-sanctioned forums. The impunity that Sukarno enjoyed as the self-proclaimed 'president for life', gave way to successive waves of tyranny in and by the Suharto government, first directed at suspected communists and then, in the 1970s, against incipient independence movements in East Timor and the West Papua region. Much of this history remains officially concealed in Indonesia. For example, the Indonesian High Court suspended the Truth and Reconciliation Commission established in 2004 to redress the 1965–1966 killings, accounts of which were also redacted in history textbooks. In so far as not a single senior officer or official has ever been held responsible for human rights violations, despite extensive efforts by post-Suharto governments to investigate and prosecute the widespread abuse, some critics have described a state of 'de facto amnesty' in Indonesia that prevails to the present moment.[51]

The 'positive presence' of modern Indonesia as an independent, postcolonial, capitalist nation not only depended upon the construction of Sukarno as an insidious communist threat (and the East Timorese and West Papua conflicts as menaces to national integrity by populations lacking legitimate grounds for self-governance), but has been one maintained by the considerable diplomatic efforts as well as military and economic aid by the United States, as it sought to secure its own geopolitical and economic interests, during and after the Cold War in Southeast Asia.[52] Lee's poetic ethics makes it impossible to ascribe to Sukarno the character of a pure and ideal heroism, even as Sukarno's leadership was crucial to the independence of Indonesia from Dutch rule. But it also depicts the modern present as unsettled and haunted by these many historical violences.

The transnational character of the 'memory work' that Lee undertakes thus reveals layers of responsibility that entangle a multitude of subjects.[53] For Lee, those who come through the explosive, murderous century are, like the subject of the 'old poem/birthing itself', haunted and burning, undone by those who cannot be assembled into citizens, human personhood, or even 'the living'. Levinas describes this phenomenological ethics towards the other as an 'approach', rather than a 'knowing', which entails remaining thoroughly open to, and vulnerable in the face of, the Other.[54] This approach towards the Other risks having everything we (think we) know broken apart in the encounter. But running such a risk is actually, in fact, acknowledging the risk that we always already run. One is not exposed because one has been exploited. Rather we can be exploited because we, and others, have already been exposed.[55] Yet, in that exposure, we might also be received in a hospitality that opens new possible futures for ourselves and for others. Literary acts such as Lee's stage, over and over again, our exposure to the Other, in ways that risk perjuring and perpetrating ourselves and leave us dismantled, so that we might respond, and respond justly, to the Other.

Acknowledgements

Li-Young Lee, excerpts from 'Furious Versions', 'This Hour and What is Dead', 'For a New Citizen of These United States', 'The City in Which I Love You', and 'The Cleaving' from *The City In Which I Love You*. Copyright © 1990 by Li-Young Lee. All reprinted with the permission of The Permissions Company, Inc., on behalf of BOA Editions, Ltd, www.boaeditions.org.

Disclosure statement

No potential conflict of interest was reported by the author.

Notes

1. Li-Young Lee, *The City in Which I Love You* (Brockport: BOA Editions, 1990), 57.
2. I build upon the work of those such as Mark Sanders (Mark Sanders, *Complicities: The Intellectual and Apartheid* (Durham: Duke University Press, 2002), 3) who, beginning with the recognition, in volume 1 of South Africa's Truth and Reconciliation Commission's report, of its moral responsibility to name 'the "little perpetrator" in each of us', theorises the social and political complicities that are simultaneously the grounds of ethical responsibilities with which intellectuals and artists must reckon. Describing such responsibility as issuing from 'the

essential human foldedness' of being, Sanders identifies literature 'in a broad sense' as enacting such 'responsibility for an other in the name of a generalized foldedness in human-being ... ' (ibid., 17).

3. Ragna Boden, 'Cold War Economics: Soviet Aid to Indonesia', *Journal of Cold War Studies* 10, no. 3 (2008): 113. Sukarno's rule also depended considerably upon economic and military aid from and diplomatic ties with the Soviet Union, who, under Nikita Khruschev's stewardship, sought to build formidable alliances with anti-imperialist nationalist movements and postcolonial governments in the Third World. Blending socialist and Islamic nationalism, however, Sukarno's relation with the USSR was a source of some unease for the military and Islamic leaders, with whom he shared political power in the post-independence era. Soviet provision of aid and interest in Indonesia was, in turn, incited by a rivalry with the United States, who had begun in the late 1940s to provide foreign aid to developing countries, especially to stem the rise of socialist movements in these nations. For both superpowers, Indonesia proved a particular point of interest because of its strategic location in relation to emerging conflicts in East and Southeast Asia (ibid., 115–23).

4. John Roosa, *Pretext for Mass Murder: The September 30th Movement and Suharto's Coup d'Etat in Indonesia* (Madison: University of Wisconsin Press, 2006), 5. However, as Roosa explains, the Suharto regime's insistence that the PKI organised the attack on the generals was foundational to its decades-long rule: 'The Suharto regime justified its existence by placing the movement at the center of its historical narrative and depicting the PKI as ineffably evil. The claim that the PKI organized the movement was, for the Suharto regime, not any ordinary fact; it was *the* supreme fact of history from which the very legitimacy of the regime was derived' (ibid., 7). Roosa goes on to provide new evidence for countering the Suharto regime's narrative of the 30th September Movement, explicitly as a 'pretext for imposing an army dictatorship on the country' and for, as the book's title asserts 'mass murder' (ibid., 22, 31).

5. Ibid., 33.

6. Bradley R. Simpson, *Economists with Guns: Authoritarian Development and U.S.-Indonesian Relations, 1960–1968* (Stanford: Stanford University Press, 2008), 12.

7. David Easter, '*Economists with Guns: Authoritarian Development and U.S.-Indonesian Relations, 1960-1968* (review)', *Journal of Cold War Studies* 12, no. 3 (2010): 158. See also Roosa, *Pretext for Mass Murder*, 15–16.

8. Warren Crichlow, '"It's All About Finding the Right Excuse" in Joshua Oppenheimer's *The Act of Killing*', *Film Quarterly* 67, no. 2 (2013): 37.

9. Cathy J. Schlund-Vials, *War, Genocide, and Justice: Cambodian American Memory Work* (Minneapolis: University of Minnesota, 2012), 16–18.

10. Kay Schaffer and Sidonie Smith, 'Human Rights, Storytelling, and the Position of the Beneficiary: Antijie Krog's *Country of My Skull*', *PMLA* 121, no. 5 (2006): 1577–8.

11. See Gayatri Chakravorty Spivak, *Death of a Discipline* (New York: Columbia University Press, 2005), 72–3.

12. Xiaojing Zhou has written quite perceptively and extensively about Lee's lyric poetry and 'prose-poetry' (as well as other Asian American poets) in a Levinasian mode in *The Ethics and Poetics of Alterity in Asian American Poetry* (Iowa City: University of Iowa Press, 2006). Zhou focuses primarily and convincingly on Lee's ethics of alterity as a response to the racialisation of the Asian subject in the United States. I consider this article a complement to her treatment of Lee's work, as well as a contribution to this special issue's broader investigation into the perpetrator on a global scale.

13. Lee, *The City in Which I Love You*, 26–7.

14. Lynn Hunt, *Inventing Human Rights: A History* (New York: W.W. Norton & Co., 2007), 26–30.

15. Samera Esmeir, 'On Making Dehumanization Possible', *PMLA* 121, no. 5 (2006): 1544. See also Samera Esmeir, *Juridical Humanity: A Colonial History* (Palo Alto, CA: Stanford University Press, 2012), 1–10, 69–95.

16. Esmeir, 'On Making Dehumanization Possible', 1547–9.

17. Ibid., 1545.

18. Ibid., 1546.

19. This is not to conflate the very divergent objectives and modes by which judicial trials, truth commissions, war crimes investigations, military tribunals and other investigative and deliberative bodies proceed. For example, while trials usually focus narrowly on identifying individual

legal responsibility for specific crimes and punishing the guilty, truth commissions focus on broader patterns of abuse and injury, often even sanctioned by the law during, for example, conditions of war. As such, truth commissions can broaden the scope of and meaning of responsibility with respect to human rights violations. See Priscilla Hayner, *Unspeakable Truths: Transitional Justice and the Challenge of Truth Commissions* (New York: Routledge, 2001), 12–14, 86–8. Nevertheless, such proceedings do usually adopt liberal international norms of criminal harm and guilt.

20. Esmeir, 'On Making Dehumanization Possible', 1547.
21. Lee, *The City in Which I Love You*, 13.
22. Ibid., 14.
23. Ibid., 15.
24. Emmanuel Levinas, *Basic Philosophical Writings*, ed. Adriaan T. Peperzak, Simon Critchley, and Robert Bernasconi (Bloomington: Indiana University Press, 1996), 14, 40.
25. Ibid., 41–6.
26. Ibid., 61–2.
27. Ibid., 118. See also Emmanuel Levinas, *Otherwise Than Being, or, Beyond Essence*, trans. Alphonso Lingis (Pittsburgh: Duquesne University Press, 1998), 86.
28. Levinas, *Basic Philosophical Writings*, 51–2.
29. Ibid., 110.
30. Jacques Derrida, *Adieu to Emmanuel Levinas*, trans. Pascale-Anne Brault and Michael Nass (Stanford: Stanford University Press, 1999), 26, 50–2.
31. Ibid., 95.
32. Lee, *The City in Which I Love You*, 18.
33. Indeed, Lee has expressly regarded this 'state of infinite referral' as a crux in his poetic practice; a 'whole universe keeps referring infinitely back … every word refers infinitely back'. See Tod Marshall and Li-Young Lee, 'To Witness the Invisible: A Talk with Li-Young Lee', *The Kenyon Review* 22, no. 1 (2000): 129–47, 141.
34. Lee, *The City in Which I Love You*, 41–2.
35. Ibid., 41.
36. Ibid., 42.
37. Dorothy J. Wang observes and warns against the tendency to read Lee as ahistorical, universalising and, paradoxically, exoticising and foreign. She argues instead that Lee's particular 'metaphorical practice' negotiates the conventional binary of the aesthetic and the social, in order to interrogate the racial forms that hail and circumscribe the representational practices of Asian American writers (Dorothy J. Wang, 2014. *Thinking Its Presence: Form, Race, and Subjectivity in Contemporary Asian American Poetry* (Stanford: Stanford University Press, 2014), 56–92). See also Timothy Yu, *Race and the Avant-Garde: Experimental and Asian American Poetry Since 1965* (Stanford: Stanford University Press, 2009), 143–6.
38. Lee, *The City in Which I Love You*, 51–2.
39. Ibid., 54–5.
40. Derrida, *Adieu to Emmanuel Levinas*, 28–32.
41. Bryan S. Turner, *Vulnerability and Human Rights* (University Park, PA: Pennsylvania State University, 2006), 27.
42. Lee, *The City in Which I Love You*, 78.
43. Ibid., 86–7.
44. Simpson, *Economists with Guns*, 4. This new historical perspective on Indonesia arises from the burgeoning field of critical Cold War studies; it intervenes in a conventional historical narrative construction of the second half of the twentieth century that centres in and on the two superpowers to the exclusion of the rest of the globe. Instead, historians and other scholars have turned to the so-called 'peripheries' to understand how military aid, diplomatic and foreign policy, and economic development in decolonising and postcolonial societies were an integral, if not *the* key, aspect of Cold War geopolitics. For an especially comprehensive account, see Odd Arne Westad's *The Global Cold War: Third World Interventions and the Making of Our Times* (Cambridge: Cambridge University Press, 2007).
45. Lee, *The City in Which I Love You*, 13.
46. Ibid., 29.
47. Ibid.
48. Derek Attridge, *The Singularity of Literature* (New York: Routledge, 2004), 22–6.

49. Lee, *The City in Which I Love You*, 19.
50. Ibid., 35.
51. Patrick Burgess, 'De Facto Amnesty? The Example of Post-Soeharto Indonesia', in *Amnesty in the Age of Human Rights Accountability*, ed. Francesca Lessa and Leigh A. Payne (Cambridge: Cambridge University Press, 2012), 263–4. This is not to deny the important, if limited, accomplishments of Indonesian human rights activists working in transnational conjunction with organisations such as Amnesty International, including the release of political prisoners, beginning in the 1970s. See Bradley R. Simpson, '"Human Rights Are Like Coca-Cola": Contested Human Rights Discourses in Suharto's Indonesia, 1968–1980', in *The Breakthrough: Human Rights in the 1970s*, ed. Jan Eckel and Samuel Moyn (Philadelphia: University of Pennsylvania Press, 2014), 195–8.
52. This investment in Indonesia was consolidated, perhaps most surprisingly given the president's reputation as a human rights advocate, under the Carter administration. In fact, in 1977, while the bureau of human rights in the State Department prepared to name Indonesia as one of the most formidable violators of human rights at that moment, the National Security Council rejected this designation ensuring substantial and ongoing aid for the ally nation. See Bradley R. Simpson, 'Denying the "First Right": The United States, Indonesia, and the Ranking of Human Rights by the Carter Administration, 1976–1980', *The International History Review* 31, no. 4 (2009): 798–826, 809–10.
53. Schlund-Vials, *War, Genocide, and Justice*, 17, 66, 122.
54. Levinas, *Otherwise Than Being, or, Beyond Essence*, 87.
55. Ibid., 55, 82.

Victims, perpetrators, and the limits of human rights discourse in post-Palermo fiction about sex trafficking

Alexandra Schultheis Moore[a] and Elizabeth Swanson Goldberg[b]

[a]Department of English, University of North Carolina, Greensboro, United States; [b]Arts and Humanities, Babson College, Wellesley, United States

This article explores the figure of the perpetrator in fictional and testimonial representations of sex trafficking, situating its analysis in the context of broader conversations about the figure of the perpetrator within human rights discourse; of feminist debates about victimisation and agency in the trafficking scenario; and of discussions in literary and cultural studies about how cultural representations contribute to understandings and treatment of victims and perpetrators of sex trafficking. We demonstrate that, rather than depending upon a single criminal figure or syndicate, a range of perpetrators from all walks of life manifest the trafficking of persons for sex. Investigating the broad spectrum of responsible parties to or beneficiaries of the sex trafficking scenario, the article argues for a more complex understanding of culpability which will, in turn, intervene in debates about trafficking that are built upon and recapitulate reductive terms of responsibility, agency, and victimhood.

Introduction

In the years surrounding the adoption by the United Nations General Assembly in 2000 of the Protocol to Prevent, Suppress, and Punish Trafficking in Persons, Especially Women and Children (hereafter the Palermo Protocol or Trafficking Protocol), a vociferous debate regarding sex trafficking emerged, born from disputes between so-called 'pro-sex' and 'anti-porn' feminists in the 1980s and 1990s about pornography and sex work.[1] On the one hand, we can read the Trafficking Protocol as an important legal instrument that builds on the success of the 1993 Vienna Conference on Human Rights, the 1995 Beijing Platform, and the 1999 Optional Protocol to the Convention on the Elimination of Violence against Women to recognise violence against women, whether public or private, as 'subject to human rights scrutiny'.[2] On the other hand, as many scholars have noted, the Trafficking Protocol privileges sex trafficking over labour trafficking as an area of concern (labour issues are more often read under the Protocol against the Smuggling of Migrants by Land, Sea, and Air, also signed in Palermo and adopted in 2000), and it conflates prostitution and trafficking, correspondingly reinforcing both normative constructions of gender as well as the state-centred carceral networks that would maintain them.[3] All four of these outcomes – the focus on sex trafficking, conflation of prostitution and trafficking, gender normativity, and punitive state sovereignty under the umbrella authority of the UN – align the legislation with colonialist agendas that would produce and regulate gender and sexuality in the service of either state authority or the authority of inter-state security networks. The Palermo Protocol draws an ostensibly clear line between victims and perpetrators in order to rescue the former and criminalise the latter by bolstering the power of border control and police operations, as well as by strengthening the regulatory role of the state over trafficked persons. Because migrant sex workers do not conform to the iconic representation of the trafficked woman or child, they, too, may become criminalised, such that the application of the law inscribes normative gender roles and oppressive migration policies, often in racially motivated ways.[4]

Like many discussions related to human rights violations, this one focuses largely upon representation: who speaks for or on behalf of trafficked persons, how the coercion and exploitation that are at the centre of the UN's anti-trafficking legislation are defined, and which, if any, structural conditions of trafficking (and its aftermath for trafficked persons) the law addresses. Since the Palermo Protocol was adopted and entered into force in 2003, real and imagined trafficking narratives have gained public traction in a wide variety of media. Scholars such as Elizabeth Bernstein, Jo Doezema, Julietta Hua, Nandita Sharma, and Gretchen Soderlund have critiqued the dominant narratives that appear in contemporary fiction and film, reportage, and human rights campaigns for the ways in which they recapture gendered and militaristic colonialist ideologies inherent in the Palermo Protocol and the state enforcement initiatives it mandates. Although we share parts of those critiques, we are also wary of the ways in which, in their efforts to recognise the agency and individual autonomy of sex workers and labour migrants, these interventions unintentionally reproduce the (neo)liberal subject – free, entrepreneurial, autonomous – as the centrepiece of law and politics and, correspondingly, elide the need for other kinds of narratives and figures to represent the very real violence of sex trafficking.

Thus, at the risk of once more placing sex trafficking at the centre of the discussion of trafficking more generally, we analyse the current debate over its representation and then turn briefly to three post-Palermo Anglophone novels – James Levine's *The Blue Notebook* (2009),[5] Chris Abani's *Becoming Abigail* (2006),[6] and Wendy Law-Yone's *The Road to Wanting* (2010)[7] – in order to make two claims: First, that by portraying complex webs of social relations, these novels erase the clear line between victims and perpetrators and, with that line, the normative constructions of gender upon which the subject, state sovereignty, and the logic of the Palermo Protocol are grounded. Erasing that line simultaneously undermines the punitive capacity of the law and reveals root causes and consequences of trafficking that remain outside the purview of anti-trafficking legislation. Second, the novels illuminate the ways in which human rights discourse and practice has been co-opted by the logics of securitisation, criminalisation, and rehabilitation, placing the concerns of the state and the priorities of various disciplinary networks above those of trafficked persons and migrants. Accordingly, the novels, each in their own way, at once betray the power of normative narratives of the sex trafficked victim in need of rescue by the state or its emissaries, and point toward the need for an expanded register of human rights, as opposed to securitisation, to address the trafficking scenario. Although the novels do not fully represent what such an expanded register of rights might look like for the subject who would claim it, they do emphasise the complex biopolitics and networks of the trafficking scenario that the law elides. Our reading of the novels suggests that their portrayal of the vast web of social inequities and interpersonal relationships in sex trafficking broadens the category of perpetrator beyond the point of legal efficacy, thereby suggesting, perhaps paradoxically, the need to shift the focus of the law from criminalisation to, rather, a guarantee of the trafficked person's rights and desires.

In both stages of the argument we wish to make, gender figures as a central analytic of power. We identify how a range of hegemonic masculinities, supported by both men and women, fuels the predatory behaviour that can harm sex trafficked persons, contribute to the ongoing devaluation of women and girls, and inform scenarios of rescue. And, we demonstrate how the Trafficking Protocol depends upon those same gendered norms, norms that reproduce the ideological division between 'good' and 'fallen' women, speciously recirculating them in the name of human rights. Finally, we examine the ways in which the novels attempt to reimagine gendered self-representation and desire (economic and sexual) and, in so doing, underscore the limits of subject positions currently recognisable within the international anti-trafficking legal framework.

Trafficking, international law, and human rights

The Palermo Protocol defines trafficking as

> the recruitment, transportation, transfer, harbouring or receipt of persons, by means of the threat or use of force or other forms of coercion, of abduction, of fraud, of deception, of the abuse of power or of a position of vulnerability or of the giving or receiving of payments to achieve the consent of a person having control over another person, for the purposes of exploitation. Exploitation shall include, at a minimum, the exploitation of the prostitution of others or other forms of sexual exploitation, forced labour or services, slavery or practices similar to slavery, servitude or the removal of organs.

Within this definition, the key concepts (and subjects of debate) are the emphases on coercion and exploitation and the link made between prostitution and exploitation. As both Vanessa E. Munro and Prabha Kotiswaran have demonstrated, this conflation of concepts, and the ambiguity of what constitutes exploitation, renders the female sex trafficked victim as the subject (or perhaps better, the object) par excellence of the protocol.[8] Although women and children designated for special attention by the legislation are entitled to 'medical, psychological and material assistance' and 'protection', given their 'special needs' (Article 6), even these clauses functionally equate the very category 'trafficking victim' with a person who has a profoundly impaired agency. Thus, the protocol's provisions for assistance and protection may also be read as forms of objectification and even coercion (particularly with regard to testifying against one's traffickers), and incarceration.

For instance, Article 6 mandates that states provide 'measures to provide for ... social recovery', which gives the law and the state that applies it authority over the physical, psychological, and social well-being of trafficked persons; while Article 8 provides for their repatriation 'without undue or unreasonable delay'. Women who are trafficked (and thus ostensibly in need of social recovery) are positioned outside the gendered societal norms of marriage and motherhood, unentitled to rights such as the right to determine where and how they want to 'recover'. Addressing anti-trafficking and migration law in India, though in ways applicable to our larger argument, Ratna Kapur notes that 'a woman whose life has deviated from the roles demarcated by these norms [of marriage and motherhood] ... is disqualified from these entitlements because she is produced as a non-member or lesser member of the nation-state'.[9] Thus, the law establishes a false opposition between normative and deviant gendered roles, leaving little space for the myriad of other ways women may understand their own economic and familial positioning other than as wives and mothers, or as prostitutes or trafficked women. Because anti-trafficking discourses figure prominently in discussions of female migration, the legislation also regulates the movement of women more broadly in the name of their (and the state's) protection.

The Trafficking Protocol, along with the Smuggling and Firearms Protocols, supplement the Convention Against Transnational Organized Crime and fall under the UN Office on Drugs and Crime, as opposed to its Human Rights division.[10] As Anne Gallagher argues about the motivations that produced these protocols, '[w]hile human rights concerns may have provided some impetus (or cover) for collective action, it is the sovereignty/security issues surrounding trafficking and migrant smuggling which are the true driving force behind such efforts'.[11] The security and sovereignty ostensibly guaranteed to the individual through the mechanism of human rights are, thus, transferred to the state, which does not claim rights but regulates access to them.

Paul Amar helps us to understand the transfer of and regulated access to rights as a political dynamic that is fundamental to the unfolding of the 'human-security governance regime': different modes of securitisation are 'explicitly aimed to protect, rescue, and secure certain idealized forms of humanity identified with a particular family of sexuality, morality, and class subjects, and grounded in certain militarized territories and strategic infrastructures'.[12] The displacement of sovereignty/security from an individual right to the state's prerogative effectively inscribes the criminalisation of those persons, such as migrant sex workers, coded as threatening to the body politic, into international, as well as domestic, law. Those in need of rescue are similarly identified according to the logic of securitisation and are positioned as beneficiaries of the state's expertise and regulatory apparatus, regardless of their desire to receive such 'gifts'. Here the paradox originally identified by Hannah Arendt of the limitations of human rights when confronted with the stateless human emerges. An update of Arendt's critique might change the title of one of her earlier essays on the subject, 'We Refugees' (1943), to 'We Migrants', as a way to capture the current human rights aporia regarding migrants motivated to move because of poverty, arguably caused by the international trade, commerce, and finance regimes as determined by the hegemonic states that control them – in which case they more rightly may be termed 'economic refugees', or by persecution on the basis of gender, which is still not one of the protected categories under which asylum may be sought.[13]

Biopolitical analyses assist us in unpacking the logics of this emerging human-security regime as an alternative to traditional forms of political sovereignty. As Roberto Esposito explains in his reading of the roots of biopolitics in political texts of the sixteenth and seventeenth centuries that feature the state-body analogy, 'what unifies these texts is the proto-functional principle that all parts of the body, including toxic germs that come to infect it from the outside, when looked at a little farther away, ultimately contribute to the body's health and safety'.[14] The Palermo Protocol functions analogously in that it provides the state with both a legal tool and a mandate to increase its power against the threats posed by those outside its borders. For instance, in keeping with the protocol's stated aim 'to punish the traffickers and to protect the victims' (Preamble), Article 5 requires signatory states to adopt laws and enforcement mechanisms to criminalise offenses as defined by the protocol. Articles 10 and 11 direct police, immigration, and border guards to exchange information and to 'strengthen ... border controls' (Article 11). Although the Trafficking Protocol includes some provisions for the 'assistance to and protection of victims of trafficking in persons' (Article 6), its emphasis is on regulation and control of the border.

Yet as Esposito also reminds us, the militarisation of borders in order to protect the body politic (or, more accurately, to protect and enhance the authority of the regime) does not simply seek to immunise the state against pre-existing foreign threats. Rather, '[a]s in all areas of contemporary social systems, neurotically haunted by a continuously growing need for security, this means that the risk from which the protection is meant to defend is actually created by the protection itself'.[15] Authoritarian power in the name of securitisation justifies itself in relation to an outside threat, such that the regime maintains a vested interest in identifying that threat and generating fear of it. In part this is achieved by collapsing the range of recognisable subject positions available for scrutiny, which not only makes them more easily consumable by the general public but also populates the categories of 'victim' and 'perpetrator' in similarly reductive ways.

Additionally, the Palermo Protocol's logic of victims and perpetrators also (re)produces the normative gendered identities upon which it is built. When these anti-trafficking discourses come to focus on sex trafficking in particular, and as a crime against women, they manifest as a means by which, in Kapur's words, '[p]art of the state's renewed efforts to reassert its sovereignty is being articulated in and through its women and women's bodies'.[16] Thus, by producing the category of the coerced and exploited victim of sex trafficking, the protocol requires signatory states to increase the policing of both its borders and of migrant/sex work(ers) who may be trying to cross them.

Our objective in unpacking this logic is not to question the very existence of sex trafficking (as scholars such as Alison Murray, Jo Doezema, and Ronald Weitzer do) or to argue against its importance as a human rights issue.[17] On the contrary, our article is motivated by the critical problem of recognising the rights of sex workers without eliding the need to address the egregious harms experienced by persons trafficked for sex. Understanding the legal framework of trafficking through the intersection of biopolitical and securitisation studies highlights the limits of the law and the cultural narratives that sustain it. As opposed to producing human rights claimants whose preferences are paramount, the Palermo Protocol produces feminised victims in need of 'physical, psychological and social recovery' (Article 6) and subject to (forced) repatriation, and perpetrators whose threat to the state, often coded in racial and gendered terms, is as pronounced as their threat to trafficked persons. These subjects, we argue, borrowing from Amar, 'should be more accurately analyzed as human-security products emerging in particular gender, racial, and transnational forms in and around military and police operations and parastatal security projects'.[18]

Discursive combatants: sex worker rights advocates and anti-trafficking activists

We turn, then, to the debates surrounding the Trafficking Protocol in order to illustrate how much of the discourse draws upon conventional narratives of trafficking and sex work that are both dependent upon notions of the liberal subject and scripted through prescriptively gendered bodies.[19] Whereas recent studies such as Kotiswaran's *Dangerous Sex, Invisible Labor: Sex Work and the Law in India* provide nuanced analyses of the different positions in the debates over sex workers as victims or agents, we sketch the broad parameters of the conversation here. For the sex worker rights advocate, trafficking and prostitution or sex slavery must not be conflated. To conflate them is to deny sex work as a legitimate form of labour chosen by autonomous subjects who negotiate national and international market conditions and maintain (or who, in calculated bets on a better future, 'willingly' relinquish) control over their bodily dispositions. Sex workers often emerge from this discourse as (neo)liberal subjects characterised by their embrace of freedom and entrepreneurship, including the choice to enter the commercial sex industry, and who need guaranteed political rights and civil liberties, not rescue and rehabilitation. Sex worker rights advocates argue that the anti-trafficking movement is nothing more than a 'moral panic' or 'crusade' launched by an odd mix of feminists and political and religious conservatives who believe that sex cannot be 'work' like any other, that the sex industry is harmful to the moral fabrics of family and nation, and that all prostitution is exploitative of women; as Victor Malarek, author of *The Johns: Sex for Sale and the Men Who Buy It*, puts it, 'prostitution – all prostitution – is not about choice. If anything, for the overwhelming majority of women ensnared in the trade, it is the ultimate act of desperation'.[20] Sex worker rights advocates like Ronald Weitzer argue that the 'moral crusade' against trafficking 'rel[ies] on horror stories and "atrocity tales" about victims in which the most shocking exemplars of victimization are described and typified. Casting the problem in highly dramatic terms by recounting the plight of traumatized victims is intended to alarm the public and policy makers and to justify draconian solutions.'[21]

According to this argument, the atrocity tale features an innocent girl (often a white woman of Eastern European descent) who is tricked, coerced, or abducted into sex slavery; is 'broken' with a combination of rape, beatings, starvation, and other horrors and is then made to serve up to 25 clients per day; is kept under lock and key in squalid conditions; does not see any of the money she has 'earned'; and is discarded when she has contracted HIV/AIDS or has otherwise been 'used up'. Sex worker rights advocates often use the word 'myth' to describe this narrative, calling it exaggerated and overblown and questioning the number of actual 'trafficked' girls and women as compared with women who make a choice to engage in sex work or to migrate knowing that sex work will be part of the bargain.[22] Some writers go so far as to question whether there is any trafficking at all, as Alison Murray does in her essay 'Debt Bondage and Trafficking: Don't Believe the Hype': 'The shadowy nature of "trafficking" may be due to the cunning of the "traffickers" or it may be because they don't exist.'[23]

Those who have decried the 'myth of sex trafficking' as fuel for a misguided moral crusade find the same level of spectacularisation and even caricature in the figure of the trafficker and john in the standard narrative. If the trafficked woman is represented as an innocent, powerless victim, then the trafficker is typically portrayed as a relentlessly cruel member of organised crime networks whose most compelling tool is violence, and the john as an 'ugly, old, bald, fat [white] man who only can get sexual satisfaction by paying for sex, often in "third world" countries'.[24]

When the story shifts to the global south, the sex trafficking scenario is often represented through what Makau Mutua has called the savage-victim-saviour (SVS) metaphor generated by the Western human rights regime: white saviour/moral crusader (typified, for example, in Gary Haugen, President and CEO of the Christian 'raid and rescue' NGO (nongovernmental organisation) International Justice Mission) rescues innocent, victimised, brown woman from brutal, brown male. Such discourse addresses trafficked persons first as passive victims and colonial subjects of humanitarian intervention, and then as criminals, all while pathologising the 'brown men' of 'native cultures' in comparison with the white men (or women) represented as rescuers (and rarely johns). Rescue, recovery, and rehabilitation efforts often perpetuate a moralising paternalism, mandating 'that sex workers give up sex work in exchange for far more poorly paid, low-skilled work typically performed by women'.[25] Thus, the 'saviour' in these conventional narratives rescues women from immorality or exploitation rather than from socio-economic precariousness.

Moreover, in most scenarios, it is men who are the perpetrators (although men and women participate in the vast networks that sustain sex trafficking; in addition, female sex tourism is well documented as being on the rise). In Malarek's dramatic terms, 'What we are witnessing today is nothing less than international sexual terrorism against women and children at the hands of men, and little is being done to stop the carnage.'[26] Combatting this 'terrorism' is the detective, border guard, or police officer whose tenacity can save the victim and seize the perpetrator (usually the trafficker rather than the john) all at once. Malarek captures the perceptions of anti-trafficking advocates who focus on the 'demand side' of the trafficking scenario when he argues that benign language like 'clients, patrons, customers, and johns' hides the fact that

> Men are the users and abusers of prostituted women and children. It is their demand for paid sex that is creating huge profits for crime networks worldwide and incentives for traffickers, pimps, brothel owners, and porn producers to entrap more and more victims … On the demand side of the equation are the men. And in demand are three key letters: m-a-n. Without men, there would be no demand. There would be no supply either: it would not be profitable for pimps and criminals to stay in this business if platoons of men weren't prowling side streets in search of purchased sex – male buyers who are willing to close their eyes and shell out fifty or a hundred dollars for a few minutes of physical bliss while deepening the misery of countless women and children.[27]

Although they stake radically different positions, both Mutua and Malarek bring the problem of categorisation to the forefront of their arguments. The SVS metaphor that Mutua finds at the heart of human rights and humanitarian discourses offers a useful shorthand for characterising the neocolonial impulses of conventional anti-trafficking narratives in their deployment of culture; however, it does not address intra-, trans-, and para-statal biopolitical networks that operate in the name of securitisation. In other words, whereas the SVS model offers a strong critique of human rights violations that are attributed to 'cultural backwardness' and that rationalise international or NGO intervention in the name of humanitarianism, it is less useful in responding to other narratives that frame trafficking in terms Amar describes as 'an emphasis on public morality, that is toward a social deviance model (or urban vice model) concerned with enforcing access to public space, reforming public masculinities, and moralizing and desexualizing urban quality of life'.[28] In those scenarios, the anti-trafficking narrative is driven not by the humanitarian but by the police officer or detective whose dedication to the public good emerges through the same 'rescue' and 'punish' dynamics as found in the Trafficking Protocol. 'Rescue' and 'punish' often serve to distinguish between normative and deviant gendered sexual identities and between sex in and outside of the home, as opposed to providing a distinction between the treatment of trafficked persons and traffickers, respectively.

Discursive taxonomies: victims, perpetrators, others

Malarek's construction of the problem as 'm-a-n' falls into the trap identified by Tristan Anne Borer, whose work is situated in the context of South Africa's Truth and Reconciliation Commission (TRC), of constructing victims and perpetrators as entirely separate groups, and of constructing members of each group in homogeneous terms. As Borer notes, '[In the TRC] the single word "perpetrator" made no distinction between the kinds of acts committed, the reasons why they were committed, their consequences or their context; nor did it distinguish between individuals who committed just one act and those whose entire operation and purpose was the commission of such acts.'[29] Putting the question of 'the Perpetrator' to the test in the sex trafficking scenario yields similar problems of definition and distinction. Who is the perpetrator? Is it the individual trafficker? Organised criminal networks? The john? If so, then how do we account for and talk about parents who sell their children, wittingly or unwittingly, into trafficking networks? About friends, neighbours, and relatives who participate in the trafficking scheme? About the trafficked girls who return to their villages after a period of time as brokers to recruit more girls? What narrative forms, available to a global audience the way the discourses of Palermo are, can represent parents, neighbours, relatives, and peers responding to a poor array of choices for their survival, as opposed to depicting them as examples of cultural degeneracy? And what about the brothel keepers and madams who enforce the living and working conditions of trafficked girls and women? Or about the police who frequent the brothels, garnering bribes and taking free sex in the process? Or the health workers that certify when trafficked persons can return to work after injury, illness, pregnancy, or abortion? Could the governments of countries that allow trafficking to happen within and across their borders be considered perpetrators according to emerging human rights norms around the responsibility to protect (R2P)?

Borer's work on taxonomies of victims and perpetrators identifies the TRC and other tribunals as major sites in which categories of identity in relation to atrocity have emerged and been refined in developing international law. For instance, one of the great achievements of the TRC was to move beyond the category of 'bystander' to the more robust 'beneficiary' when thinking of the masses of white South Africans who may not have directly perpetrated any human rights violation in relation to apartheid, but who undoubtedly benefited from the violent oppression and suppression of black South Africans. And while important critiques of the TRC show how it failed to do enough with this category during the hearings themselves, the introduction, theorisation, and presentation of the term and its presence in the TRC report's fourth volume, on institutional hearings, at least provides ground for further philosophical exploration of the concept, as well as for jurisprudence emerging in the realm of international human rights. Could this category, and others like it, be useful in other cases of egregious and systemic rights violations, including the trafficking scenario? In the remainder of this article, we turn to three post-Palermo novels – as another site where categories of identity are produced, imaginatively animated, and circulated – for the ways in which they work similarly to expand the range of subject positions within sex trafficking networks. Unlike the many formulaic fictional representations of sex trafficking, these novels complicate stories of victims and perpetrators within the Palermo Protocol. In doing so, they point to structural and ideological conditions that contribute to sex trafficking – the devaluation of women and girls; the recoding and masking of predatory masculinity by discourses of desire and virility; the state's economic and political marginalisation of minority and opposition groups; and the ways in which neoliberalism produces what Isabell Lorey calls 'governmental precarization',[30] which here includes the destabilisation of life caused by wage labour and unequal access to markets and to the rights of full citizenship.

With Borer's example before us, we turn to the novels for representation of an expanded category of sex trafficking perpetrators that encompasses actors, participants, and beneficiaries with a host of motivations for perpetuating the industry. Offering such nuanced representations, the novels disclose at once the expansiveness of the category of perpetrator as well as the need for a human rights-centred approach to trafficking that shifts the focus away from the perpetrator (and the security threat he poses) to trafficked persons (and the needs and desires they carry). In constructing this shift, the novels do not simply re-centre the victim narrative in the trafficking scenario; rather they ask readers to imagine trafficked persons' expressed needs and desires as opposed to protective incarceration or repatriation or rehabilitation according to prescribed gendered norms. The novels also, however, point toward the limits of human rights frameworks when would-be claimants are reduced to products of the human-security governance regime.

To begin, we look to James Levine's *The Blue Notebook* for a more nuanced representation of the figure of the perpetrator, arguing first that Levine opens space for a consideration of hegemonic masculinity as a perpetrator identity, a category of identity marked by characteristics into which individual men may live or may choose not to live. In this way, the novel does not indict all men as equally culpable in the sex trafficking scenario by virtue of their biological imperative as men, nor does it offer a singular depiction of predatory masculinity; rather, it reveals how, in Kapur's words, 'gender is pursued and the work that it does'.[31] Given the novel's setting in India and focus on intra-national trafficking, such representation, on the one hand, disrupts the SVS narrative identified by Mutua as one of the primary consequences of the dominant human rights paradigm originating in the West and 'applied' to the global south. On the other hand, as a novel by a white, American doctor motivated to effect change after a disturbing/inspiring visit to India (he tells of his desire 'to examine how positive action could be deployed in his protagonist, Batuk's name'[32]), *The Blue Notebook* may at first be interpreted in two troubling ways: first, as a literary gloss of the US's self-appointed role of global trafficking monitor through the Department of State's publication each year of the Trafficking in Persons (TIP) Report[33]; and, second, as a properly sentimental story that confirms the distant reader's suspicions of India's 'cultural failure'[34] as well as that same reader's (or the law's) potential as cultural saviour. We argue that the novel resists that familiar teleology to enable more complicated constructions, which we read first through constructions of gender and secondly through the lens of securitisation. Here, the systems and spaces of illegal trafficking portrayed in the novel are owned, operated, and used by Indians, as opposed to the more standard, sensationalised narrative of the white sex tourist, the brown sex trafficker or pimp, and the brown sex slave. Levine also resists the formulaic possibility of humanitarian relief offered by a white, professional representative of the global north, such as himself. Even as the protagonist, Batuk's, life circumstances of violation in the brothels and the brutal beating by a john in a hotel room that leads to her death indicate 'victimhood', her death negates what Julietta Hua describes as the 'moral tropes of rescue and redemption that ultimately work to naturalize an understanding of cultural difference that reaffirms troubling frameworks of development and progress'.[35] In place of these conventional tropes, Levine focuses on the destructive results of the devaluation of women and girls and the regulation of gender and sexuality within India. Rather than pin devaluation and regulation to cultural aberration, Levine underscores the ways in which hegemonic masculinities operate.

India is a signatory to the Palermo legislation and the 2002 South Asian Association for Regional Cooperation's Convention On Preventing and Combating Trafficking in Women and Children for Prostitution. More directly, trafficking and prostitution in India are understood through the legal framework provided by the Immoral Traffic Prevention Act (ITPA), a 1986 amendment of the original 1956 act that added criminal responsibility to the trafficker and client, as opposed to solely criminalising the prostitute. The ITPA reveals several gaps and contradictions in the Indian legal framework that are easily translated into the language of culture (as are other issues that trouble the workings of law and democracy in India, such as pervasive bribery, nepotism, and corruption). Such contradictions include the fact that under the ITPA (original and amended) prostitution is essentially legal in India, as long as it is confined to spaces defined as 'private' (e.g., not solicited within 200 metres of any public establishment). Since all public forms of solicitation are, then, illegal, the existence of the vast, highly visible red light areas in major and minor cities across India can only be interpreted as an aporia in the law's narrative, a sign of blindness or imperviousness at best, complicity, corruption, and violence at worst, on the part of the law and its makers and enforcers.

Problems such as this, when represented in media and literature, can reify what Hua calls 'developmental progress frames that pit "backward" cultures against the progress of human rights'.[36] These developmental frames, according to Hua, shape a particular 'under-standing [of] why sex trafficking originates in certain parts of the globe and with certain people and not others' – which emphasises culture as the key indicator for the emergence of such 'backward practices'. Hua argues that in the dominant narrative conventions used to represent sex trafficking, 'the backwardness of culpable cultures is measured through adher-ence to patriarchy, constructing native places as backward precisely because of their inability to grasp feminist principles'.[37]

Such frameworks, implicit in human rights legislation and the positioning of the book in the global marketplace, are undone by the absence of Western characters in the novel and the presence of more complex indicators of the causes for intra-state trafficking as well as of the 'demand' side of trafficking more generally. This is a crucial development in the litera-ture, reflecting calls from NGOs and activists to move beyond the US Department of State's 'Three R's' – Rescue, Rehabilitation, and Reintegration – all of which focus on the 'supply side' of the trafficking equation. Donna Bickford notes, for example, 'An approach to ending human trafficking which focuses only on the victim is unnecessarily limited and ignores root causes … [indeed,] the root cause of trafficking is demand … in the case of sex trafficking, the demand for bodies and orifices to purchase for sexual activity.'[38] Although as our reading below demonstrates, we concur with Bickford's call for closer analysis of customers and clients in trafficking narratives, we are wary of re-instantiating the victim/perpetrator divide. That divide both reproduces gendered norms as we have dis-cussed and fails to distinguish between sex trafficking and sex work more generally. Col-lapsing the two shifts the focus of anti-trafficking campaigns away from the multiplicitous motivations for sex work, including its roots in structural inequities (themselves often gen-dered and racialised), and toward the criminalisation of sexual desire pursued outside the 'protected' space of the home. Like Hua, Bickford argues that the common focus on women as victims in the 'atrocity story' of trafficking is reflected in the literature: 'The men (primarily) who buy the bodies of women and children are virtually invisible, and we see no consequences for them as a result of their behavior.'[39] However, while Bickford includes *The Blue Notebook* among those texts in which 'the customers are portrayed as an incessant parade of men to be serviced – few are described, most are nameless' – we argue, on the contrary, that Levine develops a range of deeply drawn male characters, all of whom figure in the calamity of Batuk's life circumstances and death; in so doing, he refuses to pit one culture against another, but rather displays a range of masculinities, ultimately indicting masculine anxieties about potency (sexual and otherwise) as a root cause of the trafficking scenario. In other words, the 'problem' is not male desire in and of itself, but the ways in which social power is scripted in and upon gendered and sexualised bodies. Significantly, the most fully developed john in the novel, and the one who ultimately causes Batuk's death, is Iftikhar, a profligate young man whose father has hired Batuk to 'teach him how to be a husband'.[40]

It soon becomes clear that Iftikhar's problem is an extreme case of premature ejacula-tion; with each time that it happens, his violence toward Batuk intensifies. This emblem of failed manhood stands in metonymic relation to other forms of male dissoluteness, also exhibited by Iftikhar: laziness, duplicity, failure to achieve academic or professional competency – all filtered through the Freudian web of desire, projection, and competition marking the father/son relationship. The cruelty, corruption, and brutality perpetrated by Iftikhar upon Batuk is matched by his corrupt scheme to destroy the reputation of Mr Vas, his father's assistant, and by the cruel competition (and competitive cruelty) among the boys who are Iftikhar's 'friends', whose vulgar boasts of sexual prowess with the various prostitutes they use belie, as Batuk notes, 'a lack of confidence and [an] immaturity'.[41] Iftikhar's violent masculinity substitutes for legitimacy, love, and competency. The illegitimate son of a wealthy businessman, Iftikhar employs sexual violence as a substitute for forms of social power: as son, husband, and future father in the joint Hindu family (a legal category whose 'authority structure is patriarchal, succession is patrilineal, and living arrangements are patrilocal', and which Kapur describes as a 'construct to regulate property ownership' rather than to define actual living arrangements[42]); as a successful businessman; and as a student and poet.

In the terms of the novel, Iftikhar's predations are both individual and grounded in socioeconomic hierarchies. For instance, Levine contrasts Iftikhar with Shahalad, the man who claims Batuk as his 'wife' after she has been trafficked to an 'Orphanage' for breaking in before she is assigned to a brothel. Shahalad adheres to the strict code of violent masculinity that organises the Orphanage by raping Batuk upon her arrival and punishing her sexually for perceived insults to his own authority. However, Levine underscores these actions as performances tied to the authority structure of the institution. Batuk recounts,

> The more I attested to [Shahalad's] potency, the less potent he seemed to need to be. In fact, within a week, he would drag me into the back room (I had learned to scream in mock fear) and there we would sit, sometimes for hours. While we sat together on the mattress, I would scream out in feigned agony from time to time or beg for 'more'. This was entirely my idea and it pleased him.[43]

The difference between Shahalad and Iftikhar is that Shahalad allows Batuk into, as it were, the secret of masculine social norms, the need to prove a violent potency even when one does not oneself want or enjoy such expression of potency. Her performance of desire and submission enables them to reach an uneasy comfort together, such that Shahalad is 'pleased' and Batuk is, for the moment, untouched. The later encounter with Iftikhar builds upon this early revelation of the function of hegemonic masculinity, revealing an escalation in brutality that, perhaps ironically, accrues to the rich, privileged characters as opposed to the poor and marginalised ones.

The various masculinities depicted in Levine's novel run the gamut: from Shahalad's performative display of masculine authority and Iftikhar's egregiously warped expressions of power and potency to Iftikhar's father's assistant, Mr Vas's, ethical positioning vis-à-vis business practice and family loyalty. Still, though Mr Vas displays a modicum of compassion in taking Batuk to hospital after she has been severely attacked by Iftikhar, he is still thoroughly implicated in the destructive masculinities indicted in the novel, as he was both the agent who bought Batuk from her brothel in the Common Street, transporting her to the hotel for Iftikhar's pleasure, and the perpetrator of violent retribution in the brutal murder of Iftikhar and his friends for their part in destroying his reputation. Finally, Levine accepts the challenge of depicting the extraordinarily troubling figure of the father who sells his child to pay a gambling debt, managing to realistically convey the father's love and connection with his daughter *and* his total failure as a father, his support of her and desire that she have a better future *and* his total implication in the system of devaluing women in the sex trade (as he himself regularly visits a prostitute, spending money the family does not have to afford himself this pleasure).

Further complicating the representation of perpetrators, Levine offers a similarly wide range of women characters who actively support, work within, are complicit with, or benefit from sex trafficking of girls and boys, women and men. These range from Batuk's mother, who arranges Batuk's 'going away party' before her father takes her to Mumbai; the attendant who washes and guards her before and after her initial rapes; the madam to whom she is bound, and finally Hita, who prepares her for Iftikhar and who is responsible, Batuk says, for 'ensur[ing] that girls like me disappear off the face of the earth without a trace'.[44]

The other two novels under discussion here similarly present a wide array of characters to challenge pat, gendered narratives of victimhood, prosecution, and rehabilitation. These novels help us to turn more directly to the role of securitisation in regulating gender and appropriating human rights discourse in relation to trafficking. Chris Abani's *Becoming Abigail*, a novella whose form reflects its protagonist's short life, moves from Nigeria to London, tracing how the institution of the family provides legal cover for trafficking the teenaged Abigail. After her mother's death, Abigail's father sends her to London (legally) in care of a cousin, who quickly rapes, prostitutes, and brutalises her, while his wife meekly looks on. Her departure is doubly coded in terms of danger and opportunity. On the one hand, Abigail's father tells her, 'He always takes one young relative back to London as well ... Imagine how lucky those children are!'[45]

On the other hand, the novella has already identified Abigail as a subject of various cousins and potentially her father's sexual predations. Wendy Law-Yone similarly ties trafficking to the family in her story of Na Ga, a member of a fictional Burmese minority group, the Lu, whose family is driven by economic necessity and social marginalisation to sell her to a local Headman as a servant: 'All that talk among the grown-ups late at night – about bad crops, bad debts, what to grow, what to sell – suddenly came together and made sense. Money was changing hands. Something was being bought and sold. Something was being taken away. I was that something.'[46] Unmoored from family and community, Na Ga experiences a series of displacements and betrayals from family members, employers, would-be saviours, and lovers, and that include being lured to a Thai brothel by the promise of work in the city. All three novels emphasise the devaluing of girls that results in them first becoming vulnerable to sexual abuse and then being transformed into 'something ... being bought and sold'; however, *The Road to Wanting* takes pains to separate different kinds of trafficking as well as to link the family's precariousness to larger political issues as opposed to personal or familial failings.

The catalyst for the sex trafficking narrative varies in each of the novels. Whereas in *The Blue Notebook*, Batuk's journey into slavery results from her father's profligacy in gambling and visiting prostitutes, in *Becoming Abigail* and *The Road to Wanting* it begins with the search for opportunity. Although Na Ga is sold as a servant at age seven, and Law-Yone clearly links the family's precariousness to their minority status as Wild Lu, it is Na Ga's decision to follow a broker's enticement of jobs in the city that directly results in her transport to a Thai brothel. This sequence of events complicates the definitions of 'coercion' and exploitation that are essential to the Palermo Protocol. Lured by the sight of a 'a broad-shouldered woman, all decked in white and gold', whose gifts include 'candy-coloured hairbrushes, gold and silver handbags and swags of glittering beads', Na Ga asks to be taken to pursue the chance of 'real freedom'[47] and to escape the monotony of her work in a paper factory. The trinkets offered by Na Ga's trafficker offer the promise of participation in the market as feminine consumer rather than labourer or product, a promise scripted as a freedom that is otherwise unavailable; however, it is that very promise of freedom that ultimately leads to her coercion into debt bondage and forced prostitution.

This larger context at once constructs a range of structural conditions that make sense of Na Ga's motivations and make it difficult to identify a single ontology or agent of coercion and exploitation. It also reveals the limits of constructions by pro-sex workers rights advocates of migrant sex workers as free agents negotiating their own passages to better lives, showing how this figure recapitulates the illusory construct of the neoliberal person imagined to be the subject of human rights, the one deconstructed by Hannah Arendt at the origins of the modern rights regime. The careful explication of the biopolitics informing Na Ga's movement reveals that the paradoxical void at the heart of the rights regime, inscribed in its most recent international conventions, is still the refugee, migrant, or smuggled person trying to navigate borders in a world untouched by the human rights dream of cosmopolitanism, still mired in a system of state sovereignty that relegates human rights conventions to mechanisms of border control.

Becoming Abigail tells a different story. Although the conditions that render Abigail prey to her various cousins' sexual abuse are undisclosed, that history provides a larger context for the forced prostitution she experiences in London. Inasmuch as the family remains the source of violence and vulnerability, the state, then, is positioned as the response to the failings of the family. Crucially, however, the narrative failure of both family *and* state in the protection or 'recovery' of Abigail, whose desire for her social worker precisely as a healing force in her life is negated by his position as an agent for the state, assigned to assist in her recovery. Perhaps it is part of Abani's purpose to represent the sexual liaison between Abigail and her married social worker as a desire that falls entirely outside the regulatory norms of both state and family. Its foreclosure, then, upon the prosecution of the social worker, leaves readers with a nihilistic sense of the impossibility of autonomy and desire for the object of human rights intervention (in this case, Abigail) – and, too, Abigail's status as a minor by virtue of age, rather than experience, symbolises the impossibility for such subjects more generally (subjects whose desires and needs are similarly constructed as outside the social and regulatory frameworks of gender and security) of obtaining the liberatory promise of the human rights conventions made to protect her.

In all three novels, the framework of easily identified perpetrator-traffickers and trafficking-victims is occluded in favour of deeply drawn sketches of the complex biopolitical and securitisation networks informing trafficking in the global context. In the case of *The Blue Notebook*, readers understand that Batuk is trafficked due to a complex set of circumstances that include both her mother and her father, and that later involves a range of complicit persons, from servants and other oppressed people (who are, not incidentally, capable of great brutality toward Batuk in the preparations that transform her into a brothel slave even as they can weep with empathy at her pain) to 'pillars of the community' and police. Without a mother to protect her, Abigail in *Becoming Abigail* is subject to the coercive power of male relatives, police, and later of social workers bound by law to 'protect' her. In *Road to Wanting*, once she has been trafficked, Na Ga is subject not just to the desires of the brothel owner and her clients, but to the state health officials who certify to her weekly health ('Being clean and safe was crucial to business', she notes) as well as to the police, who 'were constantly in and out of our rooms, now as clients, now as wardens, armed with their walkie-talkies, sidearms and nightsticks'.[48] When a special forces raid closes the brothel, its workers are first incarcerated and then turned over to the International Committee for Repatriation, in clear, albeit fictitious, adherence to the Trafficking Protocol. Na Ga's constant search for freedom in the form of personal autonomy once again founders. She comments that these international humanitarians 'were the ones who negotiated the fate of those waiting to be deported, who bargained on their behalf with officials on both sides of the border', and ultimately finds herself chosen by an American sponsor, the aptly named Will, to live with him in Bangkok.[49] The novel concludes when Will has decided to move on and *tells* Na Ga he will arrange for her to be taken back to Burma via the Old Burma Road or Great Smugglers' Highway – an appropriate route given that he is, in fact, arranging for her to be smuggled. It is at last in the town of Wanting, on the China-Burma border, that Na Ga, false papers in hand, chooses to walk across the border back to a home that no longer exists. Although the refrain of wanting and choosing intimates that the freedom she has sought for so long is at last at hand, the ending is deeply ambiguous. As Na Ga muses, 'But say, for the sake of argument, they waved me past the guard-house on this side of the bridge. Say I made it past the checkpoint on the Burmese side as well and managed from there to keep going. Say I dodged every ambush, avoided every trap, thwarted every other turn of Fate. What then?'[50]

None of the novels discussed here offers a panacea to the political and humanitarian problem of representing sex trafficked women, nor to the problem of how their representation occludes other human rights subject positions, including the right to migrate and to participate in the global economy. The three protagonists, Batuk, Abigail, and Na Ga, are predominantly legible as what Amar terms, 'parahuman subjects': 'hypervisibilized subalterns who become fetishized subjects of politics, while their ability to act in emancipatory ways is buried by multiple intersecting modes of sexual, cultural, moral, and social discipline'.[51] All three novels show that different logics of securitisation – which Amar identifies as 'humanitarian legal movements, morality campaigns, worker-empowerment efforts, and liberal sexual-rights initiatives'[52] – fail to cohere, yet they form overlapping networks which consistently regulate parahuman subjects such as Batuk, Abigail, and Na Ga. The novels stop short of imagining an alternative human rights framework; however, they offer readers much more fully drawn portraits of the complexities of trafficking than the paradigmatic atrocity tale that has received so much criticism as a determinant for the human rights response to trafficking in the Palermo Protocol.

Specifically, the wide range of perpetrator identities shows the pervasiveness of injurious masculinity across cultures, but also renders the category of perpetrator unstable except in the most egregiously violent and direct circumstances. The coercion and exploitation in the novels, rather than being solely identifiable to a person or group of persons as constructed in the Palermo Protocol, point instead to networks of familial and economic exchange as well as those structural factors that cannot be prosecuted in any court of law, but rather must be addressed through arduous social, political, and economic change over time. This epistemology in turn suggests that international human rights law should not remain focused on rescue, rehabilitation, and, criminalisation, but rather should recognise trafficked persons' rights after the trafficking event to act on their own motivations and desires – sometimes contradictory, but geared less toward entrepreneurship than to labour rights, to the economic, social, and civil rights defined by organisations of trafficked persons who should be the agents rather than objects of the law.

Notes

1. For an informative overview of recent scholarship on this debate, see Rhacel Salazar Parreñas, Maria Celia Hwang, and Heather Ruth Lee, 'What Is Human Trafficking? A Review Essay', *Signs: Journal of Women in Culture and Society* 37, no. 4 (2012): 1015–1029.

2. Ratna Kapur, 'Gender, Sovereignty, and the Rise of the Sexual Security Regime', *Melbourne Journal of International Law* 14, no. 2 (2013): 332.

3. The third Palermo Protocol, adopted along with the others, is the Protocol against the Illicit Manufacturing of and Trafficking in Firearms, their Parts and Components and Ammunition. The adoption of instruments that address sex trafficking, labour smuggling, and the illicit trade in firearms clearly positions sex trafficking within larger narratives of states' economic interests and military security.

4. Nandita Sharma develops this argument in 'Anti-Trafficking Rhetoric and the Making of a Global Apartheid', *NWSA Journal* 17, no. 3 (2005): 88–111.

5. James A. Levine, *The Blue Notebook* (New York: Spiegel and Grau Trade Paperbacks, [2009] 2010).

6. Chris Abani, *Becoming Abigail* (New York: Akashic Books, 2006).

7. Wendy Law-Yone, *The Road to Wanting* (London: Vintage, 2011).

8. Prabha Kotiswaran, *Dangerous Sex, Invisible Labor: Sex Work and the Law in India* (Princeton, NJ: Princeton University Press, 2011), 242. For a more in-depth analysis of the range of meanings embedded in the concept of 'exploitation', see Vanessa E. Munro, 'Exploring Exploitation: Trafficking in Sex, Work, and Sex Work', *Demanding Sex: Critical Reflections on the Regulation of Prostitution*, ed. Vanessa E. Munro and Marina Della Giusta (Hampshire: Ashgate, 2008), 83–97.

9. Ratna Kapur, *Makeshift Migrants and Law: Gender, Belonging, and Postcolonial Anxieties* (New Delhi and Oxford: Routledge, 2010), 8.

10. For an informative discussion of the relationship between the two protocols, see Jacqueline Bhabha, 'Trafficking, Smuggling, and Human Rights', *Migration Information Source* (1 March 2005), http://www.migrationinformation.org. Bhabha notes that the differences between trafficking and smuggling are often difficult to ascertain, especially given the conditions of 'forced labor' which may make smuggled migrancy 'forced but chosen opportunities'.

11. Anne Gallagher, 'Human Rights and the New UN Protocols on Trafficking and Migrant Smuggling: A Preliminary Analysis', *Human Rights Quarterly* 23, no. 4 (2001): 976.

12. Paul Amar, *The Security Archipelago: Human-Security States, Sexuality Politics, and the End of Neoliberalism* (Durham, NC: Duke University Press, 2013), 6.

13. Hannah Arendt, 'We Refugees', in *The Jew as Pariah: Jewish Identity and Politics in the Modern Age*, ed. Ron H. Feldman (New York: Grove Press, 1978), 55.

14. Roberto Esposito, 'Biopolitics', in *Biopolitics: A Reader*, ed. Timothy Campbell and Adam Sitze (Durham and London: Duke University Press: 2013), 330.

15. Ibid., 343.

16. Kapur, *Makeshift Migrants and Law*, 8. Kapur also discusses the far-reaching effects of the US Trafficking Victims Prevention Act (TVPA 2000, reauthorised in 2003 and 2005), includes an international monitoring system. The system subjects other countries to various levels of scrutiny and the threat of economic sanctions in order to leverage the adoption of stricter anti-trafficking and anti-prostitution laws in other countries (ibid., 116–117).

17. See Jo Doezema, *Sex Slaves and Discourse Masters: The Construction of Trafficking* (London: Zed Books, 2010); Alison Murray, 'Debt-Bondage and Trafficking: Don't Believe the Hype', in *Global Sex Workers: Rights, Resistance and Redefinition*, ed. Kamala Kempadoo and Jo Doezema (New York: Taylor & Francis, 1998), 51–64; and Ronald Weitzer, 'The Social Construction of Sex Trafficking: Ideology and Institutionalization of a Moral Crusade', *Politics and Society* 35, no. 3 (2007): 447–475.

18. Amar, *The Security Archipelago*, 15.

19. Although we highlight some of the more extreme rhetoric through which advocates stake their positions, we also note that these different positions have been subject to much excellent analysis. See, for instance, Kamala Kempadoo et al.'s volume, *Trafficking and Prostitution Reconsidered: New Perspectives on Migration, Sex Work, and Human Rights* (Boulder, CO: Paradigm Publishers, 2005) for a nuanced discussion of the ways in which the focus on sex trafficking,

and the threat to normative gender roles it represents, masks neoliberal predilections of the global labour market.

20. Victor Malarek, *The Johns: Sex for Sale and the Men Who Buy It* (New York: Arcade, 2009), xiv.
21. Weitzer, 'The Social Construction of Sex Trafficking', 448.
22. See, for instance, Jo Doezema, *Sex Slaves and Discourse Masters: The Construction of Trafficking* (New York: Zed Books, 2010), 10.
23. Murray, 'Debt-Bondage and Trafficking', 419.
24. Patrick Crough, quoted in Malarek, *The Johns*, 25.
25. Kotiswaran, *Dangerous Sex, Invisible Labor*, 223.
26. Malarek, *The Johns*, xiii.
27. Ibid., xiv–xv.
28. Amar, *The Security Archipelago*, 206.
29. Tristan Anne Borer, 'A Taxonomy of Victims and Perpetrators: Human Rights and Reconciliation in South Africa', *Human Rights Quarterly* 25, no. 4 (2003): 1088.
30. Isabell Lorey, 'Governmental Precarization', trans. Aileen Derieg, *Transversal: EIPCP Multilingual Webjournal*, January, http://eipcp.net/transversal/0811/lorey/en (accessed 15 September 2013).
31. Kapur, 'Gender, Sovereignty, and the Rise of the Sexual Security Regime', 345.
32. James A. Levine, 'The Street of Cages' (Originally published in *The Times of London*, 11 July 2009), in *The Blue Notebook* (New York: Spiegel and Grau Trade Paperbacks, 2010), 223.
33. The same year the Palermo Protocols were adopted, the US Trafficking Victims Protection Act (TVPA) became law, which included the establishment of a ranking and reporting system – tied to economic sanctions – of individual countries' efforts to address trafficking. For an excellent overview of the TVPA and the TIP Reports, see Anne Gallagher, 'Human Rights and Human Trafficking: A Reflection on the Influence and Evolution of the U.S. Trafficking in Persons Report', in *From Human Trafficking to Human Rights*, ed. Alison Brysk and Austin Choi-Fitzpatrick (Philadelphia: University of Pennsylvania Press, 2012), 172–194.
34. Julietta Hua, *Trafficking Women's Human Rights* (Minneapolis: University of Minnesota Press, 2011), 62–63.
35. Ibid., xxvii.
36. Ibid., 57–58.
37. Ibid., 61–62.
38. Donna M. Bickford, '"We All Like to Think We've Saved Somebody": Sex Trafficking in Literature', *Journal of International Women's Studies* 13, no. 3 (2012): 134.
39. Ibid., 134.
40. Levine, *The Blue Notebook*, 141.
41. Ibid., 179.
42. Kapur, *Makeshift Migrants and Law*, 46–47.
43. Levine, *The Blue Notebook*, 98.
44. Ibid., 103.
45. Abani, *Becoming Abigail*, 62.
46. Law-Yone, *The Road to Wanting*, 238.
47. Ibid., 104, 105, 111.
48. Ibid., 126, 128.
49. Ibid., 158.
50. Ibid., 221.
51. Amar, *The Security Archipelago*, 209.
52. Ibid., 186.

Index

www.ingramcontent.com/pod-product-compliance
Ingram Content Group UK Ltd.
Pitfield, Milton Keynes, MK11 3LW, UK
UKHW010020280225
455677UK00023B/718